Birth of the Conscious Feminine

Printed in the United States of America First Printing, 2018
ISBN-978-1-734-1975-0-1 Nuralight Publishing

ConsciousFeminineMedicine.com

Dedication

I dedicate this book to my mother…
who in her passion to the mystery….
her dedication to all things Divine…
and her deep love of Truth…
gave me the courage to pursue my own truth and
the strength to continue the inner exploration, despite the challenges.
Through her, I came to know my inner pole of Light…
from which I learned to fly…
once I was anchored securely.

May the Great Mother hold you in Her Light

Leonor Maria Talavera

TABLE OF CONTENTS

Table of Contents

Birth of the Conscious Feminine

~ changing the collective story of the Feminine

A new Era of Feminine Sovereignty

Leonor Murciano-Luna, PhD

Awakening the Conscious Feminine

There is a new revolution that is happening within our hearts…
It is the evolution of the Feminine Soul.
The conscious feminine is being birthed within… through every man, women
and child on the planet…
and within our very own EARTH.
This conscious feminine is the new Feminine…
a new movement of feminism that upholds LOVE as its core principle for every
being on the planet.
The Conscious Feminine begins with a shift in awareness…
breaking through 5000+ yrs. of repression of the Feminine…
restoring the Feminine within the masculine,
dark & light, body & soul, feeling & intellect….
Evolving duality into unity.
The Conscious Feminine gives rise to a new world…
one that honors the sacredness of our being.
She sees strength in our diversity…
And upholds social, spiritual, psychological, economical & political equality
for both men, women and all sentient beings on our planet.

~ leonor murciano-luna

Introduction

A NEW STORY OF THE COLLECTIVE FEMININE

What if I told you that what you think and know about yourself is set in an illusory state of mostly doubt, shame, fear and judgment? And that illusion has veiled the great mystery that lives within you, your primordial Essence. This is the mystery that gave birth to you and supported you at all times, whether you're conscious of it or not... whether you believe it or not.

Although this mystery doesn't depend on your conscious awareness of its existence, it does manifest according to your awareness of it. This primordial power has been hidden for thousands of years. Becoming conscious of it brings about what is called: 'enlightenment', which allows you to enjoy the process of life through the foundation of joy. It brings contentment and safety to your heart, regardless of the conditions you find yourself in. It' is the creative and healing force that miracles are made from, and most importantly, it gives you the opportunity to fully embody your personal power, rather than hopelessly living as a victim of your own illusions.

Through conscious awareness you get to end the game of duality, along with the cessation of pain and suffering that accompanies it. You awaken and begin to merge with an altered parallel reality of Oneness, that is inclusive, instead of divisive. And during this intensive immersion, your greatest epiphany is the simple realization that there were never two to begin with, there is only one reality!

There are many keys that unveil the mystery that gave birth to us. She's left many clues around. Most of the clues remain hidden under the guise of shame, judgment, fear and unworthiness. In order to uncover them, we must tune into the whispering voice, we must see without eyes, we must listen without ears, we must touch the depths of our souls, and there, we'll find the treasure buried within our being, in the unseen mystery of life itself.

A NEW REALITY EMERGES

How would it feel to know that you're an expression of the Divine, expressing your primordial Essence through thoughts, feelings and actions, none of which define who you truly are?

How would your life be different if you knew that there are no mistakes and that everything that happens to you has a purpose and gift? How would it feel to know that you're the love, therefore, needing love is an illusion and that all you've ever yearned for is accessible and available in this moment from your very own core?

What if you knew that your mind keeps you in fear, pain and suffering... and that you have the key to unlock the challenges that you experience in your life? **YOU HOLD THE KEY**! This has been hidden within you, but you're about to unveil it for yourself, and no one can take that away from you. You have the power within to create, consciously, a new reality, and only you can undo what has been done.

As women, this is the new story that we're weaving in the collective. This is the new story that many of us have been dreaming about. I'm here to acknowledge for you, the fact that it's possible to lift yourself from the old story of fear, shame and suffering, into full embodiment of safety, love, joy and pleasure. We can change the old, confining, collective story of the Feminine and flourish into our unique, unrestricted, radical expression of the wild Fire within. How do I know? Because this isn't just your story, this is my story. I've been blessed to experience the Grace of the Conscious Feminine. However, in order to give birth to Her highest ascent of Light, we must dive deep into the hidden wounds in our psyche. Like many, I've had an intimate relationship with fear and all of its obscured pathways, interspersed with the constant threat of terror, shame, unworthiness and hopelessness, and yet, I've made it through the threshold, and so can you. As Marion Woodman remarks in Dancing in the Flames: "rebirth to a higher level of consciousness is not accomplished by flying through the air. The ascent is balanced by the descent."[1] She is the Conscious Feminine.

There is something within you that wants to break free, and I too can feel the pulse. This undeniable pulse has been within me since I was young, something very hidden that knew the Truth and couldn't be shut down by the ever-reaching claws of fear. This primordial force is what leads you out. This is the impulse of life itself within you, the unifying light of the Feminine that guides you to a new birth. Listen quietly for She speaks softly, and yet She carries the fiercest voice you will ever know. Turn within and listen, Her wisdom is in your body, She has never left you. For it is us, who have left Her, and She is calling us back!

How to best use this book

Even though you will find intellectual concepts sprinkled throughout the pages of this book, I highly suggest that you use your body to "feel" your way through the information you're presented with, so that you awaken your visceral knowing. Rather than analyzing the information conceptually or screening it through the lens of your mind, try noticing what you feel in your body as you read it. Does it excite you? Does it bring you peace, hope? Can you relate to it? Does it stir something powerful within you?

Become aware of what resonates within your body. One of the key principles of the Feminine is the wisdom that is held in our awareness within our bodies. Through our bodies we move into other dimensions of existence, learning to feel and trust what helps you tap into your consciousness of wisdom. Listening to how something resonates within you and vibrates in your body will guide you on your path. Your body lights up and has a biochemical reaction to what you're hearing, perceiving, and recognizing. Your body sends neurotransmitters to 'alert' you and inform you. You can notice these feelings if you pay close attention to what you're feeling without any judgment of the information, or of your response. By listening deeply to these responses in your body, you're able to awaken your enteric heart connecting to your innate wisdom.

Awakening your life force through the senses in your body is part of the reintegration of the great split between our mind (masculine) and bodies (feminine). Furthermore, focus on those practices that resonate deeply; they serve to awaken the wisdom within you.

According to most spiritual teachings, at this time, we are in the precipice of a great awakening- creating a new world in which the Feminine is completely resurrected and in harmony with the Masculine, for both women and men on the planet. This is the new vision of a world in which the qualities of intellectualism, reasoning, and the material is deeply merged in a foundation of compassion, mercy, love and sacredness; where joy and pleasure in our bodies is honored as divine and both feminine and masculine are valued as two expressions of the same Oneness. We all have the opportunity to awaken our divine sacred Essence within and resurrect the Feminine consciousness within ourselves and our planet. And from our own transformation and embodiment, we can then give birth to this new world. May these words serve as part of that expansion of light and joy throughout your Being and our world.

An Invocation to Great Mother

I bow my head, heart and womb to you.
For you are the Creator & Created.
From your womb, the ten thousand things are born.
I ask that you bring me close to you, keep me in your flow of Divine Grace.
Hold me in our ecstatic presence where all veils are dissolved…
Leaving only your whispering Truth as my Teacher.
Let me drink from your cup and merge with you into the annihilation of my being,
forever and ever, dear Mother!

~ leonor murciano-luna

1
From The Beginning

FROM WHERE WE STAND ITS HALF THE STORY

We live in a world that has subtly and overtly been colored through the lens of what we call 'patriarchy', a collective culture that has been steeped in the values of masculine traits. The 'patriarchy' is this catchall field in which our experiences and values are judged through a pervasion of assertiveness, competitiveness, individualism and stereotypes. This has been the preferred flavor of dominant forces that have used their might and physical power to manipulate and create the world and society in which we live in today. These 'patriarchal' forces have been in positions of power and dominance for the last 5000 years or more, infiltrating our psyches with a biased conditioning of physical dominance, competition, independence, and material manifestation in favor of its opposing, non-material, subtle, compassionate, community and heart values.

When we began to record history through the written word, the world had already entered the patriarchy, therefore, most of what was recorded was through an unconscious masculine bias of values. This, of course, contributed to the doubting of the Feminine altogether. Many erroneously consider history to begin at the inception of the written word, which was about five thousand years ago. Therefore, the world view, through the written word, has been established through this lens of patriarchal interpretation. And as such, the written language has been given more importance than that of the un-written, oral rituals and traditions of the Feminine, which have existed since the beginning of time. Due to this unconscious masculine interpretation of our world through written word, we've lost much of this Feminine wisdom which has been passed down from generation to generation, through oral and intuitive gnosis.

As part of the patriarchal cultural perspective, the physical is valued more than the spiritual, the outer forces more than the inner forces, and (masculine) yang traits more than (feminine) yin traits. This view has led to an unequal, one-sided interpretation of our world. Everything we've learned, seen, and integrated since we were young, has been skewed through this lens of the patriarchy, leaving women and the wisdom of the Feminine hidden. In fact, artifacts that have been found before our written history (3000 BCE) were typically interpreted through the masculine patriarchy mindset, attaching relevance of war, competition and dominance to these previous cultural findings and civilizations, when in reality, these were part of matriarchal cultures, as seen in the brilliant scholarly work of Marija Gimbutas. In her last book "The Living Goddesses" Marija reconstructs goddess-centered cultures that predated historic patriarchal cultures, evident in the findings of thousands of ancient female figurines, such as the famous Venus of Willendorf artifacts dating between 28,000-25,000 BCE.

When we consider the greater implication (that most history books have been written from this perspective of the patriarchy), we realize that we've not had a very clear picture of the truth because we have been unable to separate ourselves from our place of witnessing. Our history has been imbued with a limited interpretation of events. Imagine having two people describe the same exact experience, each from a different perspective with completely opposing perspectives and meanings. We have all been personally and collectively functioning under this skewed perception of the patriarchal view, giving us an interpretation of our world only from one side. This has further anchored the imbalance in our psyches as we perpetuate this myth from generation to generation. Although we've all been told the story of our past through one-sided lens, the veil is crumbling, and many are rising and now exploring our world and its history inclusive of the Feminine perspective; initiating the dissolution of the old story.

We have to ask ourselves: "How different would my world be if my ancestors discussed the times in which intuition, sensitivity and creating life (child bearing) were sacred gifts? How different would my life be if I'd grown up in a world where women around me felt safe and secure from the time that they are born, and didn't fear the domination of the opposite sex? What would change in my world if women felt they could express their emotional sensitivities and not be judged or shamed? How would I feel if I valued my worthiness, sacredness and beauty? What would change in my world if women honored their feminine qualities of nurturing, relational connectivity to group consciousness, and their compassion, instead of hiding these qualities? How would the world be different if we honored our menstruation as the sacred life-giving process that it is?"

Moreover, my point is that we've integrated this masculine way of being, also referred to as a more yang way of seeing and experiencing the world, which is not a negative thing. The only problem is that this way of thinking has been at the expense of the feminine (yin forces), therefore, causing most of the destruction, pain and suffering we see in humanity, in ourselves and on our planet.

COLLECTIVE STORY OF THE FEMININE

As a collective, there's this common story that all women have experienced. The manifestations in each of our lives may look different, but underneath it all, the themes and conditioning of the collective is the same. Whether we're aware of it or not, it shapes every thought, emotion, action and experience we have, even influencing expectations of our world and ourselves. Until we begin to dissolve the conditioning that invisibly penetrates our being, we're powerless under its spell. Collective and personal awareness is needed in order to unravel this old pervasive paradigm.

This collective story we've lived begins with the realization of the repression of the Feminine. But what is this plague that has affected women so unequivocally? Let me explain. We all recognize that we live in a patriarchal society with values being determined by these ideals. Even though we don't speak much of this outwardly, all the signs are there. As we discussed, this collective field is impregnated with the valuing of physical strength, competition, and aggressiveness over the more subtle qualities of connectedness, intuition, tenderness, compassion and vulnerability. Women in the work force are expected to put aside their innate nurturing qualities and behave more in alignment with masculine qualities of logic and competitiveness. Shame around emotional sensitivities and intuition are just a few superficial examples of the tentacles of our patriarch system. In this way, the Feminine archetype of subtleties and intuition has been thwarted by the Masculine archetype of outward focus when establishing our wellbeing, happiness and especially our 'value'. We have lost the significance of our inner nature, our spirit, and the unseen, since this too is Feminine.

It's important to recognize that I'm not proclaiming that one way of being supersedes another, rather, it is the free synergistic expression of both of these qualities, yin and yang (masculine and feminine) within our being, that brings us deep satisfaction and realization of our full potential. We need to honor both in order to find peace and fulfillment. The key is in having harmony; honoring the subtle, unseen and spiritual dimension (feminine), as well as the physical, assertive (masculine) expressions of ourselves. Our denial of the Feminine and all things associated with Feminine qualities, has created a discontent that percolates through our existence as lack of happiness, joy and all-encompassing dissatisfaction in our lives. Furthermore, it has created severe disruption in women, manifesting as dysfunctions in physical, mental and emotional health, along with destructive relationships, powerlessness, shame, self-judgment, and an overall restriction in our ability to fully thrive towards our fullest potential.

Since the beginning of the patriarch culture, about 3000 BCE, women have been forced to live in a culture that sees them and their intrinsic qualities as second class. Throughout the years, women have had to hide their feminine qualities and adapt to masculine qualities for survival. During the 12th century Inquisition, women that displayed unacceptable feminine traits of divinatory or intuitive qualities were executed and condemned for showing their natural connections to the divine. Throughout the last few thousand years, women have not felt safe in their bodies, and even to this day have attempted to adopt the male traits for safety, survival and acknowledgement.

Women have forgotten their ways and have disconnected themselves from the oral wisdom passed on from generation to generation. As women, we've forgotten how to access and depend on the secrets from the wisdom within. Instead, we've been completely absorbed by constantly pursuing our value through material means, outside ourselves, rather than leaning on innate knowing and realization. One of the most obvious repercussions of survival has the engraved pattern of "learned helplessness" that women have adapted. In this pattern one avoids situations that may trigger a previous painful or unpleasant stimulus, to the degree that one stops trying because of fear and possibility of experiencing those painful events. Through learned helplessness, women have become victims of their own painful history, perpetuating the patterns of limitation, shame, judgment and fear.

Furthermore, learned helplessness often leads to the belief that one is more powerless than they really are, which in turn creates outcomes that are based on defeat. In many ways, women have accustomed themselves to this image of defeat, rather than identifying with their innate sense of strength and value. In my years of practice, my observation is that these unconscious limiting beliefs manifest in deeply dissatisfying, vicious cycles of hopelessness, depressed states, and even in physical imbalances in our bodies. This type of conditioning not only affects every aspect of our being, but is ultimately the root cause of our unhappiness, not just for women, but also for men.

WHY HAS THE FEMININE GONE UNDERGROUND?

There's no one to blame; we're doing it to ourselves now. On one level it may look like it all started with a masculine dominance pattern enacting on physical and religious reform, but in reality, this pattern is deeply rooted in all of humanity. Throughout history, women have adapted to this reform through submission. The fear of survival was so profound that the remnant still informs our behavior and actions till this day. This fear has become ingrained in our psyche and invisible to our conscious awareness. While it's penetrated the hidden crevices of our psyche, it's also extended outwardly permeating our every thought and manifestation.

We live in a culture that's under a tremendous amount of fear and yet fiercely denies having any fear at all, although it's evident in the great number of people suffering from anxiety. It's been recorded that one in five people have been diagnosed with an anxiety disorder in this country and if we take into account all of those that haven't been diagnosed, we come close to a quarter of our population. Anxiety is only one of the manifestations of this remnant of fear. This collective fear has forced women to deny their very own feminine yin natures, creating a collective field of suppression and repression that must be dissolved in order to step into our full potential and glory.

While we begin the process of unwinding this long history of repression and concealment, we must wonder why the Feminine went underground and hid Herself and Her qualities for so long? And why has there been so much turbulence, domination and violence? It's through the witnessing of the greater cycle of our existence, that we can even begin to respond to this question with an answer that resonates in our hearts.

If we look at the natural occurring cycles of life, inherent in every living thing are five essential stages of which the Traditional Chinese theory is based on; birth, growth, fullness, decay and death, continuing the cycle again with rebirth. This cycle is an organizing system that permeates every living thing, as is evident in our seasons, in the progression of our own lives, and even in the cycles of the moon that orbits around us. In the death cycle, life ceases and everything goes under ground to transform and revitalize itself, spiraling into rebirth and life once again. The phase of death is also associated with seasons; when things die and undergo a transformation in order to be able to birth again in a new form. In the moon cycle, this is called the dark moon phase of transformation and death, followed by rebirth. Through astrology, we can understand these cycles of the moon and other planets as they wax and wane throughout time, reenacting these cycles repeatedly.

The feminine principle, which we can refer to as the Feminine expression of Oneness, also has cycles that can be revealed to us through the study of the astrological patterns of the greater moon's 40,000-year cycle. According to Demetra George: "If we look closely at the rhythm of the moon's cycle, we may perceive that the development and flowering of the Feminine, her subsequent disappearance, and her current reemergence may be due to her natural cycle of waxing and waning phases." [1] From this vantage point the disappearance of the Feminine within our world and our psyche is part of the timing of this cycle, in which She has entered what is referred to as the Dark Moon phase of death and rebirth, lasting for 5000 years, since 3000 BCE until 2012, relatively.

George writes: "During the period of her dormancy, the images and symbols of the Goddess have been virtually absent from culture, except those occasional springs of waters bubbling up for short periods of time during various periods and places." Through her writing she supports our witnessing of the decline of the Feminine principle in our culture and the increase in masculine principles in our governing forces throughout the past 5000 years. George proposes: "She (the Goddess) entered into her dark moon phase, where she retreated and disappeared in order to heal, transform, and renew herself for another round of growth".[2]

Subsequently, through the absence of the Feminine principle, an unsafe, unstable environment was created in which the exaggerated masculine principle of dominance and competition prevailed. We call this the patriarchy. And so, we must ask: did our wise and knowledgeable ancestors, who were in tune with these cycles of life, know that the Feminine would go into her underground descent? If the Feminine principle was active in our foremothers before the descent, did they devise a great design in consciousness that would ensure the survival of women and the race during this time? How could the Feminine go underground and all the women forget their inherent light so easily?

With this inquiry in my soul leading the way, I've begun to see the gift of this collective veil of fear, shame, worthlessness and powerlessness. In many ways, it's kept us hidden and quiet enough to survive the 5000-year immersion of death. Perhaps, the creation of an illusory impenetrable energetic veil that could contain the primordial essence of light and maintain an energetic separation of light and dark, would indeed allow women to stay safe during the 5000 millennia descent of the Goddess's Feminine principles.

If we consider the Feminine principle entering the dark moon phase of descent, where destruction precedes regeneration, then a dark impenetrable veil of protection makes perfect sense. Feeling the heart-clenching gnaws of unworthiness, powerlessness and fear throughout our consciousness, as if it were real, is an effective tactic at keeping ourselves contained and small. It prevents us from saying too much or being too much, because essentially, it would appear as though we've disowned our sacred light. The veil has fulfilled its job of keeping us small in our own illusion of constriction and most importantly, keeping us safe.

While this veil may have served the purpose of protection during the prevailing times of darkness, it's no longer warranted, and nor do we have to hide our primordial essence. Playing victim to our past and identifying ourselves with our woundedness isn't necessary anymore for our survival. It's time for us to embody our sacredness as we resurrect our true power and worth in the light of our Being. This is the resurrection of the Feminine within us and our planet. that began roughly around 2012.

This resurrection of the Feminine is the foundational principle in the creation of *Conscious Feminine Medicine*™, which I'm introducing with this new body of work, *'Birth of the Conscious Feminine.'* Consequently, this body of work mirrors our own process of death and rebirth. Just like the Goddess, we dissolve in order to heal, transform, renew and give birth to a new story of the Feminine within our own Being and within our world. This is our personal and collective dark moon process, established in the foundation of the Feminine principle through a series of Sacred Initiations. *Conscious Feminine Medicine*™ (*CFM*) offers a paradigm shift in our consciousness, affecting our health and wellbeing, designed to dissolve the old constructs of conventional medicine to include the newer science of Quantum medicine; reuniting the medicine of particles with the unseen substance of primordial force and energetic realities of consciousness. CFM is the container for the resurrection of the Feminine, which is now ready to be birthed into the psyches of women on Earth. Through the principles of *CFM,* we're able to see a complete revolution of healing, not just physical, but also the deep healing that happens in our hearts and souls when we receive the medicine that we have been yearning for.

On a personal level, this journey through the shadowy terrain of fear, terror, shame, worthlessness and powerlessness has been my path, greatly affecting my heart and soul. Personally, walking through the descent and reemergence has been responsible for the many crises in my physical body via my endocrine, nervous system, emotional and immune issues to name a few. This is not only my journey, but one which many women find themselves battling quietly in their lives currently. Many of which I've had the humbling honor to work with, affording me a space to share these Feminine principles, their effects on our consciousness and implications on healing and health. I'm here to share with you these powerful Feminine principles through what is now *Conscious Feminine Medicine*™, which offers us a bridge in which to collectively ignite the alchemical dissolution of the suppression of the Feminine and give rise to the new creation cycle of the fully embodied Feminine personally and globally.

HEALING & THE EVOLUTION OF THE FEMININE SOUL

As a collective, even though we've entered the evolutionary time of resurrection of the Feminine Soul, most people are still living unconsciously. This evolutionary process has begun in many and is first birthed within. As women, we're capable of remembering the mystery of the living wisdom that is hidden within our bodies and honoring our knowing. Collectively and personally, we've become disconnected from our power; living aimlessly without purpose in this world, leaving the true world behind. It's time to recapture this living matrix along with our disembodied shadows. It's time for us to awaken our fire, joy, happiness and life force; all evident in our wild Feminine. But how do we begin to awaken to Her? We begin by listening to the wisdom in our body... in our womb, remembering that She's already living within us. This is the first secret that all the women have forgotten. By feeling it in our bodies, by listening deeply to our being, we begin the journey of restoring the integrity of our Essence.

MY STORY

As an empathic child, I was keenly aware of the emotional state of the women that surrounded me. And even though from the outside everyone seemed to live a relatively well-adjusted life, I was privy to the invisible world that was unspoken. Mostly, I was aware of the intensity of fear that underlined everyone around me and noticed how this fear affected their every thought and action. More importantly though, I saw how their joy, happiness and safety was stolen by the field of fear. I was also keenly aware of the unspoken shame and judgements that seem to surround feeling any feelings at all, especially fear. Rejection and repression seemed to be the mechanism that facilitated survival in this field of emotional denial and oppression. This seemed to be the psychic and emotional environment I witnessed around those that I loved most, and I was completely powerless against changing it.

I didn't know it yet, but my relationship with fear would be a life-long journey, not something that I could brush off or ignore. It would prove to be my worst enemy, as well as my greatest teacher. Today, I am grateful. I recognize that because of this relationship, I've discovered so many pearls of wisdom that have empowered me and allowed the dissolution of our self-imposed restrictions and illusions. Fear has been the catalyst of the greatest transformation of my soul.

When I was young, I quickly learned that it wasn't safe or acceptable to speak about my own, or anyone else's feelings and vulnerabilities. I also learned that many were unconscious to their feelings and completely clueless to what was driving them. My empathic abilities were quite confusing to me, but allowed me to have a clear sixth sense about my surrounding world, picking up on unsaid and discarded undertones to many situations. My mind equated living on this planet with suffering, and yet there was something deep inside of me urging me to challenge that reality.

In many ways, that ability to perceive the suffering in the world, especially in those closest to me, shaped my world greatly, even though there was that inner voice that refused to fall victim to the hopelessness. I'm not sure if it was my rebelliousness to questions, the status quo, or shear stubbornness that continued to push for answers of something more. Day in and day out I kept thinking that there must be a way out of the misery that others were living around me, a way out of this state of mind. I thought it's impossible for us to come here just to suffer. Perhaps the repeated hollow statements my family would constantly repeat with no further discussion or exploration: 'everything has a purpose' or 'what happens is what is always best' might have anchored some hope to embark on an inner journey of exploration, by first displaying my unwillingness to surrender to endless suffering.

To no surprise, that probably explains my choice of immersing myself in esoteric and metaphysic studies such as psychology, astrology and quantum science. But most importantly, it explains my emergence into various spiritual paths and of my unquenchable thirst for gnostic mysticism and ancient traditions. I've always had a passion for resurrecting the healing traditions that have been lost to our modern world and discovering what I call the 'real medicine of our Soul.' I knew my exploration had to be in the realms of the unseen, and I was determined to unlock the secret code, even though I couldn't find it around me.

During the last 35 plus years, I've had the privilege of studying and being by the side of a handful of transcended masters that have humbly served as my teachers. Interlaced with what I present to you here is the culmination of my personal transformational journey through esoteric teachings of Daoist, Sufi, Vedic and Christian Gnostic traditions. But most importantly, my work, personally and professionally, has been informed by the initiation of the spiritual lineages I carry deep in my heart. First, the Shadhiliyya Sufi lineage which was passed on through the teachings of my guide, Sidi Al Jamal, as well as through my blood line from the ancestor lineage of Al Mursi from Murcia, Spain. This lineage has been a powerful transformative force in my life from the moment it made itself known as a great light in my heart, in 2005. It's been the strongest path of purification that I've experienced, allowing me to continually annihilate the 'rust' in my heart, as the Sufi's would say, in order to awaken the light of my Being. Secondly, I feel very fortunate and honored to have been called to the Wu Dark Moon lineage, which has come through our honorable teacher Dan Atchison-Nevel, through the teachings of Non Somatic Extra Vessels (NSEV), which has awakened me to the Dark Moon lineage, allowing me to integrate a vast knowledge of body, mind and spirit embodiment practices. Furthermore, I feel blessed to have been initiated by the Feminine Spirit Mother Herself, bringing me the Sacred Initiations of the Feminine, since 2010, when She began her deep transformation, transmutation and distillation of my complete Soul. The Essence from these lineages have given birth to *Conscious Feminine Medicine™*.

2
Unveiling the collective wound
of the Feminine

LIVING WITH FEAR

Fear has been my teacher in many ways, as well as my worst nightmare. Unfortunately, I know what it's like to live with fear all the time; I would say it's a close cousin to shame. It's been the single most challenging aspect of my life. It was at age six that fear predominantly showed up in my life and decided to stay. It all started with a near-death experience, which I want to share with you. It took me many years to integrate all the tenets of this experience and sift through the fear, for its inherent gifts. Unlike other people that experience near death experiences (NDE), I was not instantly fearless, nor ecstatic about being here on this planet. And yet, I can sincerely say it was the doorway I needed to reconnect with the true light of my being, and ultimately, the greatest transformation of my life.

The summer before I turned seven, my family and I were driving up from Miami, where we'd lived for a year. We were heading to New Jersey, where I was originally from. During this trip, my uncle sat in the back seat with me, my mother directly in front of me as the driver and my aunt in the front passenger seat. There were only a few hours left until we would arrive at our destination. What happened next changed my life forever.

As I slept in the back seat, I wasn't aware of anything that was going on, but I remember waking up to the sound of someone calling my name, though it sounded far off in the distance, as though I was in a dream. Even though I didn't understand what was happening, or where I was, I responded to the masculine voice calling out my name.

It was the voice of a police officer outside the vehicle; apparently, I was trapped inside due to a car accident we'd had. A big tractor truck had run over our vehicle from hind side and landed right above the back portion of our car, over the vehicle, coming right up to the edge of the front seat. Therefore, the back seat, trunk and everything behind it was pinned under the tractor truck. This included me and my uncle. As a small child, I must have rolled into the foot space behind the front seat of the driver's side. I was originally in the back seat, but found myself laying down in that foot area, covered by the car seat cushions, which acted as a prevention to my body from the overhead truck.

I wasn't aware of the accident, only that I was laying down and couldn't move. The officer who had called my name asked me if I could move, if I could feel my feet, my hands? I answered yes to a few responses, completely confused. I knew I couldn't move, but I didn't really know what was happening.

Along with the sound of his voice, I could also hear my mother's hysterical cries. Over that I could hear my aunt trying to calm her down and my dog barking. All of this seemed somewhat surreal in the darkness of the moment, where I couldn't see, but could only hear. I'm not sure at what point I shifted into another consciousness, perhaps it was right after he assured me that everything would be alright, or perhaps when the loud screechy sound of the 'jaws of life' started cutting through the truck's heavy metal in an attempt to free my buried body. Nonetheless, it could've been through any point of the four hours that I was caught in that horrific trap.

I didn't really have any sense of time. At one point, I felt increasingly uncomfortable and I must have passed out. I remember feeling the anxiety and fear increasing, while paralyzed in position. At that moment, I began to have an altered experience of my reality. Everything became increasingly dark and I felt very lost and hopeless. I felt myself slipping away... return to panic... holding on to dear life... yet finally giving up and slipping helplessly into another dimension.

As my fear and terror increased, there was a sense of impending constriction around me, as if I was going through a tunnel that was dark. Still, I had my eyes open and was trying to stay conscious, but I was losing the battle. My sense of helplessness was extremely daunting, and my sense of vulnerability was excruciatingly painful. I felt I wouldn't survive. I felt like I was dying, and no one could help me. No one could reach me. As I closed my eyes, I felt terror, terror of the unknown and terror of being helpless, slipping into what seemed like death.

However, I was soon defeated and found myself letting go. I entered the darkness. I saw many terrifying looking beings of different shapes and sizes. I somehow knew that they were there to scare me, and they were doing a good job. I felt and saw all of my own fears coming to life, and all of the imagined fears that adults talk about, also came to life. It was as if people's fears and imaginations that were steeped in evil had become enlivened and I'd entered this dimension where I could see it. It felt like I'd stepped into a dark dimension of evil energy and was able to witness them all.

As I moved through this, I felt myself constricted in a tunnel where these shadows, energies and images were coming towards me to frighten me. But they couldn't touch me; they couldn't do anything to me.

Terrified to stay in the horrific space, I felt something slowly lifting me in an upward motion. There was more of an opening, and my surroundings became lighter. I slowly moved away from the darkness towards an open space with much more light. At the time, I saw four beings of light by my side moving upwards with me. The darkness fell away, as did the fear. Their faces were not distinguishable, but there was ease, peace, safety and an overwhelming feeling I can only describe as ecstatic Love combined with perhaps stillness.

This 'Love' was palpable, surrounding me. The 'Love' was an energy field that I could feel, touch and experience. It wasn't necessarily coming from any one of the angels, it was like being in an ocean of pure Love. It penetrated every fiber of my being and yet it also felt like it was my being. The Love field was everywhere. Then, I remember lying flat and floating in the air. I clearly saw myself in a physical body, but it looked and felt ethereal. I could see myself and I could feel myself both at the same time. I was surrounded by beings of light; there were many all around me.

I found myself experiencing peace. I was feeling safe and floating in this realm while all these angels were around me. I felt as if I was just absorbing all the love, taking it and basking in it. And all the light beings around me were just there, supporting me. They seemed to be attending to me and paying attention to what my body was doing, or perhaps my state. All the previous emotions were being washed away, transformed and there was no trace of any discomfort left.

This love and bliss that I felt was unlike anything I'd experienced on Earth. In that state, there was nothing to worry about, there was nothing to think about, it was just a blissful state of love.

After a short while of the floating experience, I heard a voice speak to me. The voice had no specific location, and yet it emanated from everywhere around and above me. It was soothing, understanding, and spoke words I didn't want to hear. It was a male voice, I heard.

It said to me: "My child, you cannot stay here, you must go back, it's not your time yet." Even though the voice was pleasantly soothing, my body quivered at the impact of the words and the realization I had to return to the place that I associated with fear. It was as if He was telling me that I had to return to the place of monsters, anxiety, fear and helplessness, which was essentially what I experienced on Earth most of the time. I felt panicked, I was stunned, and it took me some time to grasp the meaning of what I was being told. I resisted and remember asking again: 'But why?' Only I didn't ask it, I thought it. And the answer came from the voice again, "It's not your time," in a very loving compassionate transmission.

By then, I'd accepted that I couldn't stay and I felt devastated. I didn't want to leave the blissful state that felt so peaceful and loving. Even though I loved my mother very much, I was perfectly happy to stay exactly where I was. The beauty and love of that dimension was so enthralling and so complete that I was willing to let go of my previous life and everything I knew on Earth.

Thereafter, I began a slow and painful descent towards the Earth and into my physical body. I could see my body below me, and I could feel myself coming back into the heavy, thick energy of the planet. Even though I could see my physical body, I could also see my energetic body, which was the exact mirror copy, only not material. I could feel myself moving back into the reality, a very different reality than the one I was leaving. I quickly felt the constraints of my physical body along with the restriction of my circumstances. My body was constricted within a tiny space, immovable with intense pressure all around. This dimension felt dark, denser and harsh.

Shortly, thereafter, I remember running out of the vehicle and going towards my mother and aunt. By that time the sun had come out and it was early sunrise. Afterwards, there was a short ambulance ride that felt surreal, with me lying down again, as the abrupt sounds and movements of the vehicle overwhelmed my senses and mind. It all continued to feel surreal, moving from an experience of all-encompassing love, to the restrictions of being in a physical body on Earth. At the hospital, it was all a blur. I don't recall much of what was done there, but I do recall standing and trying to reach the tall counter after being released without any signs or symptoms of injury.

I do believe I was in shock as I didn't speak for a solid two weeks after that incident. I had no way of communicating my experience of alternate realities, nor did I feel safe speaking about it. Time went on, and although I had the recollection of the accident it-self, I unconsciously buried the memories of the near-death experience (NDE). It would be 35-years-later when I would have my first glimpse of the NDE memories. During meditation one day, the memories spontaneously began to resurface, little by little and without warning. The timing was significant, I was at a cross roads in my life, separated and considering divorce, it was a traumatic time, in which I dug deep to bring to the surface any dysfunctional patterns that were contributing to my current situation. I never imagined this near-death experience was buried there all along, but to my sur-prise, I was successful in finding this core piece.

In retrospect, I realize that the fear and terror of that experience lingered within me throughout my whole life, merging with every fiber of my being. When the suppressed memories of my NDE resurfaced, many symptoms accompanied these memories that were manifested expressions of fear in my body. The experience of these symptoms is usually referred to as post-traumatic stress disorder (PTSD) in the psychological med-ical community. I knew they were energetic memories that needed to be voiced, wit-nessed, acknowledged and reintegrated into my consciousness. The fear of dying was so traumatic for me to face that I buried it, until I had the courage to deal with it, many years later.

I believe that many of us bury traumas in our psyche because we don't have the under-standing of the deeper truth of our being, or we aren't spiritually strong enough to face some strong issues that question our life and who we are. Sometimes, we need time to detangle ourselves from our attachments to those things we think are absolutely true; who we think we are, what is safe for us, what greater power is and what God is, in order to release and dissolve the old beliefs about oneself. Sometimes, if we're too attached to the old beliefs with a solid foundation of our spiritual reality, facing old trauma can be challenging. Therefore, building our foundation of light is the first critical step in al-lowing our traumas to dissolve. Being awakened and grounded in our spiritual nature allows us to safely detach from those illusions that undoubtedly keep us stuck in pain and suffering.

Before I became aware of my near-death experience, fear had been a center theme in my life. Growing up, there seemed to be fear all around me. My family, immigrants from Cuba, felt there was no safety anywhere. There was always a great level of hyper-vigi-lance and lack of safety that determined everything we did, from where we went to how we did things. Perhaps, my families' experience of being in an unsafe country, fearing prosecution to some degree, could've contributed to this constant level of fear within us. Nonetheless, on many levels, fear was also what I associated the planet with and why I didn't want to come back.

When I became aware of the memories of my NDE, my body began to express this cellular fear. It was as if the fear had to be released, but it soon began to de-stabilize my body, creating a terrifying experience for me. My fear manifested into anxiety/panic attacks and deregulated my adrenals, nervous system, endocrine system, immune system and heart. I began experiencing terrible episodes of palpitations, irregular heartbeats, panic attacks, adrenal crises; auto-immune values shot up, my thyroid levels skyrocketed, my energy level plummeted and I had recurring obsessive thoughts of dying at any moment. My blood pressure became increasing unstable; I walked around feeling like I was going to faint all the time; my nervous system was fragile, and I would spontaneously shake uncontrollably at any given time. At one point, I looked in the mirror and I was dissolving, feeling transparent and not solid. Most of the time, I felt like I was in a dream, maybe a nightmare, where I was disconnected from my body, and this body didn't know who I was. And of course, I didn't feel safe, at all.

My thoughts were completely focused on my powerlessness and the fact that anything could happen to cause the loss of my life at any time. Under the spell of fear, I felt powerless, worthless and most of all, I criticized my vulnerabilities constantly. I judged myself for not being able to just let go of the fear, turn away, and stop listening. Most of all, I judged myself for having all the physical symptoms and not being able to heal them immediately. My thoughts of fear and powerlessness were consuming me every minute of every day.

A deep process of transformation was taking place, and it was clear that in many ways the deep fear that hadn't had a chance to be integrated at the time of the NDE was surfacing with immense intensity. During that time, I continued to engage in transformational healing work and integrative medicine practices in an attempt to move through these illusionary, yet very real processes that I found myself in.

Today most people that find themselves suffering in this way would immediately resort to quieting their symptoms through western medication. Our bodies our continuously evolving and yet many times we are too quick to label ourselves with a diagnosis that isn't a fixed state, but rather a transformational healing crisis. If we feel sad or unmotivated, we quickly label ourselves as depressed, not hesitating to take a pill for it. If we have a pain in our bodies, we quickly spring for the pain medication. If we feel fear or anxiety, we end up at our doctor's office asking for anxiety medication. We must understand that our body processes our emotions and repressed pain through our physical biology, and these symptoms may be exactly what is needed to break free from the constrictions of the past. Yet taking a pill stops the healing and releasing process within the body, locking our physical biology in a downward spiral of dysfunction and dependency.

At that time, fear was affecting and destabilizing every aspect of my body and taking conventional medication would've halted the transformational process that was in play. I instead needed to allow the fear and the symptoms to run their course while I continued the healing process. This was an opportunity for these deep-rooted patterns of fear to be witnessed and dissolved as my very own being continued to be purified of the old conditions of powerlessness, fear and shame within the trauma of my past.

I didn't disassociate from fear; my fear receptors were turned to a high level, detecting every single molecule that vibrated ever so slightly with the resemblance of fear. And so, it was. In my experience, I associated coming back to the Earth, as coming back to the state of fear. There wasn't a magic switch I could turn on or off, because to me, if I was living on this plane, I was in the fear, and there was no escaping it. So, this became the query for me... how do I experience my true light of love in this level here on Earth, where we're immersed in a dimension of fear and darkness? How do I deal with this fear? What is this fear teaching me? Why do we have fear here? And what about that experience of light and love in my body- is that something I can access?

This transformational process of fear through my physiological, emotional and mental body went on for about eight years, two of which were extremely intense. This is what many call a dark night of the soul. After many years of healing, I've finally come out the other side, with a deep understanding of fear. My body is no longer in panic, and the destabilization that fear caused in my body has been healed. There were some other physiological factors that contributed to the overall de-stabilizing of my body, but that is another story. All in all, through my experience I was able to see how deeply fear can manifest as a physical, mental, emotional and spiritual crisis in our bodies and become the lens through which we experience life.

Nonetheless, this experience took time for me to integrate in my being. Out of the many teachings of wisdom that it has given me, there are a few that stand out. First, I realized that I'd always been looking for that experience of light and love, something beyond the pervading fear. This wasn't because I had read it somewhere, or had learned it going to church every Sunday, no, this experience was in the deep recesses of spiritual memory, as it lives on in everyone's memories and DNA. It was a blessing to have tapped into that dimension of all-pervasive light of Love' early on and have it guide me.

Secondly, this experience forced me to transform my relationship with being on Earth and fear. It forced me to also confront and heal my feelings of abandonment and rejection, experienced when I was told to come back. My feelings of rejection when I was told I had to return, were not really rejection, it was a challenge. Like most people, I'd not experienced that kind of love on this plane, and so in reality, returning back to this plane, forcing me to move through the veils of fear and find the love here, was exactly the medicine I needed to heal the separation and rejection I had of being incarnated here. Eventually I was able to awaken to that blissful light within myself again, here on this plane and release my resistance and perception of only seeing fear on the planet. The belief that, that blissful state of consciousness was only possible in heaven was completely dissolved, replaced by the access to the eternal transcendent nature of our divine nature. The reality is that that blissful state of oneness is within every one of us, and I needed to come back to learn that.

Lastly, it has become my passion to share this truth with everyone I can and allow it to awaken within you, so that you too can recover your own power, love and bliss, while living on this plane harmoniously in your body. Through the avenues of spiritual healing and inner focus of connecting to our sacred Essence, I've been fortunate to break through the veil of fear and experience this reality here, in an embodied way, and I believe that everyone can awaken to this Truth. This is what healing is; the spiritual alchemy of dissolving the illusion of what we think we and arriving at the inherent Light of who we really are. I truly believe we can all access our divine light, the Essence of who we are, and break through the confines of fear, pain and suffering.

FEAR AS A TEACHER

Fear is a great teacher, probably has offered one of my most profound teachings. Even though fear brought out many intense feelings with seemingly challenging aspects, it has awakened me to a whole new reality.

Challenge comes into our lives so that we can awaken to something new, expand our consciousness and surpass our current state. Challenge forces us to break through the barriers that stand in the way of greater awareness and thus, greater levels of unconditional love. It has the potential to make us more conscious if we can learn from it. In the case of fear, we can begin to understand that fear lives in our minds and that it stems from a belief, learned judgement in our perceptual reality. It is the label we give to a set of energetic sensations that we associate with the meaning of 'fear'.

Fear moves us into the direction of Oneness, by making visible the layers of conditioning patterns that have disconnected us from our true Essential Self. Our Essential Self is the aspect of us that is Divine and carries the unconditional qualities of peace, beauty, love and much more. Fear has a way of bringing up old wounds and shadows surfacing as anxiety, obsessive thoughts, worries, concerns, etc. Through fear, our erroneous survival-based perceptions of inadequacy, powerlessness, shame and separation begin to make themselves known. Fear forces us to find a new way and confront the mental constructs which have kept these old patterns of separation and pain in their place.

Fear humbles us. It makes us realize that we really don't know everything and that we are vulnerable. It is this very vulnerability that continues to dissolve our egoic nature and lays us at the feet of our Divine Oneness within. When we are faced with our own mental limitation and surrender to the unknown, we are cracked open to the miraculous transcendent experience of who we are.

Fear appears as the challenge, but in reality, it is teaching us where we are in separation and how limited our thinking is, which creates our experience of fear itself. Fear shows us what thought or emotion is ready to be transformed and what needs to be transmuted for our highest potential. Many aspects of our Self that has forgotten the truth are in fear, which is the state of most of humanity. Fear guides us step by step, illuminating the aspects of ourselves that are ready to be transformed by the spiritual alchemy of transmutation. Richard Rudd says this about fear, "these fears lie deep within the body's immune system and create the matrix for all human initiation into higher states. It is precisely your passage through these fears that allows you to gain access to the higher levels of frequency and realization.[1]

Another aspect of fear is that it is actually just a vibration that comes into our bodies through our thoughts. It can be felt as a sensation that we label or give meaning to. We can separate the vibrational sensation from the meaning and just allow ourselves to feel the vibration throughout our body, bringing love and compassion to it. Sometimes it is easier to do this with a healer, because the fear can be so overwhelming, but nonetheless becoming aware of fear as a vibration allows us to loosen ourselves from its disempowering grip and transcend it. We will explore several practical ways to unravel fear in this way, throughout the chapters.

It is completely possible and imperative at this time that we begin to unravel and heal from the field of personal and collective fear that we have been living in. Freeing ourselves from this illusive state awakens us into the power and magnificence of our Being. This is the great change that our Universe is going through at this time, through each one of us.

AN EPIDEMIC OF FEAR

Many women unconsciously live with fear ruling their psyches in one way or another. Since the advent of religious reform and the patriarch, collective fear of survival has caused much fear in women, in which the effects are still felt today. Added to these unconscious fears are the repressive, violent, external threats many women are still exposed to in parts of the world, such as violence or sexual assault, rape, etc. Statistics from 1 Billion Rising Organization show that one in every three women will be raped or affected by violence in their lifetime. That adds up to about one billion women in the world of seven billion. Living with these tragic states adds to the collective culture of fear that inadvertently continues to affect all aspects of our Being.

Due to the repressive themes infiltrated by the reform of the patriarchy that we live in, as women, we have had to hide much of ourselves in order to feel safe, which in general, has produced great fear within our psyches. This collective fear has been passed down through our culture, whether it's conscious or unconscious, and has forced women to deny a great part of who they are in order to survive in a world of patriarchy.

In the times of the inquisition, with religious fervor strongly governing the minds and behaviors of those in authority, women were judged as heretics or witches, just for displaying their innate intuition, divine wisdom or connection with nature. We had to hide a great aspect of ourselves for survival. From generation to generation we've received the message that being who we are naturally isn't safe. Our grandmothers and ancestors knew that our survival was in question if we openly displayed our feminine qualities of intuition, gentleness, compassion, nature loving, sacredness, sexuality, direct knowing and gnosis, divination abilities and spiritual alchemy. We were in danger if we used our innate ability to see, to know, and to connect with the Divine. We were unsafe if we dared to use our sexuality and sensuality, combined with our alchemical process of transformation that lives within. All these things were: "concerns that could be interpreted as betrayal to the powers and law of the day, leading to being tortured, burned at the stake, or even beheaded." In the eyes of the authority at that time, these were all heretic or even demonic behaviors which when exposed threaten our lives. For survival, we hid these parts of ourselves, knowingly or unknowingly, under great layers of fear. In other words, we disowned these parts of ourselves, with grave consequences, which have contributed to many levels of separation and suffering.

In western countries, we have become highly functional women in a culture that doesn't outwardly seem a threat to us anymore. And yet, we're still suffering the effects of this collective repression of our feminine qualities (spiritual nature). This repression and fear-based conditioning has wreaked havoc within us and is evident in the sufferings of our body, health and happiness.

In women, this suffering ranges from minor discomforts to greater disorders both physically, emotionally and spiritually. Most of these disharmonies have been viewed as something that we must medicate in order to survive, but, medicating and ignoring the symptoms only emphasizes the problem by continuing the cycle of repression. As a western country, we have an epidemic of treating these disharmonies, solely as a physical medical condition, when in fact, it's a disharmony of our spirit. It's the result of our disconnection with our own inner Essence and thus a necessary aspect of our evolutionary spiritual process. If we want to evolve and heal these imbalances that show up in ourselves, we need to stop repressing them and allow them to surface to the light.

Here in the US, we recognize stress as a major cause of illness. In 1994, it was reported by Perkins, in the Harvard Business Review, that up to 90% of all doctor's visit were for stress-related ailments and complaints. That leaves a small amount of illness that is not related to fear, or better yet, has not been found to be related to fear at this time.

The stress that so easily manifests as disease, disharmony, or discomfort, is the cry of the repressed Feminine signaling us for help. This is the intelligence of our body exhibiting the signs of being out of rhythm and out of sync. When we continue to medicate ourselves, and reject the voice of the Feminine within us, we perpetuate the suffering of these conditioned patterns. Rather than listening and communicating with ourselves, we have become a nation that uses medication to subdue our inner voice and wisdom. We have become accustomed to rejecting and silencing ourselves, if not physically, then perhaps emotionally and spiritually.

According to the National Institute of Mental Health, about 40 million American adults have some type of anxiety disorder, and these are just the ones that have been diagnosed. Everything from phobias, to panic attacks and even low-level anxiety show up under the label of anxiety disorders, which we've all too comfortably become accustomed to living with. It's documented that 65% of Americans take drug medications daily, and out of that, 43% are mood altering prescriptions, usually related to some type of anxiety/depression disorder. When we consider that women are affected at an average of 3.5%-10% more by anxiety and fear related disorders than men, we can affirm that women are experiencing greater fear than men. Furthermore, 11% of women between the ages of 45-64 were on anti-anxiety medication in 2010, nearly twice their male counterparts, which again attests to the rate of suppression and the intensity of suffering underneath it all.

This high level of anxiety that is experienced by so much of our population is continuously fueled by conscious or unconscious fear. Fear creates various physiological changes in our body. When we feel fear, our bodies respond by releasing hormones to help us survive, for example, by sharpening our eyesight and slowing down digestion. Our heart rate increases, and our bodies prepare for flight or fight. More importantly, the presenting danger is stored in our memory by changes in the amygdala. This process may account for the collective fear that is experienced by so many women, manifesting in our higher anxiety levels.

Fear can interrupt processes in our brains that regulate emotions, which in turn impacts our thinking and decision-making, and confuses our judgments of discerning whether the danger is real or not. Therefore, the survival threat may be something that we continuously perceive, due to our history but may not necessarily be a present threat. Fear causes damage to the hippocampus part of our brain, which in turn creates difficulty in regulating fear itself. This damage may cause a person to live with fear all the time, interpreting all circumstances through the filter of fear, thus constantly affecting every aspect of their being.

Living with fear, or a constant threat of it, whether real or imagined, may weaken our immune system, digestive system or reproductive system; contributing to fatigue, depression, anxiety, ulcers, autoimmune issues, gut dysbiosis, digestive imbalances, and many other disharmonies. Emotionally, fear is experienced in many ways, including feeling out of control, chronic low-level anxiety, feelings of inadequacy, or low self-esteem, insecurity, difficulty managing pressure, unrealistic expectations of one self, unhealthy boundaries, deep unhappiness, quick to anger, irrational emotional behaviors, feeling unsettled, overwhelmed and detached from reality. Women have been known to have a higher rate of anxiety, panic disorder and PTSD (post-traumatic stress disorder) in comparison to men.

Many of those disharmonies come from the effects of Fear's disruption on our endocrine and nervous system. Through the disruption of the endocrine system we see the effects in autoimmune disorders, reproductive disorders, thyroid disorders, digestive disorders and, of course, anxiety and depression. Our endocrine system encompasses glands and hormones, which are the 'master switches' to our bio-chemical production and homeostasis within our body. The hormones secreted by these glands regulate the activity of cells and organs in our body, releasing the chemical signals that coordinate a range of bodily functions. I've use the term '*1st world feminine disorders*' for these disorders of the endocrine/nervous system that have become so common in the western women. These include reproductive disorder; gut disorders; auto-immune disorders; nervous system disorders (anxiety) and emotional disorders (depression). At the root of these '*1st world feminine disorders*' lies the root cause of the disconnection from our spiritual essence. And as our disconnection grows greater, we, unfortunately, see the epidemics of these disorders flourishing in our western culture.

According to Dr. Bruce Lipton's work in epigenetics, the cells in our bodies are either responding to fear or love. If they're responding to fear, there are biochemical reactions that happen, in which the hormones and blood are directed towards the peripheral of our bodies and our viscera system functions. When this happens, we see digestion and immune functions shut down for us to prepare for a fight or flight response. Therefore, the regular functions of digestion, immune and other systems are compromised when we're in fear.

If we consider the chronic fear that we've been in collectively, we can begin to understand the devastating, extensive damage of this collective fear on our physical systems. From this viewpoint, the perception of fear, whether real in this moment, or in the past, is modulating what our cells are doing at every moment and how much energy is available to do those things. Because we continue to perpetuate the fear unconsciously, our bodies continue to navigate this continuous assault and, consequently, continue to deteriorate. Fear uses up energy and robs it from our biological needs.

As women, whether we've had personal trauma or not, we're all collectively carrying this vibration of fear, affecting our body via the endocrine system. Furthermore, it's also affecting our behavior and our emotional wellbeing. Some of us are aware of it; some of us project it outside ourselves onto our beloveds, our government, or our outer world, but nonetheless, we're under its effects.

In the U.S. our current collective fear factor has been augmented by the aftermath of the Sept 11th tragedy, in which Dr. Lipton states: "The fear that has been propagated in the United States since 9-11 has had a profoundly destructive effect upon the health of our citizens. Every time the government advertises concerns of more terror attacks, the fear alone causes stress hormones to shut down our biology and engage in a protection response."[2]

Furthermore, with the political climate that we have been seeing, after the 2016 elections in the US, it's safe to say that now, more women and minority groups are feeling an increase in fear and stress, as they continue to hear subtle threats to their own survival by the significant political decisions being made. It seems that the overall threat of repression and chaos in our own country has been resurrected. As more Americans begin to live in an environment that threatens their very own existence, our collective fear of the past becomes compounded by live threats of the present. Undoubtedly, this unpredictable situation activates the underlying collective fear, even more.

A lot of our fear and anxiety may turn into a high level of panic, which can happen when least expected and without obvious provocation. Many times, as in my case, a panic attack can happen randomly, and not induced by any specific thoughts. Sometimes, the panic attacks are experienced through sudden flashbacks and the reliving of a traumatic memory, as in post-traumatic stress disorder, PTSD. For me, I constantly experienced physical symptoms of dying that were unconsciously triggered by my near-death experience at the age of seven. These experiences came without any warning and were not due to any conscious thought of fear. It was a physical, biological reaction, in reaction to an unconscious memory that would spontaneously sound the alarms and begin disrupting my biology. My body would react with a fight or flight response by increasing the amounts of adrenalin in my body and shutting down circulation to my internal organs, creating numbness, dizziness, rapid heart rate along with feelings of fear and terror. This is what unexpected panic or fear can do, without much notice for preparation.

If one repeatedly feels anxious and stressed due to fear, or if the effects last a long time, your body may not be able to recover to its original state of relaxation, safety and creates a new norm of anxiety as its base line. This was also my experience in dealing with fear, and through my work with so many women, I also see that as a society, this high level of anxiety is our new norm. We're constantly on the go and continue to be propelled by this level of unconscious fear.

Anxiety, as the manifestation of fear, can affect many other aspects of our body. According to Harvard Medical school, there's clearly a connection between our gut, stress and anxiety. In this publication, Harvard Medical School delineates the correlation between stress and physical illness, which includes some of these details; the connection between high, stressful anxiety and the development of irritable bowel syndrome (IBS), anxiety disorders causing loss of appetite and lack of interest in sex, anxiety increasing the risk of diabetes, high blood pressure, heart disease and coronary events.[3]

Fear, thus anxiety, creates tension and contraction in our bodies, which explains a lot of the physiological damage, including overall body pain, muscle tension and headaches, to name a few. Lower back pain is one of the most common pains that is experienced by Americans in general. According to statistics compiled by www.thegoodbody.com, it's alarming to note that lower back pain is more common in females than in males, with nearly 1/3 of females experiencing back pain as opposed to ¼ of males. And statistics show that nine out of ten patients never know their primary cause. Of course, if they're only looking for a fix on the physical level, they may never realize how much of their underlying fear and anxiety is contributing to the manifestation of the lower back pain.

BREAKING THROUGH THE VEIL OF FEAR

When we experience fear, the brain short circuits its usual way of processing information and begins reacting to the fear we're experiencing. In these situations, the brain perceives the events happening around the fear as negative and categorizes durable memories of these events as 'fear inducing'. We could say that our brain gets rewired for fear, and the events that are connected to the moment of experiencing fear also become triggers for fear in general. For example, the sights, sounds and whatever is happening around you when you're experiencing fear becomes part of the negative stimuli that will continue to elicit a fear response, whenever you come across those circumstances, regardless of the details. In psychological- physical terms, we call this Post Traumatic Stress Disorder (PTSD), in which people react to the events around the original fear-inducing situation, regardless of whether there is an actual threat in the current situation. In other words, if you fear lightening and it usually happens when it's raining, you may start panicking when its starts raining and not know why.

We must understand that women have been experiencing fear for thousands of years, around their own survival, even though it may be unconscious. This fear is in what we call the collective energy field. Therefore, many of the actions that are made daily may have its motivations rooted in deep collective fear of the past. For example, speaking in public might trigger reactions in our body of feeling unsafe, or as if our life is in danger, and perhaps the old collective unconscious memories may be flooding us, because at one time, collectively, speaking our truth would've put our lives in danger. It's understandable as to why we may get a gnawing feeling in the pit of our stomachs when we have to say something unpopular in front of a group.

Many events in our lives might have unconscious, unwarranted reactive fear responses, in which we cannot understand why we feel so helpless or so powerless. I want to propose that this underlining fear that we experience, whether its feelings of terror, anxiety, butterflies in the pit of your stomach, or plain nervousness, are mostly related to the collective field of fear we all share as women. Understanding that our brains may still be reacting to a time when our lives were in danger for speaking up, being ourselves, having an opinion, saying no, or expressing ourselves as an integrate part of the Divine, (in our power). All these experiences were causes of fear of death for our ancestors, and in many less fortunate parts of the world, still are. By rejecting fear, itself, through our rejection of the manifestations within us, we continue to propagate the rejection and repression of ourselves in our consciousness.

FEAR TRANSLATED THROUGH OUR ENDOCRINE AND NERVOUS SYSTEM

By taking a closer look at our endocrine and nervous system response to fear, we begin to see how we have been affected, thus allowing an opening for us to detangle from the web of fear I would like to delineate some of the functions of these two systems, so that we may see what the connections are with our endocrine system and the manifesting disorders rampant in us women, today.

The endocrine system is a system of glands that secrete hormones that act as messengers. Many of us think of hormones as our sexual hormones: progesterone, testosterone, estrogen and such, but our hormones aren't limited to our sex hormones, nor are they limited to any stage in life. Throughout varying stages in our life, i.e. puberty or menopause for example, they will shift and change, but remain active in our system, as we will see.

There are many different types of hormones and each hormone has a specific job to do, which in turn controls the chemical reactions in our body and the functions of our organ systems. These hormones act as messengers between the glands, signaling the varying hormonal responses of the glands themselves. Factors that stabilize the body, such as temperature and blood pressure, along with metabolism, are some of the foundational responsibilities of the endocrine system.

The endocrine system is created to respond to external stresses or to perceived external threats. Through this connection to the response of real or perceived stress, we begin to see how unconscious fear, may in fact, affect the delicate balance of our endocrine system, thus wreaking all sorts of havoc within our system.

DIAGRAM OF FEMALE ENDOCRINE SYSTEM

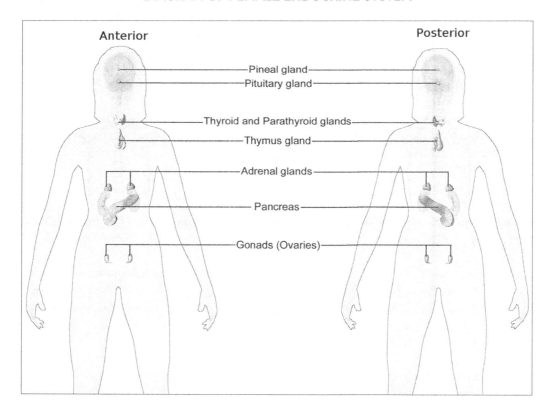

When there is perceived stress, the nervous system and the endocrine system create a coordinated response to insure your survival. When it perceives a stress response, the nervous system sends information to the hypothalamus about the stress response, which engages both the nervous system and the endocrine system. Flight or fight is a response from both systems, which creates the survival stress response in our bodies.

Our nervous system consists of the sympathetic and the parasympathetic systems, which regulate the flight or fight response, as well as the relaxation response. Together, these two systems, endocrine and nervous, react to real or perceived stress., which increases heart rate, affects gut function and inhibits digestion, increases sleeplessness, increases anxiety, inhibits the liver, kidneys and gall bladder and is generally debilitating and exhausting to your physical, mental and emotional body. Together, these two systems are connected to every single cell and action in your body, thus influencing its reactions at all times.

We must understand that either the sympathetic or the parasympathetic system can be turned on at any given time. So, if the sympathetic 'survival' system is on, the parasympathetic 'safety' system is off. The sympathetic system is the system that immediately responds to any perceived stress, bringing mostly blood and adrenaline to our extremities, in order to survive. It's our survival response. Our parasympathetic, which is repressed during stressful conditions, has the opposite effect; it releases relaxation hormones like serotonin and endorphins. Due to the chronic levels of collective fear held in our bodies, we end up with a new norm of chronic stress, which has the sympathetic nervous system fully engaged, to mitigate the stress. If we don't stop and try to engage with the parasympathetic system, we continue to experience the destructive forces of fear in our system, leaving us on guard all the time. Therefore, taking the time to disengage our sympathetic system consciously, while we cultivate our spiritual essence, is a vital important step to healing. When we take time out to relax, disengage, take a walk or smell the roses, we unwind our responses and engage the relaxation response in the body through the parasympathetic nervous system. When we continue to work nonstop and continue the flooding of our mental worrying and strategizing, we continue to deplete ourselves through the engagement of our sympathetic nervous system.

When we encounter an event outside of ourselves, the brain will determine whether it perceives it as danger of not... which of course is completely subjective to our memories. Whatever incidents we may have experienced in our lifetime, or collectively through our ancestors, our brain may register them and any associating pattern as dangerous, even though they may pose no threat in the present. In a simplified explanation, the brain sends a signal to the pituitary gland (master gland) who's function sets up the protection for your body. The pituitary gland release ACTH which alerts the adrenal glands to respond to 'fight or flight' hormones of adrenaline and cortisol, which in turn constricts the blood in the viscera, raises heart rate and directs the blood to the arms and legs. All these stress responses are happening moment to moment, within our body, and sometimes with little awareness from our conscious mind. Furthermore, this continued stress response not only leads to the above responses we mentioned, but also continues to increase immune reaction, dysfunction of the reproductive system, under or over functioning thyroids, as well as chronic low levels of depression and anxiety on a daily basis. This is the underlying cause of the '*1st world feminine disorders*' I mentioned earlier.

There is an accumulation of this collective fear that has settled in the glands of our endocrine systems, which correlate with the seven-chakra system of Ayurvedic medicine. In subsequent chapters, I've included ways in which to heal these glands and our endocrine system, breaking through the collective conditioning patterns that may be affecting you.

Furthermore, the '*1st world feminine disorders*' are the direct physical result of the overworked nervous and endocrine systems, as they've attempted to adapt to our system of fear. This is the result of our bodies attempt to mitigate and navigate the collective and personal fear inundation and survival responses that we're still carrying around in our psyche. It's through this field of fear that we've lost our rhythm and have been disconnected from our true spiritual source of regeneration. I will further discuss this loss of rhythm in chapter four, along with the ways to restore and align our rhythm again, in order to be constantly nourished, rather than depleted. Nonetheless, healing our nervous system, thus our endocrine system, is critical in our journey of changing the collective story. This is the journey of unplugging from our participation in the narrative of the ever-growing '*1st world feminine disorder*' epidemic, to living as sovereign beings in connection with our true Essence and our birth right of innate healing and health, unconditional love and blissful joy.

THREE COLLECTIVE WOUNDS OF THE FEMININE

Energetically speaking, our collective fear has given rise to the three main wounds of the Feminine: Powerlessness, Shame and Abandonment, which respectively manifest in the three, lower power centers of our body. These gateway centers of solar plexus, sacral and root have traditionally been misunderstood and regarded as less important than the upper power centers of the heart, throat, third eye and crown. But these lower centers, also known as chakras in our subtle body, are the key to embodying the Feminine in our physical body, and thus our sacredness. It's here, in the lower centers, where the collective story of fear has been stored for thousands of years and is still dictating our physical, mental, emotional and spiritual subtleties, in many ways.

As the collective fear seeps into these lower centers, blocking our own vital energy and levels of consciousness; we begin to see the wounds of powerlessness, shame and abandonment organizing through these gateways, respectively. Because these lower chakra centers give rise to our physical, emotional and spiritual disorders, we can see how impactful they are in holding the vibration of the old collective story of Feminine suffering.

In most spiritual cultures, the emphasis is on the upper power centers of the heart, throat, third eye and crown, deeming these as 'the spiritual centers' and somehow more important. But, the lower centers of the root, sacral and solar plexus, carry the secrets of anchoring our light bodies within our physical form, thus facilitating blissful levels of embodied consciousness within our physical body. It's our lower body that facilitates the union of our duality consciousness; Light energy and physical form, enabling Divine realization in our physical body. It's impossible for us to evolve our being to the highest levels of consciousness without bringing those lofty levels down into our physical body and the lower centers. This is what anchors the light and permits us to embody it, transmit it and be it. After all, we are on the physical plane of form.

As a process of the demonization and repression of the Feminine, we've associated the lower chakras with the 'lesser quality' which also relates to seeing our body, our emotional body and our sexuality as less important than the spiritual Essence of light. However, the truth is that everything contains light, even the manifested form we see with our eyes is spiritual and sacred. It's our form itself that allows us to feel and experience divinity on this plane. To continue to make a separation and label our form and our bodies somehow less than our spiritual nature, is in fact, seeing things from a distorted paradigm of separation. It's time to redeem the Feminine, as She is a representation of these vital aspects of ourselves, and in doing so, restore the value of our bodies (form), sexuality, and emotions overall, because without this aspect of ourselves, we cannot evolve to the next level of awakened consciousness.

It's within our bodies where we can feel our primordial force and open to joy and fulfillment of our Light. Somehow, this split of spirit and body, where we regard our bodies less holy than our spirit, is a continuation of the rejection of the Feminine, in all her expressions. The path of the Feminine is to embody our spirituality and not leave out the body, because the body is where we feel our sacredness. Anchoring the higher light frequencies into our lower centers, rooted in our body, is how we can begin to truly embody heaven here on Earth. Doing so allows us to feel the frequencies of unconditional love, blissful joy, peace, and safety in our everyday life, not just while we're meditating or active in a spiritual practice.

So, for many women, this collective fear has become trapped in our subtle body, affecting our glands and our biochemistry. Each of these centers hold a pattern motivated by fear, which gives rise to pain, suffering and disharmonies we experience in our body; many manifesting as *1ˢᵗ world feminine disorders* and/or deep despair in our hearts and souls. Essentially, as women, most of our dis-ease and dysfunctions are correlated with the energetic quality in these three lower centers of our body, which comprise the *Three Collective Wounds of the Feminine*. I will expand on these *Collective Wounds of the Feminine* along with their power gateways, associated wounds and healing protocols in the following chapters, but here is a short synopsis explaining their matrix and how they manifest in women.

1ˢᵗ COLLECTIVE WOUND OF THE FEMININE: POWERLESSNESS

At the location of what we call our 'solar plexus', located between our heart and our umbilicus (belly button), we find the gathering of this collective fear manifesting as the wound of powerlessness. These unresolved emotional, mental and physical patterns that we, as women have accumulated, find themselves energetically gathered into what I call the primary collective wound of the Feminine; Powerlessness.

Now, we must understand that there are two factors that converge in each of these collective wounds; personal factors and collective experience. In our personal factors we find our history of unresolved pain and suffering, along with the survival patterns created to seemingly protect us from greater suffering. Secondly, we find the collective factors, a field in which all the experiences common to a group are gathered over time, and further continued as part of that group's experience. In our case, it's the collective experience that women, in general, have experienced due to social, political and religious degradation of their existence. Each of us holds a unique pattern of wounding in our solar plexus that consists of varying degrees of personal and collective wounding, depending on our history, upbringing, karma and other factors in our lineage. When we first become aware, it's common to spend most of our time transforming personal wounding, however, some of these are feel very intense and continue to appear over and over, sometimes indicating that we're working on much more than just our personal wound, but that of a collective nature.

Now, concerning this gateway of our collective powerlessness, the disconnection from our sacredness may be experienced as a loss of Self, an inability to know who we really are. Years of denying our feelings as women, and consistently adapting our behavior according to the acceptable norm, has created a deep loss of Self and a pattern of outer dependence for our safety. Eons of adaptation for our own survival has resulted in losing the sense of who we are. Unconsciously, we've come to value ourselves based on the reaction of others, because this is what has kept us safe in the past. If others like what we say, we feel safe. For many women, being met with disapproval still triggers deep residual patterns of feeling unsafe and even powerless. These are the remnants of the collective wounding that resides in our solar plexus. Many of us feel the deep emptiness that this disconnection with ourselves has created, leaving us exhausted, constantly living our lives according to the outer radar of other people's emotions. After a while, we may come face to face with an overwhelming sense of disappointment, which breaks open this impossible expectancy that we have been unconsciously tethered to. We may be feeling the deep level of exhaustion of unconsciously trying to keep everyone outside of ourselves 'happy' and content, for ourselves to feel safe enough to exist. We unconsciously give away our power and our sense of Self to everything around us, until life begins to awaken us from this pattern. An awakening may look like a deep realization that we're are unhappy, a deep sense of powerlessness, a deep sense of disappointment, or great exhaustion.

We can experience the matrix of this collective pattern as a sinking feeling of fear, generally in the pit of our stomachs accompanied by a feeling of being stuck. There may be thoughts of insecurity about our fate, ourselves and who we are. These fears may also manifest as hopelessness, preventing us from taking an action in a proactive way. This of course, further reinforces the victim mentality of unworthiness, powerlessness and utter resignation. We may have feelings of defeat, or just pure devastation, again, resorting to an outward focus to feel value and worth. We often attempt to sedate the intensity of this wound with behaviors that may become addictive, giving us only temporary relief from our souls yearning of reconnection with our Essence. Often foods, relationship, busyness, excessive work, constant need for money and physical focus on outer fulfillment give us enough distraction to avoid being devoured by our sense of powerlessness within.

In our society, we honor the greatest distraction of all: being busy. Constantly thinking about how to succeed, or about the future, keeps us out of our bodies and stuck in our minds. Ironically, continuing our focus on 'doing' continues to feed the desperation or emptiness from which the powerlessness arises, feeding into our deep sense of exhaustion, disappointment, dissatisfaction and low level of ongoing anxiety. Furthermore, the ongoing patterns of this wound have devastating effects in our adrenals, and our digestive system, contributing to much of the gut disorders, immune disorders, chronic fatigue, anxiety and depression, we see today.

What's the medicine? Ultimately, our solar plexus is reflective of our sense of power, and our sense of power is an internal recognition of the true sacredness of our being that's not reliant on any outward acknowledgment for its value or worth. Being able to unplug from all the outer sources that we've given our power away to and coming to solely rely on that which has created us, our source and essentially our Essence for the manifestations of our needs is also the medicine. However, much of this inner power has become occulted under the veils of unresolved survival patterns of fear. The medicine is to reestablish this connection so that we can feel our true sense of Self, rather than being distracted by the layers of noise that has disrupted this gateway. Our true power is sourced from a deep connection with something greater than our limited human nature, which is always constantly sustaining us. This is our true power; power in the realization and embodiment of our sacredness and divinity. Our solar plexus is the gateway that holds our relationship to power and when it's blocked and wounded, we experience the collective wound of powerlessness. However, when it's activated, it's the very place that holds the morphogenetic field that tunes us into the great expanse unlimited power of Creation, Herself. This is what is available when we step into the Sacred Initiation of Conscious Feminine Power, all detailed in chapter [7].

2ND COLLECTIVE WOUND OF THE FEMININE: SHAME

Here, in the location of the sacral gateway, three finger widths below our umbilicus, is the reflection of the accumulated collective wound of Shame. This stores the shared fear and blaming that women have been subjected to, projected onto their feminine physical form. This is the energetic convergence place for not only the shame we've been taught for having a feminine body, but also the judgements and criticism that has been born from that shame. This inner and outer criticism, and judgment layered with shame, blocks our creative force as our sexual energy (life force), in this womb sacral gateway. This sacral gateway organically contains the creative and manifesting potencies of Creation Herself, the essence of life, which again, has been repressed with this 2nd collective wound of the Feminine.

The fear matrix in this sacral gateway consists of emotional patterns of unworthiness, inadequacy and a deep sense of self-doubt. These patterns are constantly fueled by the underlying dogmatic religious ideology of blaming women for the sins of humanity (by the famous mythical eating of the apple and subjugation of Lilith in biblical texts), further fostering a culture of objectification of women's physical form, along with demonization of our sexuality. Women have been carrying this deep wound of shame for the last 5000+ years. Our bodies, being of feminine gender, have taken the fall for the world's evil, and even though we may not consciously believe this attitude outwardly, on the collective level, this conditioning is still operating, wreaking havoc within us.

Here in this collective wound of Shame, we experience the feelings that prevent us from speaking up, driven by constant inner self-criticism. This pattern is responsible for the constant self-deprecating and judgment that we measure ourselves by at times, projecting onto other women. It's also responsible for the confined, extreme, unrealistic standards we adhere our bodies to, judging our value from the collective dysfunctional fabricated ideology of the feminine body, rather than an organic emergence of our individual form. Our sacral wound forces us to constantly seek our physical value by how the shape of our body conforms to that outer ideal, further adding to the inner criticism and judgment, where we undoubtedly fall short.

This sacral wound encourages our patterns of co-dependency that originate in our solar plexus, continuing the spiraling of self-blame and victim mentality. Inherent in this sacral wound is the belief that we aren't worthy, we aren't capable, we aren't enough and we are inherently flawed, once again leaving us open to blame and hopelessness when some outer event doesn't happen as expected.

When our sacral gateway is blocked by the filters of dysfunction, we're disconnected from the wisdom inherent in our being. Essentially, we've cut ourselves off from our life force and our sexuality, the source of Creation, Herself. Our bodies are a barometer, helping us navigate through the outer world, by deeply listening to our sensations, feelings and the ability to 'feel' the resonant vibrations. This is an aspect of wisdom that intuits, senses and is experienced in our bodies. We carry the ability to tune into the subtle realms through our body. We're a vessel of that wisdom from oneness, always available to inform us, unless we've blocked this gateway with the calcified patterns of this collective wound of shame. When we have this gateway blocked, as many women do, we tend to function mainly from our minds, splitting ourselves off from the pain, but simultaneously from the wisdom in our lower body as well. This pattern of carrying much of our energy in our minds, tends to reinforce the restlessness and insecurity of not having safety, as well as not feeling truly grounded within our own bodies.

In ancient Indian cultures, women having their menses were separated from the men, in order to allow them space during this special 'dark moon' time, to deeply listen to their bodies and receive wisdom of divinatory messages. This is the wisdom inherent in our bodies, accessed through our sacral womb. There are three wombs or chambers in our bodies: the upper womb (mind), middle womb (heart & solar plexus) and sacral womb in our pelvic region. We're accustomed to functioning from the mind (upper womb), and some of us are open to the heart (center womb), but opening up to the sacral womb has been taboo in our culture. Rarely if ever, do we tune in to our sacral womb where the pain of shame, fear, rejection and repression of the feminine, has been hiding.

This disconnection from our life force, and from our sexuality in the sacral center, re-inforces the collective patterns of blame and shame that reside in our body. Our life force manifests as sexuality and pleasure in our bodies, but is also the vital energy that breathes life into all the processes in our body. Following in the unconscious footsteps of our collective culture, we've internalized the demonization of our sexual life force and cut ourselves off from the very source of life within us. Most of us live with such a decreased life force in our pelvic area that we've decreased our blood flow and oxygenation, creating the perfect breeding ground for reproductive diseases and disorders. Furthermore, we all feel this lack of joy and pleasure in life, which in turn further accentuates our behavior to turn to outer fixes for instant, if not fleeting, moments of fulfillment.

This sacral wounding has created an epidemic of reproductive dysfunctions resulting in a nation (US) with over 15% of women that are infertile, plus the 80% of women that experience pain with their menstrual cycle. In addition to that, if we consider the high rates of hormonal medications, plus environmental factors that act as endocrine disrupters, it's no surprise that breast cancer is the leading cause of death for women in the US, ages 35-54, with over 40,000 deaths a year (compared to automobile accidents at 26,000).

Ironically, when we experience dysfunctions in our bodies, we usually turn against our bodies, further blaming and rejecting ourselves, which in turn adds to the dysfunctional pattern of the sacral wound. When we erroneously believe that we're to blame, and that we're intrinsically damaged as a result of the body's manifestation of this wound, then we unconsciously continue to negate the truth of who we are as well as perpetuating this collective wound of the Feminine. It's our choice, whether we awaken to the force of our feminine Essence, allow the patterns of fear and survival, or whether we continue to live our lives in the grips of the claws of fear.

What's the Medicine? Opening to the sacredness and life force of our sacral womb and all that it has to offer is the medicine for this wounding. Recognizing our own self discrimination, our self-deprecating words, judgements, criticism and underlying unworthiness fuels this wounding. Becoming aware of the inner self-hate, self-rejection mentality and lovingly embracing these aspects of yourself, until the pain dissolves. Knowing that while we may have a lot to learn on the personality and human living aspect of our lives, our heart of heart... our Essential Self is pure... untouched and divine. We can take responsibility for the mistakes that we make, for the times that we lash out of fear and anger, but not because we're essentially inadequate, but because we've forgotten the true blueprint of Love that is our origin, our Essence, and because we've forgotten how to speak from that love, be that love and sometimes forget it is our responsibility to uphold ourselves to that greater standard... and own it. And through acknowledgement of our mistakes, which are based on limitations, we can expand into greater levels of our matrix of LOVE, and live, share and experience life and others through that.

The medicine demands us to reestablish the relationship we have with our body's, our feminine physical form, with our sexuality and thus with pleasure. It furthers requires us to re-establish our trust in being a vessel that's always guided by the visceral wisdom in our bodies, and our ability and/or willingness to connect and respond. Furthermore, this medicine demands us to acknowledge and honor the magnificence matrix of light that we are and live through that truth, reclaiming the virginity of our Essential Self. This is the Sacred Initiation of Conscious Feminine Body Wisdom you will find in chapter 7.

3ᴿᴰ COLLECTIVE WOUND OF THE FEMININE: ABANDONMENT / ILLUSION OF SEPARATION

Our root gateway is reflective of the wound of Abandonment and Separation. This area physically consists of our perineum, pelvic floor and surrounding anatomy, imbued with the deep collective fear of feeling separate. For most of us, our mental conceptual perception of our birth into this physical dimension, is generally construed as a separation from Source, and ultimately an abandonment. Witnessed solely from the material realm, this illusion of being separate causes us to adhere to this outer reliance, in the realm of duality, leading us to greater experiences of abandonment, insecurity and lack of safety. Here the collective fear of the unknown gathers, as the accumulated struggles of our existential realities concerning birth, death, separation and oneness are accumulated.

As women, this wound of abandonment is compounded by the lack of safety we have experienced in our gender. The collective rejection of the feminine has made its home here. This root wound holds the collective memories of our culture's disrespect, repression and abuses of the feminine, often felt as trauma and terror in our bodies, related to our physical safety on this plane. Due to the abuses of our historical past, there is great density in the fear matrix of this root gateway. Years of having to suppress our emotional and spiritual natures for safety have contributed greatly to this collective wounding.

We can see the manifestation of the collective root fears not only in the corresponding anatomy of our colon, perineum, cervix, vagina, pelvic floor, etc., but also in the destabilization of our immune system, contributing to auto-immune disorders and reproductive issues, including cancer.

Ultimately, this root wounding is layered with abandonment, fear of survival, trauma and terror. This wounding may arise as a pervasive fear of not feeling physically safe, generalized anxiety, or a feeling of disconnection and isolation from the world around us. The deep fear and trauma that's held here in this root wounding adds to our feelings of not belonging. Feelings of disconnection, feeling ungrounded, and not finding ground to settle into (whether emotionally or physically) may surface. Unfortunately, when these intense feelings of fear and terror begin to surface, we often tend to further reject and blame ourselves, due to the intensity of the feelings themselves. This in turn causes further layers of isolation and alienation.

This abandonment wound may be deeply hidden, only surfacing through trauma or life and death challenges. Sometimes, this wounding may arise when we're faced with an illness that threatens our physical life. The more disconnected we are from our non-physical form dimension (Essential Self) the more suffering we may experience through this wounding.

What's the Medicine? As human beings, we're forced to live here on this plane, in physical form. Our physical safety may not be guaranteed. However, when we open ourselves to the very force of creation within us we see that our deep security and safety is in that, because that cannot be taken away from us, even if we lose our physical form. In turn, when we aren't aware of the dimension within us that lives on, it may feel very disturbing, if not terrifying to think that we just come to an end. That terror is what is accumulated there, years and generations of terror living as victims because we've been disconnected from our true Essence.

The answer is simple, we must cultivate a relationship with the unknown and trust in the mystery of life. The truth is that this mystery has given us life and that life force is what animates us. In the same way it provides for us exactly what we need on this mysterious journey we call life. Awakening and embodying our Essence, which is really this consciousness of Source, is our safety... it is our connection... and it is how we realize our oneness with all of life, Herself.

SUFFERING AS AN EVOLUTIONARY FORCE

Wanting to end world suffering has always been one the motivating forces behind my work. But somewhere along the path I realized it isn't about ending the suffering, because suffering plays a very important role in our evolution. It's about evolving the suffering... or better yet, letting the suffering evolve us. This is the role of the Sacred Initiations, but first let's unpack suffering itself.

My relationship with 'suffering' has deepened in the last thirty years, as I've have committed myself to transformation both in my personal life and professionally with my patients. And as revealed by spiritual truths, I discovered that suffering is a paradox. While suffering may look like the destructive force that breaks us down and causes us pain, it's the force that empowers us. Suffering is truly an evolutionary power; let's take a deeper look.

In the first stage of suffering we recognize it as an experience in which 'something' hasn't met our predetermined expectation, or the result is different than what we expected, whether conscious or unconsciously. This event may be challenging to us emotionally (evoking unpleasant feelings), mentally (challenging our pre-conceived idea of what 'should' be) or physically (outer circumstances are different than what we expect). There's usually some pain experienced on one or more of these levels, associated with the first stage of suffering.

In the second stage of suffering, we create a meaning from our perception of suffering and identify ourselves mentally with that meaning. When something happens outside of ourselves, or even within, we unconsciously make a statement about what it means 'about us.' In other words, because "this event" happened, therefore I must be: 'unimportant, inadequate, unlovable and/or unworthy.' And somehow, this 'meaning' that we make in these circumstances, is taken as an absolute and integrated into our 'sense of being.' The meaning becomes 'who we are' rather than just a perception about the circumstances or events.

This suffering is derived from the judgment (label) of our critical mind. In a self-centered rationale, our critical mind defaults to self-blame, in order to make logical sense about something that has occurred and is perceived as having 'gone wrong.' Children and women seem to be more susceptible to this kind of self-blame and taking inappropriate responsibility. This behavior seems to derive from a greater need of finding safety and survival, while feeling dependent on outer circumstances. We can understand how women living in a patriarchal system would default to self-blame and take excessive responsibility, in order to increase the changes of safety.

Although there's an innate quality of inclusivity and responsibility that's an integral aspect of the Feminine, we're speaking here of the overcompensation of this quality, where it becomes dysfunctional and functions at great cost to the individual. As women, this may look like taking excessive responsibility, self-blaming and consistent self-doubt in our relationship with others. In this pattern we lose the ability to experience something objectively, but rather constantly attribute unpleasant events to some wrong-doing on our part.

What if the suffering was there instead to evolve us, perhaps to show us what limitations we have identified with and to challenge our thoughts, our labels and the limiting mental construct we experience ourselves through?

What if the challenges we experience as suffering, is what happens when the Universe floods us with more light thus, flushing up the conditioning, limiting patterns and veils that prevent us from experience ourselves as true Essence and part of Oneness?

What if this thing we call 'suffering' is really the voice of the fear and survival patterns we have learned to adapt to? What if experiencing it activates the alchemical process of dissolving the very part of us that is suffering; egoic Self of separation, allowing us to merge with the Essence of Oneness that is the ground of all creation, including ourselves?

This second stage of suffering is where we often become stuck, resulting in an endless cycle of self-blame. The problem with the second stage is that in acknowledging our mistake of labeling and misinterpreting, we see the 'mistake' for who we are rather than it just being the fact that we made a mistake.

Is it possible to experience sadness, fear, grief, or any other emotion and not make yourself wrong for it? In other words, can we just let ourselves feel the emotion without needing to change something in ourselves, or 'fix' ourselves in any way?

The truth is that in life, we will continue to experience unpleasant emotions and yet, our experiences, pleasant or unpleasant, is not a statement of our value. We may feel hurt, fear, grief and a wide range of emotions without it having to be about our self-worth. Emotions are an energetic vibrational frequency that moves through us. Our value is not comprised of what we feel or experience. Our value is comprised on knowing the true Essence of our Being; our true jewel of Oneness.

The third stage of suffering is where we can separate who we truly are; our Essential Self, from our expression. If we're open to this last stage, we allow the power of suffering to evolve our expression, helping us become greater aligned with our Essential Self.

Through this evolution we're able to see the challenging situation (suffering) as the catalyst that challenges the part of ourselves that feels unworthy and activates the alchemy that dissolves that conditioned pattern that we are operating from.

When we say yes to the suffering, we realize that the suffering is a challenge to our smallness, to the part of our thinking mind that identifies with a limited and separate sense of self (egoic nature); Conditioned Self. In this way of thinking, the suffering is challenging us to expand our consciousness of 'who we think we are', challenge the negative, critical, judgmental thoughts about ourselves and evolve into our awareness of wholeness; our Essential Self.

We are all made from Essence; spiritual Essence that materializes into form. At our core, we are Love and yet in our minds, we have created an 'idea' of ourselves that functions in a state of separateness from our Essential Self (nature). This is the dance of being human (form) and being Essence (no form). We are both. And yet, at any given time we are acting from either one of these states; our consciousness of Oneness- Essential Self, or from a sense of separateness- egoic Conditioned Self. The question is where are we expressing ourselves from? And every time we are caught in suffering, we are functioning from our state of separation (Conditioned Self), in denial of our Essence. This is the opportunity to evolve from the limitation of our egoic Conditioned Self into the expansion of our Essential Self.

I use to say I wanted to end suffering in the world, I didn't want to see the suffering. I use to think that the Universe and the powers in charge were so unfair to abandon the us, human race in this suffering... leaving us helpless to this chaos. There were quite a few judgements of my own relationship with suffering. And I realize this is only one perspective of suffering, viewed from the state of separation of my egoic nature, my Conditioned Self.

I was projecting my personal suffering onto the people and the world outside of myself. It's quite a common default defense mechanism to avoid and manage our own pain and suffering. "I" was the one stuck and desperately trying to find a way out. I was the one feeling abandoned with no hope for the future. I was the one feeling angry, resentful and drowning in my own emotional turmoil. So like any good little camper with a serious rebellious side to herself, I took on the challenge of challenging what I was feeling. I challenged my feelings of hopelessness, fear, sadness, terror, grief and the thoughts that accompanied them of self-blame, unworthiness and inadequacy. I challenged the emotional and mental chaos of living without joy, fulfillment and feeling good. I challenged my own emotional and mental reality because I couldn't accept that we could be here on this planet to live constantly in pain without any redemption or grace. Somewhere deep in my bones I could feel the whisperings of love, compassion and the traces of joy and I wanted to believe in Goodness. However, not in a conceptual reality of goodness, covered by coping and toleration, but real goodness; trust, joy, love and compassion. I was willing to challenge what I was perceiving in myself and the world around me to discover the Truth.

Sure enough, I lived to tell about the other side of suffering. And I was pleasantly surprised to realize that suffering is not all there is. There is a Universe that is alive, happening always. There is goodness in this Universe that is supporting us in the force field of

Love. However, we're focused on our pain and we've been stuck there for generations, which prevents us from experiencing the goodness, the joy and the force field of Love that we are all immersed in and created from. The suffering is a what we experience when we're stuck in the un-awakened, limited field of our conditioned pattern. We feel alone, separate, in fear and in sadness. We feel disappointed, we feel hopeless and we feel sad because we're under the illusion that what will makes us happy is that 'thing' that we wanted, outside ourselves. We are attributing our happiness to an outside source, instead of the reality that it comes from within, as a state of being. What keeps us suffering is that denial of our Essential Soul nature and knowing this initiates the beginning of the 'end of suffering' for ourselves.

Suffering is not the enemy, it's not what needs to be avoided. That is the package that the gift comes in, although it isn't always clear when we're in the throes of heart ache, loss, shame or fear. Suffering is the portal that initiates the dissolving of whatever is in the way of true fulfillment.

When you begin to experience the suffering as the Universe loving you and offering you an opportunity to, dissolve that which is the true cause of pain, the accompanying deep powerlessness is also dissolved. You realize that while you don't have the power to change the circumstances outside of yourself, you do have the power to change the one thing that creates suffering: your mental, perceptual reality.

We embrace the paradox of suffering. Is it destructive or empowering? Maybe both. While it destroys our egoic nature (the aspect of ourselves that experiences itself as separate), it opens up the pathway for us to reclaim our truth of Oneness, wholeness and our Essential Nature, which is where our joy and fulfillment emanate from.

And what chooses whether we experience it one way or the other? We do. It is only the egoic nature of our Conditioned Self that experiences the suffering, gets offended, feels shame and unworthiness. We have the choice to experience suffering as the teacher that it is!

SACRED INITIATIONS OF THE FEMININE

The Sacred Initiations of the Feminine may approach us and interrupt our lives at any given moment. However, they will never reveal themselves as great initiations. Instead, they come disguised as challenges at pivotal times in our lives. These initiations seem to ask us to face something within us, some level of illusion about ourselves and our world that's keeping us small, keeping us in pain and keeping us in the limited restrictions of our conditioned patterns. However, they don't reveal to us the potential of the process that we are entering, but rather pose themselves as a great challenge to some aspect of ourselves, usually dealing with something in our immediate world.

The Sacred Initiations of the Feminine may look a physical, mental or emotional crisis that we have no choice but to address. We may experience it through loss, a health crisis or through a situation that causes us to experience great fear. We may feel like our world is falling apart, or that the foundations of our lives are dissolving. The things we'd done before to handle situations, may not work anymore, and we find ourselves at a loss of how to address the challenge. We know we're being graced by one of the Sacred Initiations of the Feminine if we find ourselves facing a great big void of 'not knowing.' This is one of the key signatures of the Sacred Initiations of the Feminine.

In the Sacred Initiations, how you dance with this field of 'not knowing' determines many factors. Do you deny that you don't know, while you exhaust yourself trying to resolve the issue and continue the facade of self-sufficiency and independency? Do you run away and deny there's a challenge in the first place? Do you toughen up and refuse to feel the vulnerability, while secretly judging yourself for this very vulnerability? Do you drown yourself in feelings of shame, self-blame, inadequacy and victimhood? Do you become angry and blame others, including the Universe, for giving you this challenge, reminding yourself of how unfair it is in order to feel justified?

How you respond to this challenge in your life, and specifically when you are faced with the field of the unknown, determines how many times you may have to repeat the process in order to evolve, how much pain and suffering you may have to endure before finally letting go and, most of all, how much misery you may find yourself in. Therefore, the sooner you can recognize what is happening and address it accordingly, the more ease you may find.

Hence, we must understand that the Sacred Initiations of the Feminine will first show up as a challenge in your life. In the subsequent chapters we'll detail each initiation and what it's asking of you. However, in general, these challenges are really challenging a thought or a conditioned pattern that you see and experience yourself and life through that is limited in some way and thus, is in the way of experiencing yourself in the truth of who you are. For example, you may have unconscious judgements about yourself and be unaware of it. These judgements about yourself may be causing you unnecessary suffering and misery. And, so, suddenly you may be faced with a disorder, say infertility, in which you start feeling all these unconscious feelings about yourself. You begin to feel these feelings of insecurity, self-doubt, inadequacy, unworthiness all because you are faced with infertility. But the truth is that the challenge of 'infertility' is really the outer manifestation of unconscious patterns within you. And consequently, it's exactly the right catalyst to trigger the unconscious feelings. Why is it important to trigger these unconscious feelings? Because as we discussed, these unconscious patterns disrupt the harmony in our body/mind and cause suffering within ourselves. Now, you may think that the cause of your pain is the 'infertility' that has shown up, but in reality, the cause of your pain is the unconscious judgments about yourself that are now surfacing.

While the first stage of the sacred initiations is confronting the challenges itself, the second stage is really facing that field of 'not knowing.' If we follow the emotional and mental turmoil that begins to surface, we quickly get to the great void the unknown, where we realize that we don't know. This is the turning point, or at least can be; we get to choose. Do we surrender what we know and admit that we don't know, and turn inward to rely on the intelligence of the Universe? This is the offering the sacred initiation is giving you in disguise. It's offering you the opportunity to step into the realization of your divinity, your sacredness, and your oneness with all of consciousness. It's offering you an opportunity of support, to manifest through you, to connect with the divine matrix of light that contains pure joy, bliss, unconditional love. Can we let go of your need to be right, your sense of separateness and surrender into the unknown to receive the wisdom of the Universe that lives inside of you?

The choice is up to you. You have free will. Life will present this to you often and you can say yes, or you can say no. You'll have many initiations in your lifetime, if you're lucky. Why lucky? Because they offer you the ability to merge with Oneness and to dissolve all the places in your consciousness where you think you're separate. The sacred initiations of the feminine are particularly focused on the collective wounding that women in particular have experienced.

The Sacred Initiations are a process that begin with the descent into the underworld where a powerful transformative, alchemical process distills us to pure Essence. There you cycle through states of challenge, vulnerability, fear, doubt, facing the unknown, acceptance, and surrender, sometimes repeatedly until you finally become a new creation. You come through the threshold of Light itself with a whole new understanding of the truth of who you are. It's only because we're now on the other side that we can understand how the old conditioning pattern was keeping us in the dark and in suffering. You have completed your Initiation and the Universe has graced you with more of Herself.

The three collective wounds of the Feminine; Powerlessness, Shame and Abandonment, all stem from the foundation of the original wound of separation from deep within our psyche. These wounds, although originating in separation, are also the doorway into the healing path back into wholeness.

As we face these Initiations that come as challenges, we allow the wounds to surface and for ourselves to feel the impressions that arise from our egoic nature of separation, guiding us into what needs to be resolved, bringing us back into our Soul's innate experience of Oneness.

The impulse of our Soul is to feel its true wholeness, which automatically challenges the places within us that identify with being in separation. Since our first experience of separation at birth, we continue to layer experience over experience of separation over this original wound of separation, until we break out of this illusion of separation and wake up to the Oneness dimension of our being. This is the first glimpse of our awakening and from here we begin the journey of the return to our innate truth of wholeness, sacredness and Oneness.

From this moment on, depending on our particular soul's evolution in this lifetime, our life's journey can be redefined by our soul's impulse to transform the unresolved places of separation into the deeper sense of Oneness within. And the deeper we merge with our Light of Oneness (our Essential Self), the more opportunity there is for us to dissolve the conditioning of separation that we still have.

If we choose to see these challenges for what they are, rather than to continue to blame or project ourselves as victims, then we say yes to the Initiation that is taking place now.

In this process of evolutionary awakening, our internal impulse of Life, Herself, continuously brings to the surface the pieces of unresolved parts of our psyche that are yearning to be known and rediscovered as inherently whole.

"As we continue this journey of awakening and healing, the bigger picture emerges, and we begin to map out the journey of our Soul in relationship to this life's existence. Ironically, we begin our journey into this plane, in the state of wholeness of our Soul, we then, inescapably move into the illusion of separation (which is a necessary step in the creation of the individual ego state of me and other - duality). In duality, we continue to experience this plane as me and other, light and dark, good and bad; until our personal soul's evolutionary impulse activates our awakening, and then our lifelong journey of rediscovering our true wholeness,[4] begins (or may even continue) if it has begun in previous lifetimes."

EXPERIENCES OF COLLECTIVE WOUNDS BY PATIENTS

Here is an example of how a patient experienced her wounds during a healing session.

Veronica Case #1

Veronica was a 35-year-old patient that came in for her first appointment, referred by a reproductive endocrinologist. She'd been diagnosed with unexplained infertility and wanted to avoid doing any invasive fertility protocols. She reported an AMH of .8 (ovarian reserve level), which is an indication of her egg reserve being low for her age, and an FSH of 11, which wasn't' too high, but considered high in the assisted reproductive model of conventional medicine. We discussed her particular signs and symptoms and I pointed out some details about diet etc. I explained to her how I worked and the importance of really looking at the psycho-spiritual underlying patterns that our bodies are communicating to us at all times, and how at that moment it seemed to be presenting a disruption in her reproductive system.

I shared with her the energetic sacral center and the general ties that it has with shame, sexuality and our disconnection from our own life force and our ability to feel pleasure or joy. As we discussed some of these general concepts, tears started to flow, which is usually a good sign that the wounds are ready for transformation and healing.

I continued to take her pulse and noticed that her right pulses were extremely weak, and so I asked if she had any issues with digestion. She said sometimes she didn't have bowel movements for four or five days. So, as I was feeling her other pulses, I felt into the energy in her body and asked about the holding pattern in her life; what was it she was holding on to and in what area of her life was this holding pattern showing up in her life? She began crying and saying that her biggest issue was that she hadn't forgiven her father for his betrayal of her mother and that every night she would pray that it would resolve itself, that somehow she could let go of the pain, suffering, anger and resentment she was still holding on to. She began talking about the pain and suffering of that experience and how it'd affected her life. This was the first piece of unraveling the old pattern directly related to the constipation. I allowed some time and space for these feelings of deep pain to arise and come to the surface, especially the sadness and buried grief that was gently melting away.

As I continued to hold space for her awareness to include all her rising emotions and patterns, she mentioned that her father blamed his actions on her, due to her decision to have a boyfriend. In his opinion, her choosing to explore and express her sexuality by committing to a boyfriend he didn't approve of, had sparked a contentious relationship with her mother, leading to his behavior of straying. Regardless of the details, we could see the layers of blame and shame that were placed on her. I could begin to see how she'd bought into the belief of being responsible for his actions and making herself wrong for having a boyfriend, and further wrong for expressing her sexuality with another. I could see the pattern of shame layering over her pelvic sacral area. From there I could also see how her constipation reflected how she was still holding on to this impenetrable pain of betrayal and abandonment from her father, in which she blamed for all of it. Because her sexuality had been a part of what she'd been making wrong in herself in this pattern, it linked in with her sacral and her ability to create, thus manifesting as infertility. There were other related beliefs in her field that created fear and kept her in this holding pattern: what if she really was to blame and couldn't trust her own body's sexuality, therefore causing more pain and betrayal in her own life? How could she bring a child into this? How could she trust her boyfriend not to betray her and leave, like her father did?

In the first powerful session, her healing was all laid out in front of us. The path had revealed itself and it was showing us the repressed emotions and hidden beliefs that had been causing the dysfunctions in her body. Veronica had taken a courageous step at beginning the healing process and melting away the deep grief and sadness of the loss of her relationship with her father as she had known it. This was an important piece of valuing herself again, and her needs, rather than having to sacrifice her needs for safety. She mentioned that she was very close to her father, and how when he betrayed the marriage, she felt betrayed as well. Furthermore, she couldn't express her feelings to him because he wouldn't allow it, so she'd buried the deep pain and suffering of the breaking of her heart, in order to still have a relationship with him. So how she truly felt around all of this, including her pain, became unsafe for her to feel, unless she wanted to risk losing his love altogether. This deep repression affected her bowels and caused a deep sense of contraction on the inner viscera.

Next, she realized that his lack of taking responsibility and total abandonment of her feelings and needs had caused a great rage within her. It was so clear that her body's response was to the shame, inappropriate blaming, the abandonment, betrayal and fear of commitment with any relationship in her life, due to the patterns experienced from the suppressed loss of her first and most important male in her life, her father. It's so fascinating to witness the unfolding in the body, and how our story is held in our bodies, manifesting in our biology. In some ways, it seems that her soul was ready to stop the pattern of shaming, blaming, irresponsibility, abandonment and betrayal that were part of herself judgment until now. By manifesting itself as a health crisis that she couldn't ignore, she could allow those wounds to surface and move through the suffering rather than repress it in order to survive, like she had done for 21 years.

I suspect that through this healing process, she will discover many things along the path of healing and unravel the limiting, painful beliefs that she's imposed upon herself in the name of survival. These are some of the possibilities that her healing may lead to:

- She will realize that there is no shame in her body, only sacredness.

- She will realize that her relationships and sexual desires are not tainted nor 'bad' in any way and do not cause suffering in others.

- She will learn to release imposed responsibility over someone else's choice and free herself of guilt and shame held in her pelvis.

- Feel safe enough to speak her truth about her experience and not have to deny her reality for someone else's love.

- Learn that her relationships with the opposite sex do not have to be modeled after her father's behavior of betrayal and abandonment.

- Restore her sense of power, versus the deep-rooted hopelessness powerlessness that she feels in relationships with the other sex.

- Her biology will respond to the detoxifying and transforming effects of all these old conditioning patterns of suffering that she has been living with for the last 21 years.

Of course, I realize that no one's healing process is linear, and that she'll move through some of these areas quickly and may not even need to move through others for her reproductive system to conceive or regulate her bowels. The above list of what is possible with her healing progress is only what was presented in the first session, in which she has opened up all these areas emotionally and spiritually that were restricted through old painful beliefs and trauma. After all, there is a deep gift in her infertility challenge; it is clearly the doorway for the healing of her heart, soul and, of course, her body.

Here is another example of how our collective fear affects our lower centers with the case from Annette.

Annette Case #2

Annette came in seeking help with her skin which was constantly breaking out, and to feel more relaxed within herself. During our session, she spoke about her feelings of loneliness and challenges she was having with her husband sexually. She felt she had to curtail her sexual desire for intimacy with him, because he didn't reciprocate in the same way, or as often. Furthermore, her skin was also a source of complaint, because she felt concerned about her excessive break outs that had occurred since getting married.

In her session, she laid down and began connecting with the anger she felt at other women, especially towards women that felt critical and gossiped a lot. She felt this in her solar plexus. She felt they were being pretentious and wanted to call their bluff. As we explored this feeling, which I knew was a projection of something within her, she began feeling the rage in her solar plexus. She voiced how angry she was at women not supporting other women, and I could intuit there was more about support and her own lack of support underneath this rage.

I asked her: Where in your life did you feel you didn't want to pretend with other people? (Usually when patients talk about something bothering them outside, there is an aspect of this that is living inside; the outside is a mirror of their inner relationships and experiences. Therefore, the importance is to focus on ourselves, and where that truth is living within our varying shadows. She answered: "my mother." She continued describing how she felt enraged as a child because her mother wouldn't pay attention to her and understand her. Her personality was very different than her mothers, and so her mother always wanted her to be like her, not leaving any room for her to honor herself, her feelings, or her voice. She saw herself having tantrums because she didn't feel heard, seen, or even acknowledged.

To no surprise, she felt this in her solar plexus, the deep powerlessness from not valuing herself and not feeling acknowledged. By the subtle rejection from her mother growing up, she felt wrong. She would also be punished by her mother, who would ignore her and be angry with her for days at time, whenever she dared to express her true feelings. She learned early on that speaking her truth might leave her alone and abandoned by others, and so she shut down her voice and learned to pretend and say, 'the right things.'

Furthermore, we discovered this pattern was being projected onto her husband where she felt fear of speaking her truth and her feelings, not wanting to risk him getting angry and abandoning her. So, the pattern was to shut down her life force and sexuality feelings in the sacral center, which was blocking her creativity, in order to survive in her marriage.

Her inner fear of abandonment and feelings of powerlessness was blocking her sense of self (solar plexus) and creativity (sacral center) and she felt disconnected with her true desires and her expression. She used to paint, ride horses, frequently visit art museums, write short stories, all of which she had let go of, in her attempt to fit in and please her new married life with her husband. Ironically, in fear of losing her husband and risking his abandonment of her, she abandoned herself, and resorted to only presenting the side of her that was in agreement with her husband's ideals of her.

Furthermore, she wondered: "How do I speak my truth, when I know others may not like to hear what I have to say, or may not be in agreement?" This was what her body was saying: Love is the bridge... we can speak our truth with love, leaving ourselves wide open, with our life force flowing... feeling our sexuality and saying whatever we have to say in love. If they don't agree, we can understand, they don't have to agree. And whatever reaction they have is their reaction, not ours to fix. We're responsible for the love we give, and to stay in that connection with our own sacredness, where we source the love. In this way we don't have to close ourselves down or pretend in order to receive the love from the outside, because we're already in the love and are just sharing ourselves with others, in this context of love. She also realized that she didn't have to seek the love from the outside; she could be in connection with source directly within and then share that. Abandoning herself wasn't an option anymore; she had pierced through the veil of dependency, no longer relying on others for her deep needs. She realized she had what she needed all along and furthermore it was her responsibility to meet her needs anyway.

In review, it was interesting how her initial response was that she was bothered by her friend's behavior and her self-imposed need to pretend. This discomfort led to the opening of a much deeper wound, affecting her solar plexus (powerlessness) and sacral center (abandonment - creativity and life force) which ultimately allowed her to heal these personal and collective wounds that were causing her emotional and physical suffering. Additionally, her skin concern was related to her inner conflict of "what face was she deciding to show to others." Within herself she felt the compelling need to pretend vs. risk being abandoned and being herself. The resolution was to rewire herself with the truth of her being, the sacredness in her sacral center, which opened up her life-force and her creativity, and using the essence of love within herself to bridge and accompany her expressions to others, so that she can authentically exists in the same space with another person of a different opinion and still be in the field of love. Love is what her soul was searching for and she now knows that it is within her.

FROM VICTIMIZATION TO EMPOWERMENT

As we witnessed in the two cases above, the healing was contingent upon the realization that they were not victims of their life, their past, or even of their suffering; they realized what they contained all along, of which they were longing for.

When we realize that our feelings of victimization stem from our mental perception of our experiences, then we're able to move out of victimhood and start taking responsibility for our life in a whole new way. Much of our victimization story has been passed on collectively, through our ancestors, whether consciously or unconsciously, it doesn't matter. We could say that our roles as victims and their inherent disconnection from sacred power allowed us to survive the threat of the last 5000 years. While this veil of ignorance may have given us safe passage through the inhumaneness of the times, it seems to me that this ignorance and ingrained fear, is now the primary cause of our decay and possible extinction. Richard Rudd comments in his book Gene Keys: "We now know that they are inherited ancestral fears carried in the DNA of the bloodlines of all human beings. We understand that they had to be there for our survival as a species".[5] Continuing the collective story of victimization does not seem like a viable option of living on this planet anymore.

Consequently, the good news is that we have a way out of this victimization. We don't to play the role of victim anymore, because we are much more than that. Even science supports us so that we can choose our lives, in more aspects than we think. There is very little that we are completely dependent on. Identified as a victim, we have no choice in the experiences of our life, yet psychology shows us that can choose our thinking and perceptions, thus shifting how we experience life. And biologically, advances in epigenetics shows us that we can even choose which DNA is operating at a given time, completely, discrediting the theory that we are victims to our DNA's hereditary patterns. Therefore, we can't deny how much power we have in choosing our awareness and consciousness, which is what ultimately determines our reality and experience. Hence, the truth is we are not victims at all, and we have much more power than most of us are aware of.

Until now, most of us feel victim to living out our ancestral conditionings and our physical disorders, we have thought our destiny controlled in our genes. While true, many of our ancestor's beliefs and physical limitations are passed down through DNA; we can still control which DNA molecules are turned on. Contrary to the popular belief still circulating in our collective viewpoints... your genetic code is greatly dependent on our attitude; beliefs, thoughts, and feelings. We have a tremendous amount of control over our genes. We can change our genes and determine which switches get turned on and off. Our DNA responds to its environment, thus shifting from turning on and turning off. While we may be born with some switches on in our DNA, we can turn them off by our 'environment'. From a quantum perspective, your environment includes your attitude, moods, feelings and even thoughts.

The study of Epigenetics, (the study of our DNA and environment) supports the notion that we are not destined to experience the same diseases or dysfunctions: spiritual, physical or emotional, inherent in our family. Furthermore, it substantiates the possibility that through the changes in our DNA, we can heal all aspects of our being and we can change the collective story to one of empowerment. Therefore, what is directly molding your body at this moment is the milieu of your energetic subtle bodies of consciousness; which includes your feelings, thoughts, and attitude. You could never be a victim of your DNA, because it's dynamic and not static... responding to your subtle fields. Below Richard Rudd, explains an aspect of this 'milieu' of our DNA; "What most people don't realize is that as a salt, DNA is a natural conductor of electricity. It is extremely sensitive to electromagnetic waves. Even a slight shift in your mood will create enough of an environmental signal to trigger a response from your DNA. Likewise, a negative or a positive thought will generate a subtle electromagnetic current throughout your body that will stir your DNA into some form of biological response. Most of us are completely unaware of how our moods, thoughts, beliefs and general attitude mold our bodies. Because of the heightened sensitivity of your DNA, everything in your life, from the food you eat to the people you live with, is co-creating your body via your attitude."[6]

Even though we aren't victims, for many years we have lived under the spell of believing that we are victims, conforming in all ways to this illusion. Our bodies have been wired through the collective story passed down from generations and generations, to respond to life as a victim, absent of our true power. But once the dark room has been lite, the secret is out, and we can see clearly. We are inherently empowered by the truth resonating within us and armed with this new awareness, we commit to our journey of exploration and excavation of this hidden jewel that promises to set us free from the old story of the collective feminine.

Although we have the power to change, we still must contend with the unconscious and conscious physiological repercussions of fear. When we experience stress, which is a form of fear, stress hormones released during this process decreases the function of our immune system. These stress hormones are so effective that they're used in the conventional medical communities to shut down the immune system in preparation for organ transplants, to reduce rejection of the organ. To comprehend this further, we have to realize that when our immune system shuts down due to stress hormones, underlying viruses that are usually held in check, are suddenly activated causing havoc and dysfunctions. Our stress response from underlying fear patterns of the past is constantly creating disharmony biologically.

Furthermore, as Quantum science shows us, the invisible immaterial realm is far more important than the material realm of form, because the form is being created by this unseen state, always. The true secret to health, healing, and wellbeing do not lie with our DNA, but rather within the mechanisms of our cell membrane and its ability to read the genetic blueprint depending on the incoming signals received from the environment. Consequently, if you have cancer programming or cancer genes, it does not automatically mean you will develop cancer, this genetic expression does not ever have to be expressed, but yet the energetic realms of emotions, beliefs, and unconscious repressions, are a greater indicator of what your body, heart, and soul will manifest.

And yet with so much power and ability to change, we must ask ourselves the question of why has the repression of women... of the Feminine still exists? What has prevented us from breaking through this holding pattern of victimhood? And while this question may not have just one answer, I believe the key ingredient in our state of consciousness, has been our deep-rooted forgetfulness and erroneous belief of our limited, separated Self. It's a self-fulfilling prophecy. Just like we have believed that our DNA has controlled us, we imagine a destiny for ourselves and then unconsciously surrender to that limited destiny, because we cannot imagine anything else. And so, the power of our consciousness keeps us stuck exactly what we limit ourselves to. We have believed that we are powerless, we have believed that we are worthless, and we have believed that we are inadequate because we are in feminine form. Becoming identified with these beliefs and the collective that continues to acknowledge those erroneous beliefs has kept us chained to them for centuries.

The truth is we've allowed it to continue. Women, as well as men, have allowed the fear to dominate and the disconnection in our being to continue, feeling ourselves living life disembodied, separate beings. Ultimately, the battle is not outside us, the battle is within. This is the battle of our own disowned parts of ourselves. We've forgotten our divine nature and have fallen victim to our separated sense of Self.

The change begins with us, taking full responsibility, waking up to the truth of who we are, anchoring ourselves in that truth and voicing our truth. The greatest battle is to challenge the limited perceptions of who we think we are. The patriarchy lives within us, it's not something just outside ourselves. It's the veil of rejection, judgment, self-doubt bundled up in fear and confusion within us. The way to change the patriarchy outside is by looking within and transforming our shadows and our greatest fears. The survival of the patriarchy depends on whether we continue to unconsciously contribute to its existence, by our subtle denial of our sacredness and divinity. We get to choose to awaken and change the story of the Feminine, through our responsibility of our state of consciousness.

When you are able
To make two become one,
The inside like the outside,
And the outside like the inside,
The higher like the lower,
So that a man is no longer male,
And a woman, female,
But male and female
Become a single whole;
When you are able to fashion
An eye to replace an eye,
And form a hand in place of a hand, or a foot for a foot,
Making one image supersede another – then you will enter in.

~ Logion 22 in the Gospel of Thomas

3
Anthropos:
Becoming the Perfected Human Being

Becoming the *perfected human being*, the Anthropos is the road to embodying our wholeness through which we annihilate ourselves into the perfection of the Divine. According to the mystics, the Anthropos; is the highest state of consciousness possible, uniting our divine nature into our physical form and making the two into one. Through the recognition of our essential nature of divinity, we can dissolve the separation of duality. Becoming 'fully human' is our ultimate, spiritual, evolutionary goal and yet in the current cultural trend of denying the mystical realm, it may seem unreachable.

In the first chapter, we spoke about the possibility of our ancestors intentionally creating a collective veil of secrecy over our true divine nature and possible hiding this Truth, even from ourselves, to keep us safe within the times they were living. If our ancestors indeed intended for us to forget our true sacred power, then I am sure they were also aware of a time of greater awakening just around the millennium corner. And so, in the path of the Sophiatic Christos, in which Mary Magdalen and other Gnostics have ignited for us, we see the road map to our spiritual awakening, culminating in the manifestation of the perfected human being; Anthropos.

The perfected human being (also known in some mystical circles as Heiros Gamos, Sophiatic Christos and Insan Al Kamal), is the flowering union of the inner duality of feminine and masculine within us. Intimately, it represents our soul's longing for the inner marriage of Beloved and Lover. As we visit this roadmap of the perfected human be-ing, we begin with the understanding that we have everything we need for this union within. Through the purification of our mind and ego, we polish the heart to be able to contain this union... where the two become one. Through this annihilation process, we begin to truly experience the divine states of our inner qualities of light. Truly a union of body and soul, feminine and masculine, physical and spiritual begin through this inner transformational process. It's here that we may come to face with the limitations of our survival patterns and the suffering they have imposed on our being. It's through this process that we move past the duality of right and wrong; yin and yang and experience the union of the paradox of duality. This exploration of the union of opposites within ourselves delivers the garden that our soul aspires rest in.

In our perfected state of being; Anthropos, the challenge is not only to recognize our divine nature but also to allow this holy aspect of ourselves to merge with our physical form (body), thereby merging the separation in our mind. This process entails allow-ing the 5000 years of cultural patriarchal conditioning to be dissolved and alchem-ized through the process of transformation itself. Therefore, we would have to pierce through the collective destructive thought patterns including the shaming our of bod-ies, the experience of sensuality and sexuality as negative or unholy and more impor-tantly we would have to break through the conditioning of believing that our form is 'less important' that our Spirit. To move into Union, we must let go of this preconceived notion that our bodies are the obstacle to experiencing Spirit, because our body is the vehicle which allows us to experience Spirit in this dimension. This is the beginning process of honoring the physical form as an extension of spiritual divine conscious-ness, thus holy and sacred. So, as we begin this process of understanding this unity consciousness of becoming one within ourselves, we will first have to have a greater understanding of the Feminine.

VISCERAL WISDOM: THE WISDOM IS IN THE BODY

In our long descent into forgetfulness, we have forgotten that our bodies are instru-ments of sensuous nature, carrying the five senses which inherently are not limited to the physical realm. What we see with our eyes, what we hear with our ears, what we touch physically can be attuned to vast dimensions of subtle consciousness, that we have forgotten about. We can see, feel, hear and perceive much more than what is available in material form.

Our bodies are instruments of resonance, constantly perceiving and responding bio-chemically to our environment. Through resonance we experience the inner vibration of a frequency, allowing us to see, hear, feel and perceive the subtle inner realms of consciousness. We can resonate with our environment, with a thought, with a situation, or to anything outside ourselves. Our body can communicate what is in alignment through resonance... this is the key to feeling good in our body. When something resonates with us, in other words the vibration of that 'thing', (whether a thought or an actual experience), is in harmony with our vibration. At its highest level, we experience joy, bliss, peace, love. It's as if that thought or experience activates the joy in our being and makes us feel good "in our body". Resonance is our bodies way of communicating and connecting with the subtle energies underlying the material forms, offering a direct line into our knowing. It's through the body and this experience of resonance, that we align our inner and outer worlds.

And yet, as a collective, many have shut down our ability to feel, leaving the body's emotions and feelings to be regarded as unnecessary and secondary to our thinking and reasoning. We have shamed ourselves and blocked most of the good feelings in our body, acceptable only when engaged in food or sex. However, reviving this disconnection is key in regaining our sacred power and becoming the 'perfected human being'.

We must ask ourselves, why we shut down in the first place. It's no secret that women connected with their Feminine power presented a threat to the established order, thereby leading the greatest craze of persecutions, witch hunting's, and burnings that the world has ever seen. Using our body as instruments to connect with the Spirit was a reason for death in our world. Furthermore, women received the collective religious accusation and blaming of the fall of man, through the biblical references of Eve's eating of the apple, and the inherent sexual seduction attributed to her actions in the garden. It seems that the collective message for women at the rise of patriarchy has been one of blame for the fall of mankind, shaming of our feminine form and distrust of our body's and feelings.

It seems that women have been taught to distrust their physical sensations, or sexuality, or even their emotions, being labeled as shameful and even demonized to some degree. Thereby resulting in physical pleasure equating with shame and by default our feminine body, our sexuality, and sensuality all responsible for the fall of mankind and ultimately unworthy of the highest spiritual Essence. And of course, this would've added to feeling too unsafe to truly explore and express our truth, our intuitions and follow the resonance (sensations) in our body. This would have contributed to the disconnection of our bodies.

The connection to our sacred wisdom is through the vessel of our body. The feminine body is one of pure sacred power. It can birth consciousness into form. It's of great holiness and sacredness. Within our body, we feel the movement and direction of divine consciousness, our Essence. It's through our body that we can feel our life force, enlivening us. It's through our body that we experience our divine nature, bliss and joy, not in our heads. And yet, collectively, our culture acknowledges and approves mainly of our intellect.

Through our body, we connect with the sophiatic wisdom through what resonates, what feels good, what is deeply satisfying, which is different than the good we feel with instant gratification. This deep satisfaction which emanates from joy and pleasure within can only happen in our bodies, not in our minds. This is the process of merging our divine nature with our form.

In turn, for thousands of years, we have made our bodies wrong, lived with the shame, limiting our impulses and our need for pleasure... for enjoyment... for feeling good in our body. We live in a culture that limits acceptable pleasure in our bodies to mainly sex and food, and our constant outer search for satisfaction. Our hearts and souls have become starved for the deep nourishment; that which only comes with an ecstatic blissful state of the union with our inner beloved. The pleasure and true joy a young child feel while exploring his surroundings somatically... is what we are missing. We're starved for this. We've become a depressed, excessively tired, joy deprived culture, which seeks momentary instant gratification pleasure in a disembodied body.

But we contain the answer. The medicine is to embody our bodies completely... fully. We begin this process by turning inward, embracing the feelings that have been calcified for so long. We begin to break through the veils that have subtly, and maybe not so subtly, prevented us from fully activating and experiencing our joy in our being. Experiencing this joy in our bodies is the result of merging our divine nature through our physical form (body), it's the process of union, merging beloved and lover.

Through alignment with our visceral resonance, we can allow our Essential Self to start piercing through the conditioning and reset ourselves to pleasure, enjoyment and feeling good. As we begin to trust our bodies again, we can allow us to be directed to the highest decisions for ourselves and our lives. If our choices activate joy (the highest vibration) then the action in question is of the highest vibration. It can be that easy, but first, we must discern between the instant gratification of just 'feeling good' and the 'true joy of the soul'. These two differ and of course, we know that not all 'feeling good' is equal. But when we feel deep joy, the kind that resonates with our hearts, soul, and with the feeling of YES in our hearts... then that is the resonance of your Essential Self (soul), and the connection with deep wisdom in your being.

13 Pillars of Conscious Feminine Medicine™

As we ascend down this path of the perfected human, we must first awaken ourselves to the dimension of our divinity and integrate that reality into our conscious awareness and our physical bodies. Let's revisit our history. As we mentioned in the previous chapters, during the past 5000+ years of the patriarchy, past cultural and religious reforms have rejected the feminine archetype, creating collective and personal trauma in women, which is at the root cause of women's physical, mental and emotional suffering today. Fear consciousness has become the operating underlying matrix in women manifesting as lack of safety, worthlessness, powerlessness, shame and rejection. This collective repression of the Feminine has engendered a personal disconnection from our sacred primordial essence (life force), greatly contributing to mental, emotional and physical health epidemics, which I refer to as '*1st world female disorders*'.

At first, it may feel daunting to confront the amount of fear and trauma that's operating collectively and within us. Shifting this destructive conditioning might seem hopeless and never ending. I know I've fallen into this trap many times. And yet, in commune with ourselves, we can hear the whispering voice of truth within, guiding us and urging us to awaken to the hidden jewel of Essence (light) in our Being. This isn't a task that we must undertake alone, although we do have to take responsibility for our healing. This is a movement, a flow, where the universal life force of the Feminine, Herself, is demanding that we end the victimization and step into a greater life for ourselves. The call to each one of us is not subtle; we hear it in the myriad of challenges in our lives, health and fulfillment. This is how She calls upon us, asking us to dare to dive deeply into our beings until we embody the truth of our jewel wholeheartedly. We do have a choice, we can keep suffering and continue to birth generations that are asleep to their full sacred power, or we can be the agents of change, beginning with healing of our heart, birthing through us the possibility, the power and magic, that we have known to be true all along.

Birth of the Conscious Feminine happens in each one of us, before it happens in our society or globally. Through the resurrection and transmission of the Feminine, we begin to remember the wisdom that has been lost; we begin to shift the light in our surrounding communities and thus our world. This is a highly intimate process of self-discovery, which engenders personal healing. Yet for each person that confronts their wounds, the wounds of hundreds, if not thousands of other women on the planet are simultaneously alchemized. At one level we are all one, and therefore our story is also a thread in the collective story. So, while we're awakening individually to our deepest truth, we're also awakening the collective and changing the story of the Feminine on the planet for all women through the law of critical mass.

The law of critical mass is seen in the 100th monkey effect, whether you believe in the controversial experiment or not, it shows us what is possible in a population when a 'critical mass' number of people adopt a new idea or new behavior. This experiment refers to a breakthrough that happens in consciousness, where the new behavior in the few is automatically, directly communicated and spontaneously adopted by the mass population.

In 1952 researching monkeys on a remote island were observed rejecting the sweet potatoes that had fallen on the ground because they were full of sand. One day an 18-month female monkey began washing the sweet potato and eating them, and then the rest of her family began to wash the sweet potatoes and copy the same behavior throughout the following weeks. What happened next surprised the observers, suddenly the next morning, all the monkeys on the island were observed doing this new behavior of washing the sweet potatoes before eating them. The change occurred overnight, so they couldn't have learned one by one. Somehow this new behavior was communicated instinctively, and it resulted in all them overnight, displaying this new behavior. And if this isn't enough, there was also another island across the way, separate from this island, in which the monkeys there, were also observed washing the sweet potatoes, with no one, in particular, showing them 'how to do this'. This was a change in mass consciousness or collective force. In quantum science, this is called the law of critical mass, whereby we begin a new behavior, and as more people start to engage in the new behavior, at some point (refer to as the tipping point), the new behavior is directly transmitted and it becomes public knowledge to all.

In the same way, as more and more women break through the old chains of fear, powerlessness, shame and, abandonment we simultaneously shift the energetics of the collective and thus influence this collective field for all women, thus bringing about the cultural rejection of the Feminine to a halt. In our awakened state of the Feminine, we will not continue to betray ourselves, nor the Feminine. As we become conscious awareness of the Feminine within ourselves, we create consciousness automatically in all those that follow and change the collective consciousness for seven generations forward and heal up to seven generations back. Therefore, our work of awakening powerfully impacts all the generations in the present, future and past. Everyone, on our planet, benefits from the healing and awakening that each one of us does. You matter more than you think you do!

So how do we get started with this massive shift of healing? Well, one by one we discover our light, anchor in it and allow all the illusory patterns to transform by the Grace of the Divine. As we awaken and heal personally, we transmit a new light and a new possibility. The personal and collective healing medicine for these wounds of the Feminine is the foundation of *Conscious Feminine Medicine*™. *Conscious Feminine Medicine*™ is a container that allows us to create awareness and step into an integrated form of being by uniting our spirituality with our physical form and becoming aware of the dance between the two. *Conscious Feminine Medicine*™ provides the tools and understanding to empower, awaken and heal women through the three principles of consciousness, spiritual transformational alchemy, and Embodiment. Through CFM you receive the *Sacred Initiations of the Feminine*, allowing women to retrieve the aspects of their souls that have remained hidden and forgotten. *Conscious Feminine Medicine*™ provides a transformational model for which women can discover the divinity in their bodies, and transform physical, emotional and spiritual pain and suffering. It offers a return to your whole Self and a way to heal the mental and emotional epidemics that stem from the disconnection of our sacredness. A myriad of 1ˢᵗ *world feminine disorders*, which I mentioned in the previous chapter, all have the possibility to heal because we directly address their primal cause of spiritual disconnection in our consciousness.

Conscious Feminine Medicine™ is based on ancient healing traditions, merged with a foundation of somatic embodiment practices, interjected with knowledge of Quantum Medicine. This platform provides us with a template in which to achieve our Conscious Feminine resurrection and transform the wounds of the Feminine.

We will begin our process of Feminine transformation and healing by discovering your full potential through the 13 pillars of *Conscious Feminine Medicine*™. This will begin the awareness process of understanding what you're truly capable of and what your full potential is. Secondly, we will journey through the *Sacred Initiations of the Feminine*, in which we begin a 5-step process of healing, transforming and embodying the medicine of the collective wounds of the Feminine. Within, *Conscious Feminine Medicine*™, you will have an array of somatic meditations, embodied practices and deep contemplations and awareness practices to unlock your full Light Signature and support the flowering of the Conscious Feminine within.

The thirteen foundational pillars of *Conscious Feminine Medicine*™ reminds us of our full potential and lets us awaken to what is possible. Reviving these core Truths in our conscious awareness creates a resonance of knowledge that triggers our forgotten memories. Our bodies hold all imprints and memories that we have experienced, personally and collectively, karmically. Therefore, contemplating these truths and reflecting upon them gives you a chance to establish a relationship with yourself around these beliefs... dislodging and dissolving the opposing restrictive beliefs of pain and suffering. As we do this, we contribute to the transformational shift of consciousness not only within ourselves but also within humanity at large and the planet, Herself.

The 13 Pillars of *Conscious Feminine Medicine*™

1. You are Divine.

2. You are the Medicine.

3. You are a Healer.

4. Activating your Trinity Womb.

5. Embodying your Sacred Feminine Form.

6. Healing the 3 Collective wounds of the Feminine.

7. Transforming the 1st World Feminine Disorders.

8. Embracing the Biochemistry of Consciousness.

9. Integrating the Universal Mothers.

10. Embracing Evolutionary Initiations.

11. Embodying Consciousness of Movement in Stillness.

12. Activating the Sacred Initiations of the Feminine.

13. Awakening to Oneness Realization.

Here is a more in-depth explanation of each pillar:

1. You are Divine: You are a divine, multi-dimensional being created from Light, having an experience in physical form. You are Light Source Essence, directly from Source, the Great Mother. As such, you contain the hidden qualities of life source Herself: unconditional love, peace, ecstatic joy, and many more. Your true natural state is one of Light & Essence, made in the image of Source, Great Mother.

2. You are the Medicine: The medicine is Source and your true nature is Source. What truly heals and what we are yearning for is Source, which we feel as Light of Love. You are this Love, and that is what transmutes, transforms everything that is void of Love. And as an embodiment of Love, you are the medicine and you carry the greatest gift of all, the true medicine. The happiness that we are looking for is within... it is your true state. You are Love, you are the medicine.

3. You are a Healer: Our physical bodies are a vessel for the pure Light Source that we are. As such, in our Essence, we can embody, transmit and direct our Essence for Healing. You aren't a victim of life, but rather a powerful being of Light, created with the ability to heal incongruent disharmonies, just by your very presence. The recognition and activation of your Essential Light is key to empowering your presence, and living in your magnificent Healing capacity.

4. Activating your Trinity Womb: The trinity womb is birthed from the primordial Trinity Essence of the Great Mother Matrix, which is the triple aspect metaphor that contains the secret of life, death and regeneration. Within us, we contain this primordial signature, expressed through the Trinity Wombs of Creative Expression, Embodied Love, and Wisdom. This Trinity matrix is accessed through our head, heart, and sacral womb areas, where they interact as bridges between unmanifested wholeness and manifested expression in our world of form. The worlds of spirituality and matter are not separate, but interwoven... and our physical form is the densest form of spiritual Essence, manifesting through these three wombs.

Our **Head Womb** is our womb of thinking and sensing; allowing our expression of creative source to manifest through our thoughts, beliefs and senses.

Our **Heart Womb** transmits the frequencies of Love, emotional states and embodied emotions.

Our **Sacral Womb** is our womb of Essence, where we experience the deep wisdom that is core to our being, and where we merge with the Infinite unmanifested Consciousness, Source of All, Great Mother.

5. Embodying your Sacred Feminine Form: Our Feminine form is sacred. Women carry the Universal Great Mother Matrix blueprint within their physical form and their energetic wombs. The womb is the primordial signature of Great Mother Source, that continues to birth form from formlessness. Our physical body is created in the form of the Great Birther; Great Mother Source. It is sacred, it is Her. Within every cell in our feminine form is the divine coding of unconditional Love, and the gift of creating, just like Great Mother Source.

6. Healing the 3 Collective wounds of the Feminine: The three core collective wounds of the Feminine have been stored unconsciously in our subtle fields, disrupting the three lower subtle body centers in women. This disruption has caused the great difficulty women have of embodying their divinity of the earthly, sensual nature of their physical body. Reclaiming our Feminine sacredness is key to embodying the Truth of who we are and healing the collective wounds of the Feminine.

1st Collective Wound of the Feminine in the Solar Plexus: Powerlessness

2nd Collective Wound of the Feminine in the Sacral Womb: Shame

3rd Collective Wound of the Feminine in the Root Gate: Abandonment

7. Transforming the 1st World Feminine Disorders: Much of the dysfunction in women's physical bodies and psyches have been created by the cultural and religious repression of the Feminine, through many lifetimes, in the last 5000+ years. This has manifested as disease, disorders and pervasive dissatisfaction in our lives. The 1st world feminine disorder is an array of physical manifestations in female bodies, that are common in 1st world countries, due to this severance between spirit and body. They manifest in women as nervous disorders, reproductive disorders, auto-immune imbalances, gut imbalances, and emotional disorders.

8. Embracing the Biochemistry of Consciousness: Our physical body is a manifestation of the interplay of the inner relationship of our subtle bodies; emotional body, mental body and spiritual body. Healing is a manifestation of bridging consciousness itself through the matter of substance, allowing the illusion of separation to dissolve. Our presence (consciousness) and where we choose to focus it on, affects the biochemistry in our body. By becoming present to the constricted, painful places in our Being, our biochemistry shifts and releases the constrictions itself, thus healing occurs.

9. Integrating the Universal Mothers: The five *Elemental MOTHERS*; Earth, Water, Fire, Air & Ether (Consciousness) are the sacred substance of all creation, including our own form. We will explore the Universal Mothers in chapter four.

10. Embracing Evolutionary Initiations: Physical, emotional and spiritual crisis are evolutionary initiations, from our loving Universe, designed to break the limiting patterns that keep us from realizing our greatest potential. At all moments, the Great Mother Universe is conspiring to support us in manifesting our greatest potential, making sure we have everything we need, in order to expand into greater levels of Her Reality of Love. Therefore, everything we experience including challenges, are out of Love... and it provides us with opportunities to break free from the wounds that bind us. The challenges force us to relinquish the unconscious patterns of limitation. The key to transcending the challenges is to recognize the unconscious pattern that is operating within you, in that particular challenge and allow the unresolved emotions of the past to transform and transmute in the unconditional embodied Love of your Being.

11. Embodying Consciousness of Movement in Stillness: We are embodied Consciousness, and Consciousness is constantly manifesting through our thoughts, emotions, and actions, as us. In Essence, we are an extension and expression of the Oneness Consciousness, constantly expressing in Movement within the greater Stillness. Feeling the dance of Movement within Stillness, allows us to transcend the polarities of duality; form and formlessness, yin and yang, mind and body, which awakens us onto our natural state of Unity consciousness or Oneness. This transcendence of duality also allows us to move into cyclical time and re-establish the primordial rhythm within our own being. This is the primordial rhythm that is inherent in all of life's process, evident in the seasons and cycles of the moon, but personally in our menstrual cycle and circadian biological rhythms.

12. Activating the Sacred Initiations: Through the *Sacred Initiations of the Feminine,* we can heal our bodies, hearts, and souls and awaken the complete potential of the Feminine within us. We're living in a special time where the Feminine is awakening on the planet through each us. The *Sacred Initiations* are a transformational initiatory experience of the Feminine through consciousness, spiritual transformational alchemy and embodiment on a personal level, thus reflecting and contributing to the awakening on the collective level.

13. Awakening of Oneness Realization: Reawakening our *Feminine Essence* within, in harmony with our Masculine qualities allows us to activate the template of the perfected human being; *Sophiatic Christos.* This is truly the marriage of ourselves with the beloved, Great Mother Source. To bring ourselves into the next evolutionary reality of Unity consciousness; where we can experience our Divine Nature in our physical body... we must reclaim the lost Feminine within and evolve our consciousness through Her. By resurrecting Her fierce compassion and unconditional love, we can create the union of opposites within us and thus transcend the plane of duality, moving into the domain of Oneness, Great Mother Source matrix.

WHAT ARE THE FEMININE AND MASCULINE QUALITIES?

As human beings, we contain both opposing energies of yin and yang; feminine and masculine respectively. These two forces are 'ways' in which we describe the particular qualities of the energetic fields and how they manifest within us. We can say that yin is relative to yang; these two don't exist in absolute terms, but in relative terms. In other words, one thing, when compared with the second thing, is classified as either more 'yin' or more 'yang'. When we use these terms to classify something, we must keep in mind that these terms are fluid, rather than fixed, and the context is always taken into consideration. For example, we can say that the front part of our body is 'yin' compared to the backside of our body, however, the front top part of our front body is more 'yang' when compared to the lower half of our front body. Similarly, we use these definitions below, to have a sense of the energetic quality, knowing that, the word yin or Feminine, or yang and masculine are not absolute, just some contextual description of the energetic quality. Furthermore, I will also note that throughout this book and in the use of the term *Conscious Feminine Medicine*™, I use the word Feminine as a synonym for the Yin quality of energy. Therefore, yin and Feminine carry similar qualities energetically.

Now, when I speak about the repression of the Feminine, I'm referring to all the qualities of the Feminine, in both men and women, that have been repressed within our culture and society. Within this book, I am addressing not just the repression of the Feminine, but the repression of the Feminine in women. This is important to note because the feminine and masculine qualities exist in both men and women. It's how we describe the duality of this energetic frequency that behaves in opposing, complementary form, born from the Oneness.

The repression of the Feminine Archetype in the last 5000+ years has caused an imbalance not just in the gender of women, but also in the gender of man. As I mentioned above, the feminine and masculine qualities are present in both genders, male and female. Within us, it's the signature expression of the one Essence within, and outside ourselves, it's the classification of the duality expression of Cosmic energy. Many of the wounds from this repression, found in women, also manifest in slightly different ways in men.

Feminine and Masculine Qualities

Feminine	Masculine
Experience Oriented	Goal Oriented
Sensitivity	Reasoning
Nurturing	Discipline
Inward	Outward
Nourishing	Independent
Surrender	Force
Allowing	Directing
Receptive	Activating
Affection	Aloof
Emotional	Mental
Empathic	Self Absorbed
Hidden	Seen
Darkness	Light
Creative	Catalyst
Unseen	Material
Restful	Exhaustive
Retreating	Striving
Slow Moving	Rapid
Being	Doing
Transformational	Multiplicity
That which holds all potential	That which activates all processes
That which all is birthed from	Catalyst for the birth
Yin	Yang

It's important to understand that the feminine and masculine qualities aren't definitive linear categories, but rather a quality of energy that performs in a way, with certain characteristics. It's said that yin and yang are considered relative, therefore defined by the relationship from one thing to another. As another example, our outgoing personality may be yang compared to our quiet meditative moments (yin), but when comparing our outgoing personality to someone louder than us, then we become yin to the louder, more animated expression of someone else (yang).

Like yin and yang, feminine and masculine qualities are also relative, even though they seem somewhat more fixed in their respective categories. For example, our emotions may be more feminine in relationship to our masculine thoughts, but within that, we have yin/feminine emotions of fear and sadness, compared to more yang/masculine emotions of anger and rage. So, feminine and masculine qualities can be used to describe two very different types of energy, the duality that comes from the oneness. They are two sides of the same coin, with ample room for interpretation and qualitative relational observation.

Furthermore, these archetypes have conditioned how we perceive and define women and men in our culture. A few decades ago, it was common for women to be restricted to domestic roles and men to function primarily out in the world. Now, we've broken these archetypical stereotypes and are continuing to progress toward outward equality. However, equality is about each gender honoring the differences and the valuing what each brings to the table, rather than having to make ourselves more masculine, and ultimately denying our Feminine nature, to be accepted. We're slowly migrating to this acknowledgment of differences as a collective, and recognizing that our sensitive, emotional natures don't have to been hidden in order for us to feel valued; we don't have to be more masculine to fit in, but rather bring all of our Self, feminine and masculine to the forefront and realize that the sensitive, compassionate, caring, intuitive nature is just as important as the assertive, thought-based, action, driven aspect of ourselves. If we continue to claim worth by excluding the feminine qualities, we continue to betray ourselves.

As part of our evolution, it's critical to realize that we're just as worthy as the men, but not because we're the same, but because we're slightly different. We must confront and heal the places within that keeps us in judgment of our feminine qualities. The denial of this difference is what keeps our world in a trajectory of destruction. The absence of Feminine qualities of sensitivity, intuition, creativity, community, nurturing, caring and oneness create a world where we're disconnected, unhappy and competing. These qualities of the Feminine are seen more in women because women were created to birth, to hold the container, to nourish the young and the families, qualities that are needed for healthy survival. It's not that men don't have these feminine qualities, but women are wired with these internally through our physiology and psychology. Women's hormones and brain chemistry support these differences, which is necessary for our roles of birthing and survival of the young. Hormones such as oxytocin, which multiplies in women's brain receptors at the end of pregnancy, make new mothers highly receptible to maternal behaviors. It's important to note that cesarean birth mothers don't receive the release of this bonding hormone, because their body's innate birthing process is interrupted with the procedure of cesarean, ceasing the innate physiological hormonal release that is wired into the organic process of birthing. Oxytocin levels cause a mother to become familiar with the unique odor of her newborn and imprints the mother with the child and vice versa, ensuring the survival of the species. Lowered oxytocin levels in males, can partly explain the more aggressive physical behavior seen in males compared with the calming response observed in females, during times of confrontation or stress. Even though it remains controversial, testosterone has been determined to play a role in the behavior differences of men and women, showing higher levels of testosterone in men correlated with higher levels of aggressive physical response and higher levels of estrogen in women correlated with higher levels of emotional reactivity, including studies showing a positive correlation to between levels of hostility and testosterone.[1]

Furthermore, these innate differences in women and men are also evident in brain activity. It shows our brains engage different parts correlated with our gender and physiology. In one experiment where men and women watched the same emotional movie, the right side of the amygdala was more active in men, and yet in women, the left side of the amygdala showed to be more active. The right side of the amygdala is in tune to the outside environment, coordinating motor actions and visual cues to negotiate our surroundings; typical of hunting behavior. While the left side is concentrated more on our inner environment of the body; producing emotional relevant content from sensor experiences and the hypothalamus' regulation of the body's metabolic and autonomic activities; necessary for the capacity of nurturing. These differences show how our gender, and thus our biology, innately respond to the world differently. However, these aren't absolutes, and while the feminine and masculine qualities can relate to higher estrogen and higher testosterone, respectively, we must keep in mind that they don't define gender. Each woman, and therefore man, contain a unique expression of feminine and masculine qualities.

And as we become aware of these inherent differences in our genders, we can begin to appreciate the extensive damage that the repression of the Feminine has had on the gender of women. As women, our bodies innately, deeply resonate to this Feminine wiring, and through this collective repression, we've been individually conditioned in making our very own internal reactions 'wrong' in some way, directly disempowering ourselves through mistrust. It's this deep-rooted illusory sense of wrongness unconsciously operating at our core that is responsible for much of our psychological, physiological and spiritual suffering.

Women have been breaking this patriarchal repression and are beginning to realize their worthiness, which is the internal shift of honoring the Feminine within. This is allowing us to steadily embody the fact that our worth is independent of our qualities, or our roles and that we don't have to hide our voice, opinions and what seems natural to us, to appear worthy. Women are awakening to the power of exposing the sensitivity, intuitive, creative, nurturing and caring qualities of the feminine in combination with the more active, assertive, physical nature of the masculine qualities and noticing the critical necessity that there is to merge these within, for our survival and that of the planet.

In ancient times, before the beginning of written societies, men and women lived in equalitarian societies as equals. These societies were sometimes termed matriarchal; but not because women ruled, but rather because women lived in equality alongside men, they were in essence, equalitarian. In these societies, both women and men had equally important roles and none was the dominant sex. Barbara Love and Elizabeth Shanklin have this to say about matriarchy society, "by 'matriarchy' we mean a non-alienated society: a society in which women, those who produce the next generation, define motherhood, determine the conditions of motherhood and determine the environment in which the next generation is reared [2]. According to Adler, in the Marxist tradition, matriarchy usually refers to a pre-class society "where women and men share equally in production and power" [3].

The Feminine and Masculine archetypes were in harmony with each other and men and women displayed this through their relationships and harmonious interactions. Dr. Page states in her book *The Healing Power of Sacred Women*, "Here women were considered sacred from their inherent link to the Divine. Mother Earth was honored for her abundant fertility and cyclical episodes, such as seasons, were respected as essential for life to evolve." She continues, "They knew that women possessed powers far more potent than physical strength, financial wealth, and man-made laws. These forces include fearlessness in the face of death, the ability to purify and transform, the power to create life, the gift of inspiration and most importantly, the power of love. These qualities mirrored those of the 'Great Mother', who had been worshipped for tens of thousands of years before the appearance of the patriarchy."

The Feminine archetype reflected in the state of women's lives, was well and alive back then, and for many reasons our cultures then shifted away from the equalitarian type society to what we have experienced in the last 5000+ years. Women have forgotten what it is to be a sacred woman, and more importantly their direct link to the phases of birth, death, and rebirth that is carried in the mysteries of their feminine form.

The sacred connection represented with Mother Earth in the Feminine archetype, is also reflected within the body of a woman. This cycle relates to the macro and micro cycles of life. The macrocycle of life on the outer can be seen in the seasons, the moon's orbit, and the natural rhythm of birth, maturation, and death, in all of creation. The moon's 29½ day orbit is an outer representation of a woman's monthly cycle of menstruation. This cycle permeates all aspects of our life and informs all living processes. It is the rhythm and dance of nature, itself.

Our body's cycle, just like the moon's cycle, is divided into three aspects; death, rebirth, and manifestation. In the female body, we experience maiden, mother and crone stages. As we experience our monthly cycle, we're in rhythm with the cosmic rhythm of the Universe. Our individual menstrual cycle mirrors the moon through the same cycles of death (the release of the physical lining, as well as emotional and mental purification), rebirth (our innate renewed ability to conceive every month and bring in new visions for ourselves, family and community), and manifestation/conception (the ability to transform spirit into matter within our body and give birth).

The value of becoming conscious of the Feminine as an archetype is not just about the integration of the feminine qualities, but it is about syncing with this cosmic field of the universal rhythm itself that is consistently giving birth to the material realm. This lost connection with the Feminine, can be traced back to 500,000 years ago at the Neanderthals burial grounds. Evidence shows us that the Neanderthals would bury their bodies in fetal positions, facing an east-west position with red ochre sprinkled all over their bodies. They saw themselves as part of the continuum of life, an extension of the greater rhythm of the Feminine, coming from Mother Earth. The east-west burial positions were in honor of the cycles of the sun, of day and night, replicating the sun's rising and setting position. The red ochre (Earth paint) used at the time of death symbolized the return of the individual back to the womb of Mother Earth, in the color of blood, from which one is born.

The Feminine was also traced throughout time, in women, as the nurturers of the young. Women were seen as an extension of Mother Earth in their responsibilities of provision. As Mother Earth provides for all of her creation, women provided for the young that were born from them. This direct unbreakable line between women, the Earth and the Feminine, was revered and honored by ancient cultures featured as early as 30,000 BC where we have seen the emergence of the countless sculptures of the Mother Goddess carved from stone through the Pyrenees in Spain, all the way to Siberia. At this time before history, women embodied the mysterious and nurturing powers of nature, herself. There was no separation between a woman and the Feminine archetype, which in many ways represented power over man (humanity), power over life and death, and power of the mystery Herself. This correlation of Feminine and women predominated for over 30,000 years, from 35,000 BCE to 4,000 BCE, in which the Earth and women were revered as Sacred, and interestingly, it was also the time in which peace reigned for thousands of years.

The Venus (mother goddess) figurines discovered throughout the near and middle east, from the Pyrenees to Siberia, have further suggested the worship and rituals of the Goddess throughout the Paleolithic period. In 1908, the famous Venus of Willendorf was excavated in the Danube valley, Austria. In total, some 144 such figurines have become discovered, which are between 3 cm and 40 cm in height. In September 2008, archaeologists from the University of Tubingen discovered a 6-cm figurine woman carved from a mammoth's tusk, the Venus of Hohle Fels, which dates to at least 35,000 years ago.

After the end of the ice age, 4,000 BCE, with the advent of the Neolithic agricultural revolution, the Goddess culture was not able to prevail. Women began to be treated as objects, the appearance of warfare was seen, and the paradigm shift towards patriarchy was well underway. In Egypt, around 3,000 BCE, we see the mythological introduction of Osiris, the first male deity. Then around 2400 BCE, a series of aggressive invasions took over Egypt by invaders that introduced the concept of dark being evil and light being good, along with the establishment of a supreme Father deity. Around 1900 BCE through 1500 BCE women lost their right to choose their own partners at will, and children became members of the father's kin, instead of the mother's, as had been the custom. By 1570 BCE we see Patriarchy completely take over, where women are constantly treated as objects, and the honoring of the Feminine quickly becomes a taboo and therefore hidden in the society. It is around this time, mid-1500's BCE that the last of the Feminine matriarchal societies ceased to exist in Crete (Minoan culture), as they were radically and forcibly taken over by a new power of warriors, led by patriarchal rule.

In the time of the ancient Sumerians of Mesopotamia and the early dynastic period of Egypt, around 3500 BCE, there was not much history committed to written form. After that, written history made its appearance concurring with the advent of patriarchal domination. It's been easy for cultural analysts to conclude that history was patriarchal because they had based their assumptions on the available writings that only revealed the current patriarchal societal, political and cultural view. The previous matriarchal norm that had been observed since the beginning of time had vanished before writing form began. It is now becoming clear that since the beginning of time up to the advent of 'written history', matriarchal and egalitarian cultures prevailed, yet leaving no written history behind that is easily detected. Therefore, the earlier artistic, creative flourishing of matriarchal and egalitarian societies, has been easily dismissed by historians in the past. However, things are changing. Due to the overwhelming archeological, cultural and symbolic discoveries in recent years, these Goddess cultures of our history can no longer be denied.

In general, we've experienced this overall Patriarchy rule, roughly since 4000 BCE till now, a little over 6000 years, and yet we can still see remnants of matriarchal societies at the heart of these hidden cultures. In China, we have the Mosuo culture, near Tibet, which is described as matriarchal [4]. In their culture, women are head of the household, inheritance is passed down through the female line, and the women in their communities make business decisions.

In India, there is still some evidence of matriarchal and matrilineal communities recognized in their national constitution as 'scheduled tribes', which have been known to be more egalitarian [5]. In Vietnam, the role of women in their culture can be traced by the indigenous cultures influenced by matriarchal customs, such as women ruling over their tribe as in the AU CO tribe. These tribes have a double kinship system, which combined matrilineal and patrilineal patterns of family structure and assigned equal importance to both [6].

Native Americans have roots in matriarchal societies and sexual equality. The HOPI, for example, operate as equalitarian. HOPI women participate fully in political decision-making and still are matrilineal, acting as the female principle activated in women and Mother Earth, as its center source [7]. In their tribe, they have the Clan Mother, which has the power to overturn land distribution decisions made by the men if she felt it was unfair [8].

On the other hand, the Iroquois Confederacy, which combines a few Native American tribes, operates under the constitution below, which have women as their center focus. It was formed in 1000-1450 CE and recently transcribed from verbal to written form in 1880:

"In our society, women are the center of all things. Nature, we believe, has given women the ability to create; therefore, it is only natural that women be in positions of power to protect this function... We traced our clans through women; a child born into the world assumed the clan membership of its mother. Our young women were expected to be physically strong... The young women received formal instruction in traditional planting... Since the Iroquois were dependent upon the crops they grew, whoever controlled this vital activity wielded great power within our communities. It was our belief that since women were the givers of life, they naturally regulated the feeding of our people... In all countries, real wealth stems from the control of land and its resources. Our Iroquois philosophers knew this as well as we knew natural law. To us it made sense for women to control the land since they were far more sensitive to the rhythms of the Mother Earth. We did not own the land but were custodians of it. Our women decided any and all issues involving territory, including where a community was to be built and how land was to be used. In our political system, we mandated full equality. Our leaders were selected by a caucus of women before the appointments were subject to popular review... Our traditional governments are composed of an equal number of men and women. The men are chiefs and the women clan-mothers... As leaders, the women closely monitor the actions of the men and retain the right to veto any law they deem inappropriate, our women not only hold the reigns of political and economic power, they also have the right to determine all issues involving the taking of human life. Declarations of war had to be approved by the women, while treaties of peace were subject to their deliberations." [9].

Upon this foundation, we move forward and create the resurrection of the Feminine, not against the masculine, but as equalitarian, each bringing our gifts forward. A vision where both the masculine and feminine are complimentary to each other.

I often find myself being asked, "Why focus on the women? It seems that both men and women have lost something and have something to regain in the Feminine. While I absolutely agree, the focus of my work for the past 20 years has been primarily on women and the history, effects, and healing of the Feminine. My personal absence of focus on the men, doesn't mean that it's not needed for both genders. However, I do believe that as we bring the attention of the wounds that have haunted women for thousands of years to the forefront, we open a greater conversation and opportunity to heal at the core. I believe this is a story that has to be told.

SOPHIATIC CHRISTOS: MARRIAGE OF DUALITY

As we look towards the resolution of the collective and personal repression of the Feminine, we come across the mysterious concept of the Anthropos, the perfected human being. The Anthropos means to become fully human. The process begins by fully integrating the Feminine and Masculine principles, but most importantly, it creates union from the state of human duality that we live in. It's a shift in perception more so than in anything else within us. Cynthia Bourgeult writes this about the concept of Anthropos, in the Messages of Mary Magdalene;

"Obviously, there is far more at stake here than simply integrating masculine and feminine principles within one's finite humanity. The integration takes place on a cosmic scale and is accomplished through learning how to anchor one's being in that underlying unitive ground: that place of oneness before the opposites arise. Some traditions would call this the "causal level." However, one defines it, its origin is on the vertical axis, in a realm and mode of perception far more subtle than our own. It has less to do with what one sees than with *how* one sees; it amounts to a fundamental shift in perception.

When this level is attained, either by sudden spiritual insight or by a long, tough slog through the minefields of ego, a person becomes "a single one" (in Aramaic, *ihidaya*: one of the earliest titles applied to Jesus): an enlightened or "fully human" being. The union of opposites Jesus is speaking of really pertains to the union of the finite and infinite within oneself, or the bringing together of the vertical axis with the horizontal so that there is "one Heart, one Being, one Will, one God, all in all." When this happens, the world does not pass away, but one is able to live in it as master, re-creating its external forms ("making one image supersede another") out of the infinite generativity of the One."[10].

The Anthropos is the way that we merge our bodies consciousness with the sacred, divine aspect of our being. They're one; we just experience them as separate. It's the reunion of body and soul, body and spirit, feminine and masculine. This is the process to wholeness, to realize our full divine human potential and reality, here in this body now. And in doing so, we embrace the process of resurrecting the Feminine qualities alongside our Masculine qualities within our psyche.

The process of becoming whole and experiencing our unified field of Oneness as the 'Anthropos' is a process we can describe as dissolving the ego states of illusion and distilling our consciousness to experience the Essence of light that we are. Normally, we experience and identify who we are with our feelings, our thoughts, beliefs, and the roles that we play. Such as being a mother, sister, wife, doctor, artist etc. While these are things we experience and roles that we play, these are not things that we are. These are our thoughts, emotions, beliefs and actions all experienced by our sense of individuality, through our ego.

And our Essence is of Light; which is really the same as this consciousness of Oneness. However, from consciousness of Light, we then uniquely express varying vibrational frequencies known as universal qualities. These are the core fractals of light vibration/

frequency coming from the Oneness, which makes up all form, including ourselves. These Universal qualities are in everything... and every form distills down to a quality or combinations of qualities. We humans carry our human traits and are essentially created from Light in the form of Universal qualities. Our journey of enlightenment (realization) dissolves our human traits so that our Universal qualities of Light can be expressed. This is a process of the dissolution of our ego-conditioned states of separation, leaving us with the purification of our Light of Oneness. This is the process of becoming the perfected human being, Anthropos.

CONTEMPLATION WITH THE 13 PILLARS OF CONSCIOUS FEMININE MEDICINE™

To begin your contemplation with the 13 pillars of *Conscious Feminine Medicine*™, first, sit in stillness and allow your mind to clear. You may do this by taking a few breaths into your lower abdomen, letting your body settle and your breathing slow down.

Secondly, have a journal ready and begin your contemplation with each of the 13 pillars. Once you have settled your body and mind with breath, begin the inquiry into each pillar by first reading the statement of each pillar in the chapter and then reading the corresponding inquiry below. If the inquiry doesn't interest you, you may expand your conscious journaling to include one of these inquires instead:

What is your current relationship with this pillar statement? Do you believe this is possible? Have you had an experience that relates to this pillar? Do you have strong reactions within your body, either positive or negative, when you read this pillar?

After you have read each pillar and written consciously, from the deep heart, let yourself take a few extra minutes, in silence, breathing and just listening to your heart. Sometimes, we may have some wisdom coming through from our state of presence. If so, let yourself add it to your conscious contemplation.

For all the pillars listed below, make sure to read the full statements of these pillars in the chapter before contemplating the inquiry.

1. **You are Divine** - How are you honoring your Healership as a woman?

2. **You are the Medicine** - Can you feel the medicine of your Being, residing in your core?

3. **You are a Healer** - Can you feel the healing potential of your being? Let yourself reflect on your body's ability to heal itself through the activation of the Light that you are. What does that feel like?

4. **Your Trinity Womb Center** - What does it feel like to become present to your Trinity Wombs in your body, feeling your direct connection with your Spiritual nature?

5. **Embodying your Sacred Feminine Form** - How does it feel to become present of the inherent perfection of the physical Feminine form, embracing the sacredness in your biology, emotional waves, intuitive awareness and mystery within?

6. **Healing the 3 Collective wound of the Feminine** - Begin by exploring your relationship with each one of these wounds in your life. This will begin the transformation and the Sacred Initiation in each center, respectively, as you reclaim your Feminine Soul from each.

7. **Transforming the 1st World Feminine Disorders** - What physical and emotional imbalances have been challenging you>> Let yourself sit in reflection and listen deeply to the underlying emotion that is calling out to be heard, acknowledged and seen. Journal what you discover as you do this.

8. **Embracing the Biochemistry of Consciousness** - Contemplate your emotional, mental and soul body through Breath and presence, bringing awareness and space to the reality that you are consciousness and it is living with you right now. How does it feel, what unwinds within?

9. **Integrating the 5 Elemental Mothers** - How does it feel to know that the Universe cares and sees you?

10. **Embracing Evolutionary Activations** - Can you accept that the challenges that you have faced have been out of love. Can you see the gift in it?

11. **Embodying Consciousness of Movement in Stillness** - What is your relationship to stillness?

12. **Activating the Sacred Initiations of the Feminine** - Are you ready to let go of the collective and personal wounds and experience your greatest brilliance?

13. **Awakening to Oneness Realization** - Let yourself feel the perfection in your Being and surrender everything you think you know into this Light of your Soul. How does that feel to you?

4

Vessel as Sacred Temple

Our Physical Body is the vessel,
the Sacred Temple…
where the in-breath of Spirit creates
form from formlessness.

YOU ARE THE MEDICINE

Women that have been tested positive for breast cancer genes have been making radical decisions to remove their breast and all the surrounding tissue to limit their chances of getting a cancerous diagnosis later. What these women do not know, in making this decision is that diseases in our physical body, like cancer, are not just determined by the physical matter such as cells, tissue, particles and so on. There is a whole other world of energy and consciousness interacting and affecting the physical plane of matter. This world of energetics can be addressed, so that we can create health, rather than just avoiding disease in our physical body, at the end of the spectrum. By not acknowledging the causal level and energetic world of consciousness, which is scientifically supported by Quantum science, we continuously make hasty decisions with our bodies and perpetuate the story of powerlessness. In this fashion, we continue to support the false illusion of merely treating the physical body solely, while we ignore the underlying interplays of our being, thus preventing real healing from occurring on all levels.

Quantum science has brought the interaction of the unseen world of energetics into visible reality, and these foundational principles explain the underlying interplay of energetic values revealing the real natural relationship of the unseen (consciousness) with the seen (matter). Through the vast understanding of Quantum science, we can recognize the significance of the practical teachings of ancient traditional healing wisdom, that have been dismissed from our contemporary experience of medicine. From this perspective, our health is created from an intricate dance between the seen and the unseen worlds, culminating in a harmonious state (and sometimes inharmonious state), in what we call body. This 'body' or form is a mere reflection of the energetic interplays of consciousness themselves.

Quantum medicine, along with epigenetics, have empowered us with the ability to break through the constrictions and illusions of material, conventional medicine and has opened us up to the myriad of interactions of higher consciousness. This unified field of consciousness is what we sometimes refer to as God, Divine, Oneness, Spirit, or Source. In this paradigm, we are inspired to transform and create shifts, which intrinsically result in healing, harmony, and health. By embracing Quantum Medicine and epigenetics, we no longer must stay victim to our circumstances and our physical bodies. We can rise to claim the power within, with active participation and active responsibility in our expanded awareness of the inner dimensions. Although to some degree, we're still at the mercy of ultimate consciousness (the unified field), here, we explore more meaningful choices over our state of mind, which directly impact the manifestation of our body's health, as we shall see throughout this chapter. In this model, our happiness doesn't depend on avoiding disease and relying on something outside ourselves for happiness, but rather accessing a dimension of consciousness within us that innately contains the ability to heal and to return disharmony to harmony. Along with its myriads of expression that make up our subtle bodies, we soon realize that we are the map and our consciousness is the true map that leads us to our healing. Let's explore.

Our happiness, harmony, and health stem out of the interactions brewing in our energy levels, including our states of consciousness. This very fabric that we are made from determines what we see and experience as our body. In the Quantum model, we realize that we're not separate from our consciousness in our energetic self and that any thoughts of separation are illusions of the ego. Thus, we also realize that what we are searching for outside ourselves exists within us all as our Essence or our Essential Self. Health and healing are a byproduct of activating and awakening to this Essence dimension. What causes us disharmonies, challenges, and/or diseases in our bodies, mind, and emotions, is rooted in our disconnection from our Essential Self. Within quantum medicine, you realize that all imbalance is related to a spiritual imbalance and that everything arises from consciousness itself, including ourselves.

The Quantum Field is the field we relate to as consciousness itself, with properties of the interplay of the energetic fields themselves. We're composed of these energetics fields, and it's crucial to understand these fields, subtle bodies of energy so that we have a greater understanding of our energetic terrain. Understanding the terrain of consciousness and the interrelationship of non-form and form will empower us in our transformation and our evolution of the Feminine Soul.

Quantum medicine was first brought to our awareness through the work of Albert Einstein in his famous equation $E=mc^2$, which explains that all matter is compressed energy in one form or another and his discovery of the Quantum field. From this perspective, we can derive that our bodies are, therefore, a solidification of energy into what we see as form. Quantum Medicine is the field of medicine established by the principles of Quantum physics. It's the bridge between the old paradigm of material, conventional allopathic medicine, and the traditional energy medicines of the world. It incorporates an understanding of the functioning of these traditional energetic medicines and allows us to integrate them into modern medicinal practices. We no longer can deny the existence of the energetic world of consciousness and its interplay with our material world, and our physical world, as we know it.

Through the principles of Quantum physics of Non-locality, Entangled Hierarchy and Discontinuity, we can scientifically acknowledge that all of life is not just a physical phenomenon, but rather an interplay between physical matter and non-physical matter. The existence of this unified field of consciousness, also known as the quantum field, empowers us in knowing we have a choice in creating our health and most importantly offers us a myriad of possibilities for healing. One of the most important acknowledgments of Quantum medicine is that our consciousness plays an active role in the creation of our physical material body through the morphogenetic field (Sheldrake 1981) and as mentioned, it recognizes that our body is not entirely explainable in terms of solely material biology. It substantiates the knowledge that the ground for all being is Consciousness. While it's important to acknowledge the physical material components of disease; cells, genes, and structures; it's equally important to look at the underlying field of consciousness and energetic realms that are influencing the signals for physical manifestation. Therefore, what we think our beliefs, feelings, the mental, emotional and soul level imprints we consciously and unconsciously identify with, directly communicate with the subtle morphogenetic (blueprint) of our physical body, dictating every single cell and function in our body. According to Sheldrake, this subtle morphogenetic field exists around each biological morphic field (which is highly acceptable in the biological arena), from which groups of cells go on to form a particular physical form like our cardiac tissue, or liver, etc. In 1980, Sheldrake studies suggested that there is an energetic field surrounding these morphogenetic fields, in which he terms subtle morphogenetic field, and which passes down 'energetic' tendencies we see in families with the same resonance. On the physical level, Sheldrake's theory offers a biological-energetic explanation of why families experience the same emotions or develop the same behaviors. These subtle morphogenetic fields are not limited to time and space, therefore being informed by accumulated collective conditioning of our ancestors, or past lives if one believes in that. According to Sheldrake, the subtle morphogenetic fields inform our DNA and perhaps may also signal which DNA turns on or off.

Furthermore, the subtle morphogenetic field seems to biologically explain the collective effects of our perceptions and conditioning from our past. In other words, it shows that there is a measurable biological field that correlates with the collective beliefs that are passed down from generation to generation, further molding our physical form of cells, organs, and biochemistry. Thus, most of our transformational work will be to resolve this collective conditioning, which directly affects our present state and experience of life itself; physically, emotionally, and mentally.

According to Dr. A. Goswami, consciousness is the ground for all being. This consciousness may be known to us by other names such as the unified field, unity consciousness, Source, Spirit, or God. Our emotional, mental, soul, subtle bodies and matter, are all quantum possibilities of consciousness, all derived and created by Consciousness. The form is just denser manifestation of consciousness.

Universal consciousness (unified field, Source, or God) is the beginning from which all else stems from. Universal consciousness is not individual, but is a unified field between all forms and formless phenomenon. Consciousness cannot be plural; it is one. There is one consciousness, and we're all interconnected in this consciousness. This consciousness is the source from which our physical body is manifested, and where everything in the Universe is created. This process of creation is referred to as downward causation by Dr. Amit Goswami, in which Consciousness becomes denser and denser as it manifests into varying forms of creation; such as our emotional body, our mental bodies, our soul and the densest begin our physical body. The downward causation model does include all forms in the Universe, not limited only to the creation of human beings. We will discuss these subtle bodies in greater detail.

This source of consciousness is also experienced as the force we know as Love. This is a force that brings things together, that unites and contains gravity. This is the force of Love that we associate with Divine Intelligence and the Law of attraction, moving through all of creation, not just limited to the conditional human love that we experience. Love Consciousness is the source that connects us all and what we transmit to each other in relationships. Eckhart Tolle tells us that Consciousness can be experienced as Love and all of Love is rooted in the same Love, even though it is evident that we do not experience the same love with all people. What changes in the Love we feel for some people and not for others is the intensity of this Love, but not the actual Love itself, because all Love is this stream of consciousness. When two people mirror the same intensity of Love for each other, then it can be said that they 'love' each other and sometimes choose to be in an exclusive love relationship with each other. Thus, what we're experiencing as this connecting factor of Love is Consciousness itself.

In the quantum model of consciousness, Dr. Amit Goswami defines this model of 'downward causation' which means that everything is derived from Consciousness (Love) itself, and then Consciousness flows creating from the subtlest to the densest of form. Therefore, we begin with an unmanifested unified field (universal Consciousness), from there, our subtle bodies are created from the most subtle, to physical form; secret, soul, emotional, mental and physical. Even though I will be working with a slightly expanded model from what I have shown here; I wanted to point out the difference between this quantum medicine model versus the more conventional allopathic medicine model which most of the scientific and medical community still adhere to. This downward causation is precisely the opposite of the allopathic medicine model, which is based on upward causation. The model of upward causation begins with form/matter and its parts; cells, atoms, molecules, and neurons, which create our physical body and from our brain, the Consciousness is created. In this allopathic model, our brain gives rise to Consciousness, or at least the idea of Consciousness, putting our brain as the central creator, in a sense. Everything here has physical causation, and there is no room for Consciousness to be a primary cause, placing Consciousness as the result, basically making it a manifestation of our thoughts, rather than the source of all phenomenon.

The Quantum model empowers us and enriches us, allowing the mystery of Consciousness, Herself, to be at the core, giving us infinite possibilities of creation. Embracing this paradigm shift of Quantum science is so powerful because, amongst many other things, it allows us to directly influence and have choice in our lives and our creation, rather than being at the mercy of only our perceptual reality of our minds.

From this Quantum perspective of consciousness, I would like to mention two other principles relevant to quantum medicine, which directly reflect the interaction on these subtle levels. The first is the principle of non-locality, and the second is entanglement. In simple terms, the theory of non-locality confirms that energy can be in two places at the same time, and it can influence the outcome of a matter. Non-locality explains the interaction of matter and energy. As described in Bells theorem, energy, or quantum particles are not limited to any time and space. It states a single un-separated state or field still govern two quantum particles that are apart in space. In other words, it acknowledges that there is a more significant state, field, or Consciousness that proves to hold these two particles together, and it is not limited to time and space as we know it. Energetic matter seems to be infinitely mutable, and can be in two places at once, as well as being able to move backward in time, being connected by a field of Consciousness, that is invisible to the eye, Therefore, energy is continuously interacting with itself through energy fields and as matter, influencing the outcome of matter even if they are in different locations. This concept of non-locality explains how healing is possible even when the helee is in a different location than the healer, and how energy moves between them as varying vibratory states or frequencies. It also speaks to the consciousness shifts, and changes we know are possible between generations, including past and present generations, when one engages in healing on the collective levels.

Secondly, another aspect of non-locality is quantum entanglement, which demonstrates that two particles somehow remain in contact with each other no matter how far apart they are, influencing each other. This explains how intention can affect energy and the outcome.

Through non-locality and quantum entanglement, we can understand the underpinnings of the phenomenon of intention, prayer, and long-distance healing. The phenomenon that while one person is praying in one location and a second person at another location, has reported great healing is due to these effects of non-locality and intention. The person praying sends their intention energetically, which in turn affects the energy of the person it's intended for, through space and time. In healing work one person, while consciously connecting to the Universal Consciousness of the Unified field, can influence the healing through the transmission of Consciousness itself, of another person in a different location, which shows the principle of entanglement. This is all-important because it substantiates the energetics fields of Consciousness and shows how the energetics states of Consciousness are available and how they interact in the arena of transformational healing. In conclusion, Quantum medicine substantiates that everything (every form) starts with Universal consciousness and then moves down into our various bodies of energy, finally forming the physical body. Thus, the physical body is a reflection that we can see on the subtle bodies of Consciousness and true transformational healing is inclusive of all the levels of existence, not just our physical.

YOU ARE THE MAP

Quantum medicine identifies several subtle energy fields of consciousness from lightest to denser, resulting in a form (matter). There have been many systems, throughout time, dedicated to understanding the interaction of the subtle bodies of reality. These range from the astral, causal, buddhic, atmic, monadic, morphogenetic, gate centers or chakra system, meridians, extraordinary vessels, and the nadis, to name a few. Furthermore, Daoist, Vedic, Buddhic, and mystical Christianity all have interconnecting energetic systems explaining the mystery of the subtle realms, which is supported by Quantum science. In my explorations, I have worked with a great deal of these subtle bodies exploring the intersection of where and how they correspond with each other. You will find that the teachings of *Conscious Feminine Medicine*™, (CFM), incorporates some of these subtle bodies, that I feel are critical to our evolutionary process of awakening.

Within the CFM system, we explore the interplay of the 7 Gateways of light (chakra centers), the Sufi subtle bodies, the morphogenetic field, the pre-Daoist extraordinary vessels, and Trinity WOMB centers. These fields directly act as intermediaries between un-manifested consciousness (Oneness or the Unified field) and manifested consciousness (form or body). Below we begin exploring these subtle fields listed above, and in the next chapters, we will expand our discussions to more significant of energetic Consciousness that are critical to our evolutionary process; the 5 Universal Mothers (elements of water, fire, ether, air, earth), Feminine and Masculine polarity of duality (Yin And Yang) and engaging our Essence through the Heart Portal.

In exploring the roles of these subtle bodies, we first must understand that these subtle fields are all denser aspects of our Essence, our source Consciousness, and as such contains many of the perceptual imprints of our past. These subtle bodies are intermediaries between our form and our Essence; the interplay between our humanity and our divinity. These subtle bodies are mechanisms that temper the realm of light (Essence) into form (physical body). This interplay is also where our perceptual experiences of our past, our beliefs, our memories, and all unresolved pain and suffering is stored, giving rise to our distinct sense of self we call Ego or Conditioned Self. I discuss this Conditioned self in more detail in other chapters.

Being the holding stations of our psychic material, along with our unresolved pain body, the subtle bodies quite often are blocked and somewhat polluted with all this energetic material, that obstruct the light of our Essence (of Consciousness) to shine through. These memories and energetic material housed in our subtle bodies is not only our material but also the composite material that is passed down from generation to generation, culturally, socially, politically, and karmically. Therefore, beliefs that have been the foundation families, or groups of people, are all 'stored' in our subtle body, as part of our identification, mostly unconsciously.

As we discussed earlier, our thoughts and beliefs directly affect our physical body, therefore, and by understanding our subtle bodies, we can begin to see how the energetic material stored here can continue to affect our biochemistry and our physical body. For example, unconscious grief, loss or suffering can manifest blockage of energy in the heart gate center, affecting the thymus gland, disrupting the physical functioning in that part of the body, possibly contributing to breast disorder. Many times, unconscious feelings of powerlessness reflect in the lower gate centers contributing to imbalances in vital energetic flow in our solar and sacral centers leading to digestive or gynecological disorders. As we'll see, these levels of conditioning and identifications all affect the subtle bodies in particular ways, which in turn blocks our Essential Light and our true expression as human beings. Our evolutionary journey is one of transforming the unresolved energetic veils and truly begin to experience and identify ourselves with our Light, rather than with the limiting aspect of our Egoic self. We are here to allow our true Essence (Love) to shine through. Let's take a closer look at the subtle bodies that are directly correlated with these veils of conditioning.

MENTAL BODY

The mental body is the field that houses our thoughts, beliefs, and perceptions of our conditioning. These thoughts and beliefs that we hold as absolute Truths in our consciousness live in this realm of our subtle bodies. We accumulate most of our experiences through our perceptions, which involve our thoughts and thus our mind. Through our perceptions, we experience the world around us. Once we have decided on a perception, our mind turns it into a belief, unconsciously hidden from our conscious mind and our awareness. After that, how we see the world is colored through the lens of that belief, and in turn, affects how we feel. What we think and how we feel create specific biochemical reactions in our physical body, which always carries the potential to dysregulate the harmony of our system. Thus, our conscious and unconscious thoughts and beliefs are constantly interacting with our emotional and physical states, either creating harmony or disharmonious reactions.

For example, women may carry within their mental body a belief of not being good enough. A woman might have experienced growing up in an environment that limited what they could do, how they should act because of their gender. This can create an unconscious identity belief of "I am not good enough because I am female." As this statement becomes an unconscious belief, which conditions the experiences we have. This is a common and robust belief associated with most women, and many women still carry that belief within their mental body (which we discuss in later chapters), without even being aware of it. In another example, when a woman is faced with physical health challenges, and they may begin to attribute their health challenge to their value, again concluding that perhaps they have this health challenge because 'they are not good enough becoming identified with this thought about themselves.' This thought isn't really who they are but now they see themselves this way and become limited to their potential due to their limited view of themselves.

Many times, we conclude thoughts about ourselves and our situation, that isn't based on truth, but rather on a perception of our reality. Unfortunately, this reality is altered by the unconscious thought and beliefs that have been living in our mental field from a very early age. It's believed that our mental body is created during the years of 14-21. At this time, our karmic, societal, cultural, and family lineage beliefs are anchored in our mental body, becoming the conditioned veil that we see and experience ourselves through in the world. This continues until we begin our self-transformation of dissolving the calcified conditioning in our mental body. To a large extent, these mental conditioning patterns contribute our overall unhappiness and suffering.

EMOTIONAL BODY

Our emotional body is the subtle body that stores the unresolved and emotional patterns of our past. It holds all past conditioning related to our emotional experience, whether this lifetime or others. This subtle body is continuously adapting to our mental stimuli. Thoughts create specific emotions, and those emotions trigger biochemical changes, which we generally categorize as "stress." Stress is a catchall word for responses in our system that bring up unconscious beliefs or behaviors. When we experience stress, we can learn from these reactions, because our reactions are telling us precisely what unresolved pattern is ready for healing.

In her book, "Molecules of Emotions", Candice Pert[1], shares with us that emotions have related receptors to particular emotions and that the more consistently one experiences a particular emotion, the more receptors, to that emotion, are produced in their body, which in turn lessens the number of key receptors needed for people to absorb vital nutrients. The implications of this are that as we collectively and personally are wired to default to particular emotions, such as hopelessness, powerlessness, abandonment, anger, inadequacy, etc., we further deteriorate our health and wellbeing via the inability to absorb key nutritional elements. Therefore, collective experiences such as victimization and our responses to it, do contribute to the state of our physical and emotional wellbeing. Pert gives us an in-depth, biological understanding into the interplay of emotions and our physiological responses, demonstrating how our habitual expression of anger, sadness or hopelessness, may contribute to a biological deterioration and dysfunction in our body via the receptors in our genes. Therefore, breaking through these habitual emotions that we unconsciously default to, whether it runs in our family of origin or not, is key to our healing and wellness, on all levels.

Emotions can also be understood as an energetic flow of vibrations that requires expression and release from our bodies. Many women, along with many men, have been conditioned to repress our emotions and interpret our emotions as a sign of weakness, when it's an innate mechanism to regulate our biology. Many of us have learned to suppress our emotions in order to avoid rejection, ridicule, and or even worse fates, as institutionalized or branded as 'lunatic,' irrational or unfit. Many of us have created our fear of emotions, believing that they will overcome us, control us and make us do 'irrational' things. And, yes, while emotions can be compelling, especially if we've repressed them for very long, we can process and resolve these strong, repressed emotional states in a safe, contained manner. Our emotions are not the enemy, they're the energetic flow of expression that is vital to our wellbeing, and our expression as human beings.

When emotions aren't expressed, they are in turn repressed, and denied and this affects our network pathways, blocking our vital energy of Qi. When we attempt to block the unpleasant emotions, this blocked Qi (vital energy) ends up as a filter in our emotional field, dulling all emotions; our pleasant emotions, as well as the unpleasant ones. In turn, our inability to feel our elated states of joy and contentment causes us as much damage as repressed levels of unpleasant emotions.

What is interesting is that most people feel that expressing sadness, grief, hopelessness is contributing to negative thinking, and they classify it as a 'bad' thing that may contribute to a 'bad' outcome. However, what is not understood is that expressing our emotions, positive or negative, pleasant or unpleasant, is important to maintain our health and our wellbeing. When we're always in a chronic state of any particular emotion, such as, anger, sadness, hopelessness, etc., and react in this way to our daily life, it is the chronic states of emotions that interfere with our wellbeing and ill health. Expressing our emotions when we feel disappointment, sadness, fear, etc. is key to allowing this energetic field to flow within us.

Secondly, it's also the repression of these emotions that create biological imbalances and contribute to ill health and wellbeing. For example, not willing to look at unprocessed grief, rage, anger, fear, etc. either because we may not be aware of it, or due to self-judgment about having these 'feelings.' It's the repression of these emotions, usually due to unconscious fear, that creates the greatest dysfunction. And the reality is that at any given time, we're being affected by these unconscious emotions that may be part of our lineage, our ancestors, our cultural upbringing, or our perceptual realities.

As women, we carry many generations of repression in our emotional body, which has been compounded by our need for safety and survival, and this repression affects every one of us, even if individually we express our emotions well. Collectively, we've inherited our ancestor's fears and shame, that stand juxtaposed with our inherent desire to express. So in many ways, we see the scars of this phenomenon in the epidemics of thyroid issues that women experience, affected by their inability to express their true feelings and emotions freely. Furthermore, under the collective guise of 'not wanting to hurt others,' we do not speak our truth and continue to suppress our emotions and feelings, perpetuating the collective repression and shaming of our emotional body.

As women, biologically, our emotional body is much more expressive than that of a man. Higher levels of estrogen contribute to this difference in women. Our emotional body is an integral part of our being, allowing us to process varying stressors on all levels. Inherent within us, as women, is the ease of being able to move energy through our emotions and release our pain and stressors. We also find hormones in our tears, so that when we cry, our bodies are releasing and balancing our hormonal biology.

Most importantly, our innate relationship with our emotional body is critical for our survival as a species; it allows us to access deep levels of compassion, empathy, and care for others. We're wired this way, as primary caretakers and birthers of the next generation. It's the way of the great Mother Feminine energy.

Sadly, in the last few thousand years, we've lost touch with our emotional body, losing touch of our 'care' for others, for ourselves and our planet. The mothering aspect of the Feminine has been repressed, along with our emotional sensitivities. Our emotions allow us to feel the pain so that we can empathize, and from this, great compassion is born. When we dull or shut our emotional sensing down, we shut down our hearts and our care for others. We begin to see the world as something separate from ourselves, entering a paradigm of us versus them. This is the biggest challenge we have inherited from our patriarchal culture.

Of course, to men, the emotional body is not as visible, their biological tuning to higher testosterone levels do not automatically give rise to more significant yin emotions, such as compassion, and empathy, even though they are more than capable of feeling and cultivating these. For them, it is easier to suppress these emotions and lead with their intellectual faculties, rather than with the heart. The world of the patriarchy has been modeled in this way, leading us to the deterioration of the world we see now. Is it possible to live in a world that doesn't have empathy or lead to compassion for others? Yes, it is, we're seeing it now, full of wars, hatred and 'me or them' mentality. It's a world that leads with monetary profits over social care. However, it is not about leading with only heart, although that would not be a bad start. Ultimately, it is about leading with both, heart and intellectual ability, feminine and masculine, yin and yang. It is about genuinely leading with compassion, care, and human decency.

Ultimately, the expression and thereby healing, of our emotional body is a doorway in which we enter the inner realms of our Essence. It's the road in which we may experience the higher blissful levels of the heart, which lead us into the Divine realms. If we don't pierce through and heal our emotional body, then accessing these divine levels within us, become limited as well. Whether the emotional state is experienced as pleasant or unpleasant, at the root, these emotional states derive from the energy that is attempting to move through us, seeking the light. Blocking this energy affects our ability to feel deeply, whether positive or negative emotions. Therefore, if we block our anger or our sadness ongoingly, we also lessen our ability to feel any emotion, not just the targeted one. Healing our emotional body opens us up to feeling more, pleasant and unpleasant, and frees the underlying energetic blocks that cause dysfunction biologically.

Furthermore, once our energetic pathways are clearer from unresolved emotional debris, we can more easily access the higher states of our heart. These are the states of bliss associated with being in our Essential Self and Presence. Intending to access our blissful spiritual states while ignoring the unresolved emotional turmoil (shadow side) that lives within us, becomes something known as 'spiritual bypass.' Similar to positive thinking, it focuses only on the 'good feelings' continuing to repress and deny our pain, therefore perpetuating the very same, collective paradigm of Feminine repression that we are trying to breakthrough in the first place.

So, as you can see, our emotional body is our ally, not enemy. It's here to experience this physical realm that we live in. It's part of our humanity. We all have this emotional body, even though women are wired biologically a bit differently than the men. Let's begin our journey by honoring this miraculous body of emotions, releasing the shame, fear, and rejection we have associated with it for so long and returning it to the sacredness of our body.

SOUL BODY

Our soul body correlates with the distinctive design of our spirit, the spark of light that you contain, from the Universal Consciousness, our Essential Self. This is your particular body of light that is unique to you, and created from Divine Essence, Source. This is what many call your higher self. It holds the ultimate design for each individual as well as the fundamental universal qualities that create your Essence. Through the soul body, we can communicate and receive from the Universal Consciousness/ Undifferentiated wholeness. The soul level is the first level that we feel the oneness of our Spirit. Here, we can feel the collective energy field of all women, and of any other group that you identify with. Great healing work can be done by connecting with this level and beyond. This is the last level where we are individuated from the Essence of the Divine. Even, though there can be trauma and wounds on the soul level, we can also experience the great peace and universal love and many other universal qualities that exist on this level.

There are many collective wounds that women carry on the soul level, as well as on the emotional and mental level. The high levels of fear that have been experienced by our ancestors, and all women on the planet, have been anchored in the soul level. As we receive more and more light from our awakening process, we find ease and transmutation of these collective veils, allowing our true light to emerge in greater quantities.

As human beings looking for our evolutionary expression of our divinity, we want to live in the soul level expression of our being or even aspire to move into the more delicate, subtler levels of divine consciousness found beyond our soul level. It's said that in the Soul level, our Light signature is written in our hearts, in the form of the Universal Qualities that we are carrying. These are the qualities that we are meant to bring forth in humanity during our lifetime. Some of the Universal Qualities are compassion, love, peace, freedom, and justice, to name a few. Living in our soul requires us to transform the denser emotional and mental body, dissolving our conditioning and ego-attachments from our Conditioned Self.

It is in the soul level of our Being, where we enter the Oneness of our Essential Self, and feel the respite from the denser vibrations of chaos, turmoil, suffering, and struggle. We may still feel these emotions now, but slowly, as we awaken from the illusory effects of the denser world, we can transform the root triggers of these emotions within us. The process of awakening and living in our soul is the process of transformation itself. Although living in our soul does not guarantee us an existence without challenges, we do have access to the dimension within us that connects with higher consciousness, Herself. The soul dimension is the access of consciousness that is peace, unconditional love, and safety. Having access to this dimension, eases the pain when we're confronted with unpleasant realities or triggers in our lives. We begin to understand that the reality of Consciousness is the core of every manifestation in the world, including ourselves and we begin to trust that no matter what we may experience in the moment, we can fall back on to a higher reality of Love. We may vacillate between the pleasant and unpleasant, each time anchoring into our embodied soul. Our body has a roadmap to this consciousness, and so the process begins, back and forth, as we recalibrate our neuropathways and our complete body to our true Essential Self of our soul.

THE SECRET OF THE SOUL

The secret in our Soul is the dimension within us that is the pure light of our Essence. This is the breath of the Divine, Oneness. At the soul level, there is still identification with the separate "I" of our Conditioned Self, here in the secret of the Soul, there's only Oneness, pure Light of Undifferentiated Wholeness. This is the dimension of the unified field of Oneness. As we continue this process of transforming and accessing our most profound dimension of wholeness, we finally land here in the Secret. This is the dimension where our hearts are cleansed, and we can see and experience the world as one connecting field of Love. This is the dimension where our separate sense of Self unites with the greater wholeness. In the Sufi tradition of mysticism, the Secret is the place in which the heart is cleansed of the desires of the egoic self, as it gains greater intimacy with the Divine Essence of God. A quote from Meister Eckhart describes the process well.

MEISTER ECKHART

"As the soul becomes more pure and bare and poor,
and possesses less of created things,
and is emptied of all things that are not God,
it receives God more purely, and is more completely in Him(Her);
and it truly becomes one with God,
and it looks into God and God into it, face to face as it were;
two images transformed into one.
Some simple folk think that they will see God
as if He(She) were standing there and they here.
It is not so. God and I, we are one".

7 Secret Gateways

In the next few pages, I have outlined specifically, the seven Gateways and its corresponding elements, so that you can viscerally experience them. These gateways, also known as 'chakras' are spinning vortices that are the intermediary doorways that bridge undifferentiated wholeness to our individual Essence signature. These are also space holders and containers where we are constantly receiving the pure light of Consciousness. This light of undifferentiated Conscious further comes in as descending heavenly forces of yang and the ascending earthly forces of the yin, synonymous with feminine and masculine, which are then processed, assimilated, incorporated, and discharged through these seven main gateways. Each of these gateways, respectively affecting specific glands, organs, and all of our matter, as well as having specific influences over our subtle bodies of emotions, mind, and soul.

Inherent in our energetic anatomy, are these seven gateways that offer us the bridge to access and manifest an expression of Divine Consciousness, here on this plane. Therefore, each gateway, at its purest, highest vibration is an expression of Consciousness Herself, moving through us, and capable of manifesting here in our experience of life. However, the manifestations of these high states of consciousness in our expression depends on how much unprocessed, unresolved conditioning may be blocking any gateway.

Therefore, becoming aware and transforming the energetic patterns that may be contained in any of these seven gateways allows us to embody the finer expression of Light more fully.

These gateways are critically placed in specific areas of the body and correlate with emotions, thought themes and mental constructs, personal beliefs, and all physical aspects of our body. Our conditioning and personal beliefs stagnate the light that is able to move through theses gateways, first creating blockages energetically, secondly, contributing to physical dysfunction in our bodies. The gateways are essentially a map of our psyche, where unconscious material we call conditioning accumulates, obscuring the expression of our pure Light.

For our purposes, we want to understand these gateways as a field that holds resonances and themes that may affect our subtle bodies and physical body. Therefore, by addressing a belief that relates to a particular gateway, we may simultaneously heal issues that might be manifesting in physical disorders as well as emotional struggles. Here, we start to see how intertwined our physical or emotional struggles are with any of the gateways. Activation of these seven gateways allows us to access the conscious signature each one of them offers us, empowering ourselves to express and embody greater levels of Light consciousness.

As I mentioned in chapter one, the three lower gateways are where the Feminine holds the greatest wounds in our Feminine bodies. I won't repeat those wounding's again here, because we will be working with these lower gateways specifically during our Sacred Initiations of the Feminine. However, I don't feel that these lower gateways are less important than the upper gateways, even though they have been ignored and devalued in traditional spiritual alchemy. It's in our humanity that we have been wounded, not in our spirit and working to heal the pain and wounding that we carry in these three lower gateways, is the way to unite with our Essential Self. Focusing only on the higher gateways, those above the heart, in an attempt to connect with our spiritual essence, only further contributes to 'spiritual bypassing,' neglecting our humanness, our emotional body and the shadows that we have accumulated. If the lower three gateways are containing unresolved emotional conditioning and trauma of our human experience, we cannot fully merge with our greater Essential Divine Light.

Below is a synopsis of each energy signature and the aspect of our Light Self it correlates with. The blockages or conditioning that we may have accumulated in these particular gateways directly translates into disharmony and dysfunction in our health, wellbeing, and ultimately limited ability to embody these Consciousness Signatures.

In many spiritual cultures, chanting is an effective way to activate, purify, and restore the integrity of these gateways, and thus their corresponding affiliated elements. In chanting each sound vibrates at a frequency, known as toning, affecting the vibrational frequency of each gateway. When a vibrational frequency is experienced that resonates with the frequency of that gateway, there is a harmonious effect upon the gateway, and thus clearing the old calcified energetic components that create a blockage and wounding. In this spirit, the Sufi Arabic Universal quality is listed under each gateway, for one to dissolve and heal the obstructions in each gateway.

Furthermore, it's important to note that for women, these gateways significantly affect the corresponding gland; which also act as an intermediary in creating health and healing in our physical body. Attention to these glands is key in restoring harmony in our Feminine body. I would say that many of the components of the physical body that are affected by "hormones" are connected to these gateways and their corresponding gland. Therefore, when working with these gateways, always envision the gland that it corresponds with, it is vital for health and healing.

The Sacredness of Our Body

Our Body…
It is not the obstacle,
to the waves of
Bliss of our Spirit…
Our Body…
is the vehicle
which allows us to
experience the
Bliss of our Spirit.

~ leonor murciano-luna

CHAKRA/VITAL ENERGY CENTER
Diagram

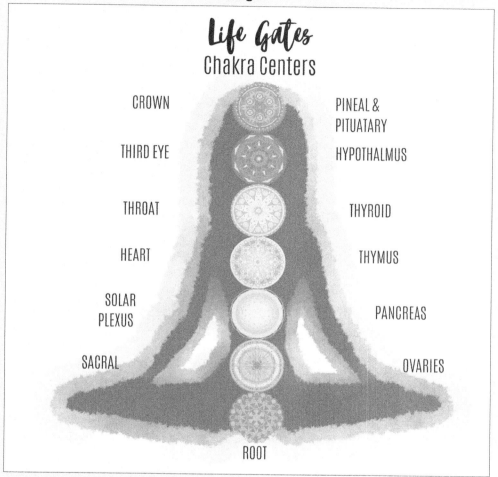

CROWN   PINEAL & PITUATARY

THIRD EYE   HYPOTHALMUS

THROAT   THYROID

HEART   THYMUS

SOLAR PLEXUS   PANCREAS

SACRAL   OVARIES

ROOT

Root Gate of Primal Life Force
Vital Self

The Root Gateway is the primary source of feeling secure and safe here on Earth, by accessing our Vital Self. Our Vital Self contains the primal life force that sustains us, that invigorates us and makes us feel safe and secure on this physical plane. As women, we've had a traumatic history of unsafety, violence and survival trauma that is contained collectively in this gateway. As we heal these wounds, the turbulence clears from our root, prompting our ability to feel secure and rooted in the Feminine, feeling grounded in the solidity of Her Earth element.

Sufi Universal Quality: Al Rafi (To be uplifted and rise above; spiritually evolve).

Physical and Endocrine focus: Perineum, pelvic floor, cervix, yoni (female genitalia).

Breath: In through the NOSE, out through the NOSE.

Element: EARTH

Essential Oils: Sandalwood, Vetiver.

Planets: Saturn

Chakra: First Muladhara; Base; Color: Red. Also, pale pink to deep blood red.

Sound: LAM (repeat 7 times in cycles of 3 or 7 to activate this Chakra.)

Physical Correlations: In women, most of our perineum, pelvic floor and cervix area remain unconsciously contracted with fear. Chronic urinary tract infections, irritation with our female genitalia, lower back pain, sciatica, rectal tumors/cancer, depression, and immune-related disorders are all associated with the closing of this gateway.

Psycho-Spiritual Reflections: This root gate being located at the base of the spine, relates to our most basic survival needs and our sense of **belonging, being rooted and safety.**

When rooted, we feel secure and confident. When we aren't rooted, we may feel impressions of lack of safety and scarcity, resistant to coming into form, lack of trust in the Divine, feeling abandonment from the Divine and more. Fear, terror, and functioning in survival mode all correlate with trauma in this root gateway, including fear of death and fear of survival.

The inability to access our parasympathetic nervous system, through the nerves in the sacral bone is also correlated, which includes continuing to function in anxiety. This gateway directly leads us to the connection with Mother Earth and our ability to open to the love, support, and union with the Feminine aspects of ONENESS.

Sacral Gate of CREATION
Creative Self

Our Sacral gateway correlates with our Creative Self. At its purest expression, it streams the creative force that manifests all forms into being. When we can express our Creative Self, we enter the dance with Life, Herself, diving deeply into Her mysteries. In our Creative Self, we experience ourselves as a perfect expression of the Creative aspect of Consciousness, Herself. Acknowledging the perfection and sacredness inherent in every living 'thing' including ourselves. Embodying our Creative Self means surrendering deeply to the creative impulse of life within us, letting us freely engage in Her dance of life. As women, it is here in our sacral womb gateway that we surrender to the mystery of our Creative Self when we witness Life be born within us. This is the greatest potential of our Creative Self, the ability for Consciousness, Herself, to birth life through us.

Sufi Universal Quality: Al Hayy (Life itself)

Physical and Endocrine focus: Gonads and Ovary glands

Breath: In through the MOUTH out through the MOUTH.

Element: WATER

Essential Oils: Clary Sage, Jasmine, Sandalwood, Saffron.

Planets: Venus

Chakra: Second-Svadhisthana- Sacral; Color: Orange; all shades.

Sound: VAM (repeat 7 times in cycles of 3 or 7 to activate this Chakra.)

Physical Correlations: Chronic lower back pain, sciatica, gynecological problems, infertility, polycystic ovaries, endometriosis, hormonal imbalances, menstrual irregularity including cramps, urinary tract infections. This gateway is in our reproductive area, right below our umbilicus and metaphorically connected with the birth of all aspects of our being and our creations. It relates to our reproductive hormonal functions of estrogens, progesterone, testosterone and the reproductive system.

Psycho-Spiritual Reflections: In this womb area women have carried the brunt of the collective shame we have experienced of living in a female body, in this patriarchal system. The constant shaming, blaming, and judgment opposed upon us is mostly held here in this gateway. The very fact that women are the birthers of new life into the world has threatened our existence in the patriarchy, adding to the shaming of our gender. In response, women have hidden their creative abilities and their ability to Creative Self, in fear of persecution or of their life.

The excessive amount of hyper focus in our culture to restrict our feminine looks to one single acceptable expression is an example of how suppressed the Feminine has been in our culture. The impression of shame, guilt, and judgment with one's own body and our sexuality are all contained here, disconnecting us further from our sacredness, holiness, and union with the Creative Source of Life.

Solar Plexus Gate of EMPOWERMENT
Sacred Power Self

The Solar gateway relates to our sense of Self, our internal idea of ourselves. At the highest vibration, this gateway connects us with the sacred power that comes from experiencing ourselves as a vessel of Creative Flow of the Universe and as Consciousness Herself. As we open to this truth in our Being, we feel the power that is released from being rooted in this knowing. However, this center also contains all our conditioning of what we have 'thought' ourselves to be and how we've valued or devalued our sense of self.

The Solar gateway contains all the judgments we hold against ourselves on the mental/emotional plain. As women, we've identified mostly with inadequacy in our Feminine form. We hold much of the fears and insecurities of our Feminine form in this solar gateway and the corresponding physical and emotional components. This gateway is associated with our self-esteem and our sense of personal power. When in balance, we feel capable and confident in manifesting our goals and desires.

This solar gate, along with our adrenal glands, are greatly affected when we feel powerless, helpless, and flawed in some way. When our sense of self and our value is limited to our human attachments and our limited roles and personality, we end up exhausting ourselves and our adrenals trying to accomplish, by using our will, rather than in connection with greater will. Most of us are caught in this perpetual "doing" and have disconnected from the internal rhythm of "doing and being." The key to bringing balance and harmony to the adrenal glands and recalibrating this gateway is twofold; first, we want to root our Selves in identifying with our Essential Self, (the perfected light of our Soul) and allow the Conditional Self (the egoic aspect of our separated identities) to evolve. Secondly, to reestablish the rhythm of our Being, by being, instead of continuing the imbalance of doing to achieve in the outer.

Sufi Universal Quality: Al Bari (Defines where we carry the Essence in our Soul Level and our own individuation.) (the perfection in our form).

Physical and Endocrine Focus: Pancreas and Adrenal glands.

Breath: In through the MOUTH out through the MOUTH.

Element: FIRE

Essential Oils: Bergamot, Juniper, Ginger

Planets: Sun

Chakra: Third-Manipura- Solar Plexus; Color Yellow; all shades.

Sound: RAM (repeat 7 times in cycles of 3 or 7 to activate this Chakra.)

Physical Correlation: Adrenals and pancreas glands are affected by this solar plexus gateway. In the adrenals, we hold the imprints of fear, survival, and power-lessness from being faced with the constant outer need for approval for survival. In the pancreas, however, we hold the longing for the sweetness of life, juxtaposed against our constant outer temptation to search for that sweetness outside our-selves, followed by continuous disappointment.

Gut and digestive disharmonies, gastric or duodenal ulcers, colon intestinal prob-lems, pancreatitis/diabetes, indigestion – chronic or acute, anorexia or bulimia, liver dysfunction, hepatitis adrenal dysfunction. Diabetic tendencies, blood sugar imbalances. Functions of insulin, blood glucose levels, digestive enzymes, cortisol, DHEA, dopamine, epinephrine, and norepinephrine. Adrenal dysfunctions, cell metabolism, anxiety, and mental and physical restlessness.

Psycho-Spiritual Reflections: Patterns of unworthiness, powerlessness, and shameful sense of self. The ability to free ourselves from restrictive patterns of limitation of our mental and emotional bodies and empower ourselves by em-bracing our sacredness. This gateway is correlated with our ability to trust our-selves and believe the truth of what we are made of, the perfection in our Soul. When this gateway is blocked or affected, we may experience powerlessness and frustration. Chanting Al Bari allows us to open to the perfection in our form and to the empowerment, we may feel by embodying that perfection in our Soul.

Heart Gate of LOVE
Compassionate Self

Our Heart gateway, located in the center of our chest, and holds the imprint of unconditional Love and Compassion that derives from the highest state of Consciousness, Herself. This is where we tune into the unconditional Love that underlies all of creation. From our Heart gateway, we see only love and feel in union with all of existence. We can understand the mistakes that we make and that others make because we can feel the compassion for our humanity and all of Life. We lose all sense of competition, scarcity, or need to protect ourselves because all we see and feel is the field of everlasting, unconditional love. The conditioning that is held in our heart is experienced as profound sadness, grief, deep hurt, and loneliness. Painful experiences of the heart create a barrier between them and us, anchoring our feelings of differences within, and isolating us further from the love of others. At its densest vibration, we may contain self-hatred and self-rejection here, feeling unworthy and underserving on the true Essence of Love. This heart gateway relates to our ability to connect with ourselves as Essence and discover our true Compassionate Self.

Sufi Universal Quality: Al Qawiyy (overpowering strength)

Physical and Endocrine Focus: Thymus gland.

Breath: In through the MOUTH, out through the NOSE.

Element: AIR

Essential Oils: Rose, Neroli, Jasmine, Helichyrysum.

Planets: Venus

Gate center: Fourth- Anahata-Heart. Color: Green; all shades

Sound: YAM (repeat 7 times in cycles of 3 or 7 to activate this Chakra.)

Physical Correlations: Congestive heart failure, heart attack, mitral valve prolapse, cardiomegaly, asthma/allergy, lung cancer, bronchial pneumonia, upper back, shoulder, breast cancer. The thymus secretes thymosin, which helps the body distinguish cells that belong in the body and those that do not. When our conditioning and unresolved pain blocks this heart gateway, it may minimize the thymus's ability to protect the body, and our defenses may be weakened, contributing to dysfunction in our immune system, and immune-related disorders. Consequently, the integrity of our lymphatic system, involving our spleen, lymph nodes, and other lymphatic tissue is dependent on our thymus and therefore, this heart gateway.

Psycho-Spiritual Reflections: Our heart gateway is significantly affected by our inability to forgive past hurts and the suffering of ourselves and others. Disappointments, as well as grief and loss, play a significant role in the health of our heart and related systems, we mentioned above. Being able to forgive and accept our journey in life, where we can fully rely on the divinity within is an important part of healing our engaging the highest vibration of our heart gateway. Ultimately, Love heals our wounded hearts and the pain of the past, however, we must be willing to take that first step in opening up to a new possibility.

We must be willing to have faith in something greater than our own limited experiences.

Throat Gate of SOUL EXPRESSION
Expressive Self

The throat gateway is in the throat area and related to our ability to communicate and express directly from our Essence, our Soul Consciousness. At its highest vibration, we can embody the true Expressive Self that is one with Consciousness, Herself. We realize that we're a vessel, being continuously directed by the One and that the sound we use through our words and our voice are creative expressions and extension of the life force here on this physical plane. Collectively, for women, this throat gateway has been blocked with great fear and terror, due to the fear of survival that has been instilled from our culture. Women have been terrified to speak our truth, and therefore, it has remained energetically blocked in order to ensure safety and survival. This imprint of fear has given rise to the epidemic of thyroid and thyroid immune-related dysfunctions. The restrictions we feel, and collectively still carry in our DNA, coupled with the inability to speak our truth manifests as constrictions here in this gateway. Moving through this paralyzing fear, speaking the truth of our feelings without swallowing what needs to be said is important in healing the imprints of this gateway.

Sufi Universal Quality: Al Jabbar (power to act in the world and the restorer)

Physical and Endocrine Focus: Thyroid gland and para thyroid gland.

Breath: GENTLY... In through the NOSE, out through the NOSE.

Element: ETHER

Essential Oils: Blue chamomile, sage, hyssop.

Planets: Mercury/Jupiter

Gate center: Fifth- Vishudda – Throat. Color: Blue; all shades.

Sound: HAM (repeat 7 times in cycles of 3 or 7 to activate this Chakra.)

Physical Correlations: Raspy throat, chronic sore throat, mouth ulcers, gum difficulties, joint problems, scoliosis, laryngitis, swollen glands, thyroid problems. Functions and regulations of thyroxine, calcitonin, T3, T4, parathyroid hormones, and the health of the thyroid itself, is all governed by this gateway.

Psycho-Spiritual Reflections: Issues of self-honesty, being able to express our most authentic desire of self, me vs. them, and expressing our voice is an important key to this gateway. Trusting and honoring our unique Universal Qualities and how we express them in life, rather than seeing ourselves as failures due to not being like someone else, is also a key factor in bridging the power of this gateway in our beautiful feminine vessel.

Third Eye Gate of TRUE VISION
Visionary Self

This gateway is located between the eyes, and is the center of insight, vision, and deep connection with the inner worlds of consciousness. Through the third eye gateway, we can see the many levels of consciousness that exists, beyond the physical manifestations. We can also see the world of possibilities and become aware of the subtle energetic bodies at play, behind the physical world we are accustomed to. Here, everything is possible, and we also become aware of the divine intelligence that is managing everything is that is happening in our world. Due to the repression of the Feminine, there is an imprint that has resulted in an obstruction of this gateway, that manifests as a sense of hopelessness, self-doubt and a veil of pessimism, tainted with fear instead of Love. The third eye gate has the potential to open us into seeing the worlds of the unseen and the mystery, HERSELF. It gives us the ability to perceiving the varying subtle forms of light upon light that is at the foundation of all manifestation.

Sufi Quality: An Nur (the light)

Breath: N/A

Physical and Endocrine Focus: Pituitary gland

Element: N/A

Essential Oil: Helichrysm,

Planets: Uranus

Gate center: Sixth- Ajna- Third Eye. Color: Indigo.

Sound: OM (repeat 7 times in cycles of 3 or 7 to activate this Chakra.)

Physical Correlations: This gateway affects our glandular system entirely, because the pituitary is the master gland and regulates all other hormone production in our bodies. The fact that we so much fear and terror veiling this gateway, explains the fact that so many women have hormone imbalances of one kind or another. The glandular system is the key system in women's bodies that regulate function and maintain harmony within all our systems.

Psycho-Spiritual Reflections: This gateway gives us the ability to open our vision to the reality that underlines all the manifested worlds and allows us to envision a greater vision for ourselves and our planet. Through the activation of this gateway, one is freed from time-bound consciousness. At this time, many of us are awakening and purifying the veils that have obstructed our third eye gateway and envisioning a new reality for ourselves and our planet, while creating health and healing in our Feminine physiology!.

Crown Gate of CONSCIOUSNESS
Cosmic Self

This gateway is at the top of our head, at the crown and opens to the Light we receive from the ONENESS/ Source/ Divine. Together with the opening in our Root gateway, we can step into the higher purpose of our vessel as an intermediary, receiving the Yin and Yang light frequencies of Heaven and Earth. The crown gateway connects us to pure consciousness and cosmic consciousness and assists us in remembering the truth of who we are. For women, receiving the Light frequencies through the crown as we allow it to merge with the Yin energies of Mother GAIA, is key in the embodiment of the highest frequencies of cosmic consciousness.

Sufi Universal Quality: Al Hadi (the guide)

Physical and Endocrine Focus: Pineal and Hypothalamus glands

Breath: N/A

Element: N/A

Essential Oils: Frankincense, Myrrh, Neroli,

Planet: Neptune

Gate center: Seventh- Sahaswara- Crown. Color: Violet; all shades.

Sound: OM (repeat 7 times in cycles of 3 or 7 to activate this Chakra.)

Physical Correlations: This gateway activates our brain, activates the hypothalamus and pineal gland, continually creating new neuropathways, and signaling our body to new organizational patterns. The hypothalamus works closely in conjunction with our pituitary master gland, signaling the release of hormones throughout our system. The regulation and dysregulation of this biochemistry within our body are greatly affected by our thoughts and the limited collective patterns we have been subjected to. Clearing these old pathways and creating new patterns of relating to ourselves and to our world, which includes the Truth of the mystical dimension, is key to opening ourselves to the full potential of full realization of our Being.

Psycho-Spiritual Reflections: The crown gateway opens us up to the greater possibilities of the Light beings that we are. What we spend time thinking and contemplating affects us significantly in our ability to activate new neuropathways and awaken to new levels of consciousness. Cultivation that involves activation of these gateways and realization of other levels of consciousness are the needed strategy in order to break through the old collective patterns and anchor ourselves in the reality that is in alignment with our highest Truth.

If you could get rid
Of yourself just once,
The secret of secrets
Would open to you.
The face of the unknown,
Hidden beyond the universe
Would appear on the
Mirror of your perception

~ Rumi

TRINITY WOMB CENTER

Now let us look at another subtle vital system, the Trinity Womb Center that encompasses our Head, Heart, and Sacral areas. These are powerful energy vortexes within our own body and psyche. The previous seven gate centers are contained within the Trinity Womb Center. In pre-Daoist cultures, these are also known as the three dantiens, even though they are quite different in nature.

The Trinity Womb Center reflects three distinct energetic wombs that respectively encompass our upper, mid and lower centers. The ancient, mystical power of the trinity (3), which has strong esoteric associations with the Feminine and the cycles of the moon, is held in the matrix of our wombs. We can say that these three phases of the Feminine, are living within us through the Trinity Womb Center.

Let us remember that our bodies are designed as vessels continually being infused by the creative energies of Consciousness, and as such, this pure consciousness is manifesting in the physical dimension as our bodies. The Trinity Womb Center (TWC) is another interface between that undifferentiated wholeness of Consciousness, Herself, and our manifested form (bodies). In the vortexes of our Sacral womb, Heart womb and Head womb we receive and process the energetic frequencies of the ascending earth energies (Feminine/Yin) and descending divine energies (Masculine/Yang) into our vessel system for creative distribution and manifestation.

In the TWC, energy is stored, processed, transformed, received, and transmitted. These centers act as intermediaries between the subtle realms and our physical manifestation. They influence everything from our energetic function, psycho-emotional aspects, and physiology. The TWC is a creative vortex in which the pure stream of primordial force enters each particular womb and fuels a new creation.

Aside from their metaphysical, esoteric aspects, the TWC also contains amazing physiological pathways which indicate an independent brain in each of these centers. Of course, we know that in our head womb, there is a brain. However, studies now show that the areas of the heart womb and the sacral womb contain a large number of neurons that allows it to be considered an independently functioning brain, without the necessary interference or acknowledgment of our head brain. Therefore, our heart and sacral wombs are capable of processing completely independent of thoughts and head brain activities. And yet we live in a culture that has consistently relied only on our thinking capacity, at the expense of our more embodied heart and womb experiences and expressions. In our collective repression of the Feminine, we have severed ourselves from the use of these other two lower wombs, relying only on the limited functions of our intellectual realm. We may even say that as a culture, we have begun to open our heart womb consciousness, evident by how much compassion we see in the world, or through others. However, we remain mostly, a society that is entirely devoid of connecting with our Sacral womb, which is our connection to the formless dimension.

Let's unravel the mystery of the Trinity Womb Center. First, we have the head womb, located in our head, housing the brain, the pineal gland, pituitary, and hypothalamus gland. This space is where primordial energy generates creative thoughts, beliefs, thinking, and intellectual capacities as a whole. In our culture, we value ideas and reason, above feelings, intuition, and the unseen realms. Nonetheless, this is a valuable part of the trinity, where our primordial energy comes in and ignites creative, inspirational thoughts and ideas. The danger is when we become dependent on only this womb, growing out of balance with the rest of our trinity and disconnected from accessing the full range the ONENESS in our being.

Secondly, we have our Heart womb in the visceral cavity. This center is our emotional center, which at its highest vibration allows us the ability to feel unconditional levels of Love; universal love, peace, compassion, mercy, etc. Our unprocessed pain and suffering blocks the ability for us to feel more significant, more profound levels of LOVE from primordial source and thus prevents the stream of flow from our Heart womb to ourselves and outwardly towards humanity. Activating this Heart womb center allows us to open ourselves up to the generous flow of primordial essence and feel the light of LOVE in all its manifestation flooding ourselves and our lives, transforming all other levels of experience. In doing so, we open ourselves up to the constant outpour of unconditional love from the universe.

Last, we have our Sacral womb center in the pelvis, related to Spirit and Breath. Here we access the formless dimension of undifferentiated wholeness, and Consciousness, Herself. Through this womb, we're infused with the knowledge that we're much more than just our physical form; the formless dimension of our Being. This is where we can tune in to receive the wisdom directly from Consciousness/Universe. In our Sacral womb, we feel our 'gut feelings' and more importantly, our true knowing. As women, being cut off from our Sacral and Heart Womb has for the past 5000 years, has created much trauma and dissatisfaction within our very souls. Activating our embodied senses and the formless dimension of our spirit through our Heart and Sacral Wombs are an intricate part of awakening to our complete power as human beings.

By bringing awareness and consciousness to the Trinity Womb Center, we awaken our potential powers of creation and vital source within. Thoughts are energy, and by focusing our thoughts, we awaken the hidden secrets in the quantum field of the TWC. Bringing our focus on the TWC further activates the potency of Universal Consciousness to dissolve the old conditioning patterns that cloud the emanation of the pure light, purifying our ability to transmit even greater light through our being, via the Trinity Womb Center. This is part of activating our light bodies.

As we activate the TWC, we become aware of the interplay of Consciousness within us, through its myriad of subtle signals and guidance, that is always occurring. We become more aware of the relationship and role that Consciousness is having in our lives and how it directs our lives. Our inner faculties become awakened, and our ability to hear the inner dimension is heightened. As the Trinity Womb Center becomes activated within us through our awareness, we can feel the stream of Universal wisdom clearer, and it becomes an essential element of our inner guiding system. Listening within and our ability to tune into what 'feels' right and what 'resonates' with us becomes clearer, thus, helping us make decisions from an embodied place, rather than just from an intellectual, mental awareness. We can be led by the deep wisdom in our bodies, through the awakening of the TWC. Our Trinity Womb Center helps us to go beyond our superficial egoic needs, and truly follow a path that is in alignment with our soul's desire. It helps us to reestablish the trust with our bodies again, realizing that through the vessel of our physical form, we access the invisible, powerful sacred realm of our Being.

The Trinity Womb Center offers us an integrated dimension of experiencing our body and our existence. Using this Trinity Center, we can embody the primordial essence and the creative flow in these various dimensions we call wombs. In our Sacral Womb (lower) center, we awaken to the wisdom of our spirit and our Essence, feeling the core of our vital force. In our Heart Womb (middle) center, we access the womb of emotions along with the unconditional Love that underlies all of creation. Here we have an opportunity for forgiveness and endless compassion. Finally, our Head Womb (upper) center gives rise to thoughts and creative ideas, as well as the five senses we experience at any given moment. This is also the womb of imagination.

As we become aware of these womb centers, we enter a dance with life itself, becoming steeped in the richness of the subtle layers that are always interacting. We can witness the depth of the mystery, which is manifesting as ourselves. Awakening to these womb centers creates vibrancy in our health, relationships, and all aspects of our lives. We feel the aliveness of feeling deep happiness and fulfillment as we reconnect with the unseen subtle realms of our Being. It's time to dissolve the hidden doorway of forgetfulness and open to the full power of the Light in our Trinity Womb Center.

OUR SHADOWS CREATE OUR STORY

We all see the world through the special colored glasses of our imagination, in combination with our conditioning from our past experiences and the personal meaning we have given it. While there is collective conditioning; the overall common responses experienced by groups of people, towards an event or events that take place, most of us attach mental meaning to our personal experiences, thus creating our own 'stories' about why things are happening. Intertwined within these stories are value judgments about ourselves, other people, and the world at large. Often, when experiences in our lives do not fulfill our needs, we personalize these experiences and assign blame to ourselves for these dissatisfying events. These layers of self-blame accumulate, gathering all sorts of illusory justifications as to why unpleasant things happen to us all who have underlining themes of self-blame, unworthiness and/or inadequacy, within them.

As a child, wholly egocentric, this is one of the foundational ways in which we begin to make sense of the outer world, especially the things that are not so pleasant. To feel some level of control, in a world in which we have no control, we attempt to take responsibility for external events, believing that if somehow, we were different, we could change the external outcome. This leads us on a barrage of unconscious attempts to continuously alter how we behave, or what we do, to control our external circumstances, and ultimately feel powerful, important, safe, and happy. This, of course, sets us up with the illusion that if we were only 'good enough' we would have everything happen to us that was pleasant. Secondly, it continues to anchor the belief that we are inadequate. Couple this with the social and cultural bias we have all been living under towards shaming and labeling women as the weaker sex, and we create a powerful conditioning story that continues to disempower ourselves completely. These 'stories' are rooted in our perceptual reality; what we believe to be true. These are the stories we must dissolve to live our greatest magnificent reality.

When we experience an event in our life, such as a parent leaving us for good, emotional abuse, physical abuse, or even sexual abuse, etc., we create a "story" about the meaning of that incident. The story is our way of understanding events that produce pain and hurt; it's is also a way of attempting to gain control of situations that we have no control, to avoid suffering. This happens not only with horrific events in our lives but also with minor but hurtful, unpleasant events, such as not being heard, acknowledged, validated, warmly caressed, adequately fed and nourished, when young. Unfortunately, the 'story' that we create only works for a short period, helping us cope with the immediate pain and suffering. After a while, the 'story' represses the pain and suffering, unconsciously justifying the idea of being inadequate. It also locks away the painful, unresolved emotions derived from our perceived meaning of the situation, keeping the memory alive but stuck in layers of our consciousness, as if it were true. This becomes the colored lens of our perceptual reality that we, perpetually experience life through, not realizing that we have created our own biases that we continue to live from, continuously provoking the pain and suffering of our past.

Keep in mind that what causes us the painful emotional states of suffering is 'the meaning' (story), we have given those events. There's no doubt there are various levels of pain; physical pain, emotional distress, etc., and so, in any event, there may be physical pain associated with the event, if someone is physically abused, of course. But what I am referring to as suffering is the emotional pain that we carry, due to the meaning we have given the event. This suffering is prolonged by the shaming and self-blaming attached to these stories. In other words, we may view a situation of a parent leaving us and attribute an egoic response of meaning such as, 'they left us because we were unworthy." The truth is that it's not their absence that becomes the most significant pain; it's the meaning (story) we've given it, that creates our suffering.

According to Freudian psychology, human beings are mostly geared toward preventing pain and seeking pleasure, thus the pleasure principle. Therefore, in our search for happiness and avoidance of pain, we get stuck in trying to make sense of what happens to us, to regain control and avoid the pain. This impulse dictates the need for our minds to create the 'story' of the painful events in our lives, to ultimately gain control. However, the stories themselves become the source of suffering within us.

So, when we begin to unravel the 'stories' that have governed us and become calcified in our being, we begin the empowering process of freeing ourselves from the illusive beliefs and realities that have caused the real suffering.

These 'stories' aren't just personal but are also collective. For women, there are general beliefs that we've assimilated as truths, because many of us have experienced these same realities within varying outer circumstances. This is the foundation of the three collective wounds of the feminine, in which all women have experienced or been indirectly influenced due to the collective culture bias. These 'stories' become calcified in our beings, affecting everything from our biology, our emotional nature, and negatively dictating our behavior, even if we're unaware of them. They live in our psyche, personal and collective, and influence our thinking, our expressions and the choices we make. At the root cause, the stories are responsible for epidemics we see, and, moreover, for the continuation of suffering in women.

The stories contain the 'shadows' that we've repressed about ourselves, because we've so desperately ingrained in our being, judgment, shame and responsibility for the suffering. And while there is truth to the statement that we're the cause of our suffering, it isn't for the reasons we think. We're the cause of our suffering because of our ignorance, not because we're wrong or unworthy. We're the cause of our suffering because of our inability to live from our divine nature and light. We've contributed to the suffering through our perpetuation of the lies we've been told. Perhaps, as we mentioned before, this perpetuation was needed in order to survive, so when I say we have been contributing to it, it's without any judgment. However, it's important to realize the stories that we're living from, and the impact they've had on us, to liberate ourselves and unplug from the conditioning that has repressed us.

As we have referred to above, the 'story' carries our wounding, which is the part of ourselves that is locked up within an energetic structure, that isn't voiced, heard, seen, nor acknowledged. This part of ourselves we hide, deeply forgotten to our conscious mind, though still holding the original pain of the unresolved event. We hide it because the pain reminds us of the story of not being good enough, or it tells us we're wrong in some way. Yet ironically, it's is facing these shadows within ourselves with love, that allows us to transform and heal the unresolved past. The paradox here, is that what we think is giving us pain and making us suffer (the pain with), is really what will liberate us, if we dare to face it directly.

The cultural conditioning shaped by the repression of the Feminine in our culture, has given rise to these stories and the deeply painful wounds that they carry. When we address the collective and our personal story, we pierce through the collective veil called the 'Maya.' Maya, is the Hindu name for the distortive veil in which humanity sees through, which prevents us from seeing our true eternal nature. This is also what mystics refer to as 'being asleep until we wake up' and become conscious of the eternal reality within.

In relationship to our stories and our shadows, our subtle bodies are the bridge that connect our inner world of belief to the external, physical world of manifestation. In other words, the subtle bodies discussed as our Gateways, Trinity Womb Center, emotional body, mental body, etc. are the intermediaries that receive the finer vibrational frequencies of the primordial light which allow the direct alchemy to create form in all aspects; cells, organs systems, skeletal structure, blood etc. These subtle bodies are in constant flux, responding to the greater frequencies and light codes of the Eternal. Thus, working directly with our subtle bodies allows us the deep transformation that is available for us to liberate our complete Being.

By understanding the biology, and the unseen factors that affect our biology, we can start to understand the complexities that affect us as women and see the pervading damage from years of fear-related stress, which women have endured for thousands of years. This is the cause of the epidemic we see rising in these '1ˢᵗ *world Feminine disorders*' I mentioned earlier. The longer we perpetuate the old story we have been living in, the longer we continue to limit our abilities to thrive to our fullest potential. Below are three charts that show us three variations in our thinking and our choices. Follow each chart around the arrows, to understand some of the choices we might be veiled from.

CYCLE OF LIMITED HEALING

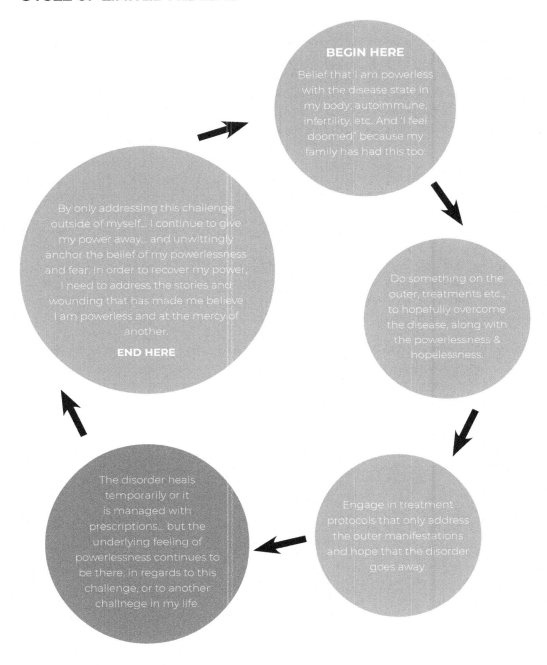

BEGIN HERE

Belief that I am powerless with the disease state in my body; autoimmune, infertility, etc. And "I feel doomed" because my family has had this too.

Do something on the outer, treatments etc., to hopefully overcome the disease, along with the powerlessness & hopelessness.

Engage in treatment protocols that only address the outer manifestations and hope that the disorder goes away.

The disorder heals temporarily or it is managed with prescriptions... but the underlying feeling of powerlessness continues to be there, in regards to this challenge, or to another challnege in my life.

By only addressing this challenge outside of myself... I continue to give my power away... and unwittingly anchor the belief of my powerlessness and fear. In order to recover my power, I need to address the stories and wounding that has made me believe I am powerless and at the mercy of another.

END HERE

CYCLE OF FULLY HEALING

BEGIN HERE

Belief that I am powerless with the disease state in my body; autoimmune, infertility, etc. And "I feel doomed" because my family has had this too.

By only addressing this challenge outside of myself... I continue to give my power away... and unwittingly anchor the belief of my powerlessness and fear. In order to recover my power, I need to address the stories and wounding that has made me believe I am powerless and at the mercy of another.

END HERE

Do something on the outer, western treatments etc., to hopefully overcome the disease, along with the powerlessness & hopelessness.

NEW REALIZATIONS

In turn, I realize that to own my power I have to do these 3 things:

1. Realize that I have the power to change my DNA and what I experience in my body and how my body functions.

2. Secondly, address the underlining pain and conditioned shadow that has contributed to the disharmonies by embracing these repressed aspects of myself that hadn't been acknowledged, loved, expressed in the past.

3. Treat the physical body, while I shift my mindset and allow the healing of my wounded self.

NEW OPTION

Realizing these deeper beliefs that contribute to my form are held in my DNA and can be switched on or off depending on my attitude (what I believe) and the 'story' I tell myself.

THE PHYSIOLOGY OF HEALING

Let's reconsider what healing really is. Healing is truly an evolutionary process that we're all undergoing, to one extent or another. Many of us are awakening to our Divine dimension and Essential Self. For that to happen we must simultaneously break through the conditioning and illusory 'Maya' that we spoke about earlier. To the degree that we can surrender to that process, is to the degree that we are entering our healing process. Thus, healing is the ongoing process of awakening to our divine nature within our physical form.

There are various aspects of healing, and some of us are consciously pursuing the dissolving of these conditioning patterns, so that we can embody our fullest potential and union with our Essential Self. Others may be awakened as a result of the challenges and suffering in their lives. Nonetheless, healing occurs in the same way for all of us.

In the healing process, what's ultimately healed is the place where we've experienced the wound the pain. When the places of calcified conditioning come up for healing, we witness a dissolution process take place, in which we can shift perceptions, from our egoic nature to the truth of our divine reality. In healing, we recover all those lost parts of ourselves that are ultimately intertwined with the stories and wounding of unresolved trauma within our fields. When we dare to open to the places within us that are in pain, that feel rejected, judged, alone, unlovable, inadequate, we ultimately reclaim our Essence and the 'judgement and pain' of this past event dissolves. This is the true healing, when we surrender who we think we are; our past unresolved experiences of pain and judgements within and thus simultaneously we open up to the light of being, the primordial source within us, our Essence Self.

Once we're able to face our vulnerabilities and feel safe enough to allow these repressed cellular memories to come to the surface, we begin to be part of this great transformation that takes place in the dissolution of these stories into the pure Essence of Love.

We could also understand healing through the terms of vibrational frequencies, where we can see frequencies on the spectrum from denser vibrations to higher vibrations. Denser vibration are frequencies usually felt in feelings of fear, grief, sadness, anger, etc., and then on the other side of the spectrum we have the higher frequencies of love, joy, elation, bliss, etc. As we feel these, you can see that sadness, for example, feels heavier, and joy feels lighter. Therefore, when we think of healing in terms of vibrational frequencies, we could understand it as transformation that happens when we invoke the higher frequencies of love into the places of pain, fear, sadness (denser frequencies).

In actuality, the whole planet is created from sound and light. According to Sufi metaphysics, the Absolute (Divine) creates frequencies of light that contain motion which in turn creates the various planes of existence. Therefore, nature, animal and human kingdom are all manifestations of these vibrations, as are our thoughts, emotions and physical body. This is the study of the Universal Qualities of light, of Sufi esoteric knowledge. Many of these subtler frequencies aren't perceived by our natural faculties, but, nonetheless, affect change within our system and causes subtle changes within our emotional, mental, and soul level.

Another unique quality to vibration is that contained in vibration itself is sound, a unique quality of tone that makes it, its own distinct creation. As these tones of sound mass together they create unique manifestation, each different in nature, according to their particular 'tone.' Each tone creates a light, some audible through what we know as language.

In mystical terms, each syllable in our words has a affect because of its unique vibration. This is the foundational understanding when we use sacred language and chanting for healing through their vibrational frequencies. Healers and mystics have used the effects of sound for our mind, emotions and spirit and have used it effectively in many practices. Sound has great influence on the muscles, circulation, nerves and all substances in our body. In fact, our bodies, being almost seventy percent water, act as a great resonator of sound itself. Not only is sound contained in our cells, atoms and glands, but our body's very existence is dependent on these vibrations of sound itself.

In our bodies, sound can kill viruses by identifying the frequency at which an object (virus) naturally vibrates; resonant frequency. And sound can also modify our DNA. In 2011, the Russian biophysicist Pjotr Garjajev was successful conducting an experiment in modifying DNA using only sound and light frequency. They transformed frog embryos into salamander embryos by transmitting the DNA.

In terms of frequencies and sound, it's important to understand that our thoughts also carry vibrational frequencies. And it's these vibrations that are at the forefront of epigenetics, the study of how our DNA is affected by our vibrational environment. So, because sound vibration can transform our DNA so radically, the use of specific thoughts (which carry vibrations), chanting, sound instruments and so much more, can all be powerful allies in the process of healing.

As we know, there are many healing practices throughout the world, everything from shamanic healing, to sound vibrational healing, to healing with our mind and intention. The great mystics and ancient healers used sound, dance, movement and intentions, to obtain altered states that resulted in healing on many levels. Many of the ones we'll be exploring are contain the sound and light codes carried in the Universal Qualities of Sufi traditions.

Furthermore, in soul healing there's a process that takes place that encompasses three key principles. These are the three key principles of true *Feminine Healing,* as well as *Self-Realization.* While *Self-Realization* is a life-long process, ultimately, it's the consequence of healing the stories of separation, that stand in the way of awakening to our Essence. These three foundational principles below, are woven throughout the map of *Conscious Feminine Medicine™.* However, before we discuss those three key principles, let's explore the foundation of somatization, which gives us a deeper understanding of the embodiment of Feminine consciousness, versus, visualization which is its masculine counterpart.

A Word about Somatization

As we engage in these healing processes, and especially in the healing process that I created called 'Soma Presencing,' I need to clarify the meaning of somatization and its role in healing. This process of 'Somatization' is the process we engage in when we become aware and perceive our experience from the level of the inner world of ourselves, rather than the outer. In other words, this is the experience of tuning into our bodies and feeling our subtle fields of emotions, thoughts, sensations, and even wisdom rising from our inner world of consciousness, that is all contained in the form, of what we call 'body.' Our bodies can be experienced on many levels; we can experience our emotional body, our mental body, our physical body, and every element in our body has consciousness. Therefore, somatization assumes this level of consciousness is actual in our bodies, and we can 'tune in' and become aware of any area or form in our body, through our consciousness.

When we place our consciousness in a particular area, say our liver or our solar plexus; it begins to expand, remember the adage that says, "what we think about, expands." Therefore, according to quantum medicine our consciousness allows things to shift and to bring our consciousness to the unresolved calcified stories in our bodies, allows us to first, become aware of them and become conscious of these stories, the restrictions and what is being held there cellularly, therefore, giving us a choice. Secondly, by focusing our consciousness in an area, it allows it to begin to be seen, to unwind and transform from a state of unresolved separation and pain to a state of love and light, thus healing. In this somatization process there is a response from the body to the brain, when we 'tune into' a consciousness within ourselves. We're in the process of listening to the body, the inner body, within the inner worlds. This is quite a different process than visualization, in which we engage in 'doing' through mental thoughts of directing ourselves to 'let go' release' relax' bring light' etc.

Visualization is the more masculine, yang aspect of engaging the imaginal realm, while somatization is the more yin, feminine way of directing our consciousness and allowing the intelligence in our body to dissolve, transform, transmute and align us to our Essential Self. While it's true that even when we engage in the visualization and we stimulate our bodies with a particular image, we're still creating a favorable biochemical response, a reduction of stress hormones and ultimately a return to a more harmonized wellness state in our body. However, one of the most crucial differences lie in the fact that somatization can unwind the body and dissolve the root core calcified constriction, allowing the body to organically return to a higher vibratory state of union. Within a visualization, our minds are guiding the process, in which we are only limited to what we 'think' we need. In somatization, we're surrendering our power to the intelligence in Consciousness, Herself, that organizes and gives us life to begin with. Somatization allows the presence of Oneness, Source or ultimately Essence, that which is undisturbed, to direct the show, allowing us to receive way past what we 'think' we need to heal, and opening us to heal on divine levels that we may be unaware of, or lack the understanding of. It is the soul healing process that acknowledges and defers to our inner foundational Essence of Consciousness, rather than to what we, as limited human beings, think we know best. The word somatization can most eloquently and simply be described in Bonnie Bainbridge Cohen' s book, 'Sensing, Feeling and Action,' where she writes: "I use this word 'somatization' to engage the kinesthetic experience directly, in contrast to visualization which utilizes visual imagery to evoke a kinesthetic experience. Through somatization the body cells are informing the brain as well as the brain informing the cells."[2]

Even though I have slightly amplified the use of somatization to include the direct involvement of our Essential Self and the correlation with consciousness, in healing, I am respectfully expanding on the amazing work that Bonnie Bainridge Cohen has pioneered.

The Three Key Principles in Feminine Healing

1. Awareness Consciousness is the first healing principle of Feminine Healing. The first step is to become aware of something new. That new awareness can be a new way of thinking, or a new awareness in our field. But awakening to something new and allowing a new consciousness is key to opening ourselves to having a greater expanded experiences of reality. Awareness challenges what you take for granted and allows the space for a shift to take place. If we're fixed and don't allow any new consciousness to enter, then we're closed to all other possibilities. Consciousness, whether in the way of a new concept or in our experience of the present moment, is the first door that allows us to open to healing.

2. Transformational Alchemy is the second key healing principle. Transformational Alchemy takes place from the alchemical process on the spiritual realm. It's not something we 'do' it's something we allow to take place. The alchemy is the dissolution of one vibrational frequency into another. It happens when we allow our conscious energy to resonate into a receptive frequency with the intention for healing. To move into this space of spiritual alchemy, we must surrender what is present with us and submit ourselves into the emptiness and 'not knowing' abyss. From this place, the light can come into our darkness, the place of limitation that we were experiencing at the beginning and something new can be created. In this place, we encounter Fear as the gate keeper, as we consider surrendering to what we've known till that moment. Once we pass the test of facing the gate keeper, we slowly enter the dissolution of what is, while we 'die' to the old and give rise to the new. This too is the process before you die' known to the mystics and occult traditions. The death that's referred to is the death of the egoic state, of the old ideas, concepts and 'story.' From here, we can open up to many seemingly conflicting realities at once, as we learn to expand our hearts to contain greater levels of consciousness and Truth.

3. Light Embodiment is the third key principle in Feminine Healing. The process of embodiment is one of letting ourselves fully express the light of our Being, as well as the Universal Qualities that are in our Soul. By embodying these qualities, we evolve into being, feeling, and full expression of Being these rather than just having a concept, or a mental construct of these lofty ideas. Through the process of embodiment our bodies can shift, heal and complete the process of transformation into a new experience of ourselves as complete human beings.

Healing further asks us to be willing to change the story and to let something else be born in its place... a greater truth, without knowing what it is. In many ways, healing asks us to surrender into a place of 'not knowing' first, and enter into the unknown, so that we can allow for something new to be born, but not from our known mind which houses only our past, but from the unknown, which is in our heart... in our soul. This unknown makes us very uncomfortable, as human beings we like to be in control and know, but if we restrict our solutions to our minds, then we continue to receive the same limited information as before, because our minds create from what we know, rather than from the great potential that is only possible in the unknown dimension of Consciousness, Source.

Our minds are generally limited by what we've known and what we've experienced. We read, learn and challenge ourselves to learn new things by educating ourselves. But there's a greater place within our own being that we can derive wisdom from, which doesn't originate in our minds, but rather originates in our deeper dimension of our Essence, the place that is closely connected with undifferentiated wholeness and the source of the Universe.

To do this, we have to let go of what our egoic mind thinks is right, and our sense of being right and move into a place of 'not knowing;' of being empty, as the Daoist would say. In so doing, we surrender our minds to our hearts, and allow ourselves to let go, detach from the story and everything that we know, letting inspiration and wisdom come into our empty being. This is a great leap of trust and faith. This allows a new creation to come in and arise within us.

OUR EVOLUTIONARY TRANSFORMATION

When we speak about transformation, we're speaking of dissolving the conditioned and calcified energetic patterns held in our conscious, unconscious energetic and cellular bodies, that block the essential light of our Being (spirit), which is LOVE. We all have these blockage patterns; they've been established within us for survival; it's part of our egoic self. As we awaken to our deeper dimension of truth and wisdom, the consciousness or awareness of this truth, automatically continues the process of transformation within us. Once we awaken to the deeper dimension of ourselves and continue to surrender our lives to it, we simultaneously dissolve the layers of egoic constructs through which we have experienced our lives. In our evolution of awakening, we vacillate between states of being in the bliss of the Oneness and being in the restrictions of our egoic states of duality. We move continuously back and forth as we become freer and freer of the constriction of our past woundedness and slowly anchor ourselves in the higher realms of our Being. We realize more and more that the wounded conditioned definitions of Self that we have been identified with all along, are the actual veils that keep us from truly merging with the beloved within, with Source of Oneness/ LOVE, and living out of our Essential Self.

The transformational alchemy process is the purification process that polishes and dissolves these mental constructs (stories) of what we 'think' is true and delivers us into a new consciousness of extended possibilities. The transformation purifies our veils; the illusory manifestations of our conditioning, rooted in deep levels of the protective fear that we're collectively enmeshed in. The process of transformation refines our senses, thoughts, emotions and even our physical body, shedding the layers of conditioning that we have called "ourselves." It's a process of shifting from an identity limited to our minds and logic (masculine), to one that includes undefinable experiences of subtleties of heart and soul dwelling in the unknown mystery (feminine). If we don't submit ourselves to the alchemical process of transformation, we cannot fully embody the essential qualities of Light that exist in our Being and fully integrate the Feminine. However, we can, and many spiritual paths do indeed reach altered states of consciousness and enlightenment through the mind, but in so doing we leave out our heart and our vessel; the Feminine experience of Spirit in the physical body. This type of enlightenment or union with our divine nature is incomplete, causing a level of separation and rejection of the Feminine in the material. This is essentially what has happened with the spiritual approaches that have come before this time, where our sense of merging with the Divine has carried an inherent separation and rejection of the Feminine, which is seen in the negation of the body, and the material realm, Herself.

However, when we commit ourselves to the alchemical transformation of our heart and surrender to the three key healing principles of *Feminine Healing; Awareness Consciousness, Transformational Alchemy & Light Embodiment,* we find ourselves in the evolution into the "perfected human being," capable of experiencing both Feminine and Masculine qualities without separating from our Essence in the Unified field of Oneness.

An important part of transformation and purification is to take responsibility for the places in us that are in separation and experiencing other; such as our actions of anger, sadness, rage, grief, hopelessness, etc. All of these are examples of our reactive pain body, that respond when we're acting from a place of separation within ourselves. The unresolved pain in ourselves reacts when we speak to others out of anger, react in judgment, put ourselves or others down, and when we feel unworthy or shameful. These are the opportunities we must transform our separation and heal our hearts by taking responsibility for our shortcomings and realizing that our reactions point the way to the unhealed places within us. These are the moments when we can see that we aren't in the Love and meet these reactions from ourselves with compassion, rather than judgment, because judgment perpetuates the state of separation, thus our pain. These opportunities are constantly available when we embark on this transformational journey of Self-Healing and Self-Realization.

When we spend time in Essence, the eternal dimension of our Self, the other conditioned patterns quickly dissolve through this process of transformational alchemy. That's why spending time in cultivation, mediation, chanting, reflection practices and energetic practices where we are tuning in to the higher dimension of Consciousness, helps to transform our own conditioned patterns. While this is one way of indirectly evolving our state of Consciousness, there is also a direct way of dissolving conditioned patterns and stories, by facing them directly and using the sound and light codes, activations and ancient healing practices that are part of *Conscious Feminine Medicine*™.

For the greatest transformation, we need to be willing to be with and feel all our states; the pleasant and unpleasant. The old calcified survival patterns of fear, grief and pain that are held in our psyche and body all need to be transmuted with the unconditional Love, that wasn't received at the needed time. We must be willing to let the unresolved feelings express themselves and be heard, be accepted without judgement. The process of being heard, witnessed, acknowledged with acceptance and love, creates in itself the alchemy needed for transformation and transmutation, and ultimately healing.

The truth is that our suffering is based on the illusion of separation; our suffering is experienced from the egoic nature of ourselves (the part of ourselves that experiences life as separate from Oneness). Therefore, the one that suffers is the ego. Nonetheless, suffering is valid. To on this plane and have individual experiences, we have created an egoic nature that experiences itself as separate from Oneness. Having an ego is part of being a human being. However, when we have ego's that have forgotten completely about our Oneness dimension, then we create unnecessary suffering in our being; because we deny the truth of continuity of life itself. Therefore, the goal is to be in our unique expression, with feelings, individual thoughts and our creative impulses while being anchored in our Oneness dimension, realizing the greater magnificence of our Soul. Ultimately, suffering itself is the tool that helps us evolve by showing us where (in our consciousness) we are still in separation and in pain.

Women carry the healing within their being,
through their direct access to the Feminine within.
But as previous chapters show, we have been disconnected
from our own Essence and rhythm.
Beginning the process of healing starts with recalibration of our being and bodies
to the inner and outer cycles of the Universe,
awakening to the 5 elements and reclaiming union with the 5 Elemental Mothers.
Using the collective wounds of the Feminine as our opening,
the Universal Great Mother begins to activate the life force within our being,
restoring the foundation of that which has been hidden and forgotten,
the Feminine, within us.

~ leonor murciano-luna

5
Women as healers

WOMEN WERE THE FIRST HEALERS & SHAMANS

Legend has it that the WU Healer's lineage, a lineage I've had the honor to be associated with, was among the very first 'cave women' shamans, that lived up in the mountains, coming down to join society only when their community was in need of balance, healing and harmony. These women drummed and danced, bringing harmony and healing through their physical vessels, using their connection to Primordial Essence to transmit healing needed for the tribe, the community or individually. These tribes of women existed around 38,000 years ago at the beginning of civilization. Thereafter, many tribes and medicine shamans have been recorded throughout early civilization. Women by nature are Shamans. Their bodies attuned to being a vessel that receives Spirit and transforms it, resulting in either healing, childbirth or transformational manifestation of Creation, Herself. The teachings passed on from the Wu Healer lineage has been passed on orally onto my mentor and Chinese Medicine teacher and doctor, Dan A. Nevel, from which the NSEV (Non-somatic Extraordinary Vessel) practice has come about.

Living in an unbalanced male dominated society, in the advent of patriarchy, men are predominately the ones to communicate with GOD. On the surface, this is how history has been generally interpreted, however, through deeper observation, the ground-breaking written work by Marija Gumbutas, Ph.D.,[1] and Max Dashu [2], has shown us that this rise of men's relationship with Divinity is a new phenomenon, only occurring within the last 5000 years, compared to the Goddess culture that has existed throughout Paleolithic and Neolithic times. In Layne Redmond's book, "When the Drummers were Women" she shows us that feminine power and spirituality has been the fabric and the norm since the beginning of time, even though not much of our literature has revealed this side of history. And as many of us are aware, the time for the restoration of the Feminine has come, and with it the truth about how the Feminine has been hidden throughout our history.

In earlier times, men weren't the intermediaries; the shamans, nor the healers. Undoubtedly, it's been the women. And even the male shamans of a later time wore traditional women's clothing to perform ceremonies and other sacred rituals. Then why has our literature consistently connected men with the Divine? The answer seems obvious; showing men connected with the Divine, gives them the allure of power that patriarchy has tried to strip from women. According to Max Dashu, "images, oral traditions and historical descriptions show women as invokers, healers, herbalists, oracles and diviners, ecstatic dancers, shapeshifters, shaman journeyers, and priestesses of the ancestors." She goes on to say: "The Chinese Wu were ecstatic priestesses who danced to the music of drums and flutes until they reached trance, receiving Shen (spirits) into their bodies, healing and prophesying under their inspiration, speaking in tongues and swallowing swords and spitting fire." [3].

From a historical aspect, we can argue that the World was Feminine first as the first signs of life on the planet were reproduced asexually. Even more interesting, is that scientists now believe that the "EVE" first genetic ancestor of all women, lived 143,000 years ago, way before findings for the genetic first man of "ADAM" only 59,000 years ago, according to the findings of Peter Underhill, at Stanford University in California. Although our culture has been living with a creation story that attributes life to a Male God giving birth to the first man (ADAM), which then produces a woman from this man.

Biologically, for the first five to six weeks of embryonic development, all fetuses are attributed the X chromosome only, and after that the Y chromosome is activated for males, as well as having the X chromosome inhibited. All embryonic life begins with ovaries, which later descends to form the male testes, if one's gender is male. Therefore, scientifically and phenotypically speaking, in the womb, becoming male is a development from the female form and yet our culture insists on maintaining creation stories that depict the exact opposite that continue the illusion of having female gender born from male gender.

Furthermore, we discover hidden information about the Feminine body that has been buried deep in the archives of our unconscious; the ability for women to conceive on their own. Over a hundred years ago, the famous biologist, Jacques Loeb realized and publicized this statement in relationship to parthenogenesis, (the ability for women to self-conceive), "the male is not necessary for reproduction, a simple physio-chemical agent in the female is enough to bring it about." In 1933, Dr. Walter Timme, an endocrinologist presented evidence to prove that self-conception was a scientific possibility for women, further explaining that in some cases the female reproductive organs can produce living spermatozoa and impregnate eggs in the same body, fertilizing it without the use of the external male. These claims are all speaking about the long-kept secret of women having the ability to self-conceive, 'parthenogenesis.'

While parthenogenesis has been acknowledged within the scientific community regarding the animal species, it hasn't been embraced in application to humans, regardless of the scientific discoveries by these geniuses. And yet these 'immaculate' conceptions have existed throughout our history. According to the secret esoteric knowledge, virgin births such as that of Mary's birth to Jesus Christ and other well-known visionaries such as Buddha, Moses, Leonardo de Vinci, and Plato may have been all born in this way of 'parthenogenesis.' While science is slow to actively pursue the in-depth investigations into the ancient mystery of parthenogenesis, there is quite a lot of evidence to show that parthenogenesis is an ancient primordial form of conceiving without the need for the male counterpart.

In Marija Gimbutas book, 'the language of the Goddess' she states that, "the parthenogenetic goddess has been the most persistent feature in the archeological record" referring to all the discoveries Ms. Gimbutas made and recorded during her time. In her book, 'Virgin Mother Goddesses of Antiquity,' Marguerite Rigoglioso Ph.D., explores how many of the goddesses of the Olympian pantheon were virgin mothers who birthed entire creations without the assistance of a male consort. As we explore and begin to look at history through the untainted lens of the patriarch, we realize that much of history has revered the Feminine, as Creator, primarily supported by the markings on pottery, the artwork in caves and the rituals used at death and birth. All of these leave us a very full and rich depiction of a world where the Feminine, and women in general, played an essential role in the creation of life itself.

Whether we believe that parthenogenesis is possible or not at this time is not important here, however, what needs to be considered is the remembering of the unique and sacred relationship that women and the Feminine have had with the essence of life, since the beginning of time. Furthermore, these immaculate births all point to the mystery that is innate in the womb of the women, where the Feminine transforms life itself, through Her magic. Through these observations, we begin the journey of restoration of the Feminine soul within our won sacred Feminine form, unraveling this mystery and honoring the magical imprint of creation itself within us. Hidden in the story of our ancestors and underneath all the noise, we feel the pulse of the Feminine rising in our awareness and in our consciousness, giving the seeds of Truth the presence needed to break through the illusions that we have been fed.

WOMEN WOMB CONSCIOUSNESS

Women are the bridge between the worlds. We carry the Essence in our womb, not just spiritually but biologically. In the womb, women bear the essential codes of Life, which transforms spirit into matter. Our womb consciousness serves as a bridge from the Divine realm into the physical realms. The energetic frequencies of Love and Compassion are magically activated in our womb consciousness and seeded in the wombs of our offspring. Our physical and energetic womb is the receptacle of this Divine Essence, passed on from generation to generation. Our womb is the bridge between the worlds, birthing compassion into each new creation, one birth at a time.

The word "Womb" in Arabic has the same root word as compassion. In the holy text of 'the Quran,' 'Rahman' is one of the most stated names of the Divine, naming the Divine as the Unconditional Compassion, 'Ar RAHMAN.' In our womb consciousness, women carry this Universal Light code of unconditional compassion, intimately connecting us with the Essence of the Divine, related in the holy books. Outwardly, our womb is seen as the 'Rahman,' that compassion, that essence of LOVE from which life itself is created.

Women are gifted with the mystery of birthing Essence directly into our world. Our wombs are created in the image of the Feminine face of the Divine, the blueprint of Mother Creation, Herself. We're the midwives of the new generation, holding in our womb consciousness the new codes of ascension, and activating them as we remember and begin to embody them. As humans, we swim in that matrix of Love and are continuously supported by that Essence. We've never been separated from that core Essence, but through the imprints of our conditional perceptual realities, we have forgotten. Becoming aware of this Truth allows reality to awaken within us.

Men also carry this Essence in their being, but in slightly different ways. In the Feminine form of a woman's body, she carries the codes that manifest the Divine Feminine, that which conceives, and which creates. In this way, women are made as a mirror of the Cosmic Womb. Her vessel, as well as her physical womb, carries the imprint of the greater Cosmic womb of Creation, Herself.

In the evolution of our Feminine soul, it's critical to recognize the body as being as important as out spirit. Self-care for the body and soul is a key element in healing our Feminine wounds. When we continue to doubt ourselves or feel shamed in our responses because they arise from our senses, rather than from the intellect, we've fallen into one of the shadow wounds of the Feminine. On the other hand, counteracting that with the recognition that deep within you, you carry the Essence and that this Essence is Divine Source itself, then honoring that which arises from that (your emotions, your intuition, your knowing) becomes easier to accept. Learning to trust ourselves and experiencing ourselves as sacred is the beginning of the restoration of the Feminine within us.

Up until the last 5000 years, we've lived in awareness of the Feminine qualities in creation, and yet to us, they seemed to have been hidden since the beginning of time. But in the grand scheme of things, one thing could not be altered; the correlation between women, the moon and the mysterious ways of their cycles with birth. This is something that couldn't be denied, nor altered.

In the 1960s, a man by the name of Alexander Marshack, [4], found a piece of bone near the Nile, which was close to 30,000 years old. He went on to find other bones, stones and goddess figures in Russia, Spain, Italy and Czechoslovakia that had unusual notches carved into it. After studying these numerous finds, he concluded that these markings were the first attempts at keeping a record of time through actual indication of lunar cycles.

Later, the carving of 'Venus of Laussel' 22,000-18,000, [5], in France was discovered which clarified even more, the culture of the time. The goddesses figure carved on the rock was holding a bison horn on the right hand with thirteen lines, which was determined to either be the thirteen days from the visible New moon to the Full moon, or the thirteen New Moons of each yearly cycle. But along with that, her left hand was upon her welling womb, showing the correlation between the phases of the Moon and the cycles of the womb. It was clear that the mystery and power of the spiritual realms had been embodied in the Female form.

If you look for this symbolism today, you can see evidence of the images of Mary, mother of Jesus in any catholic church, standing on the crescent Moon. Here we see the Moon becoming the symbolism for the Goddess, or the Mother, governing the tides of the sea and the tides of the womb. And in many languages, the words for Moon, month, menstruation have either similar meanings or common root words. The early calendars were measured from New Moon to the next, giving thirteen New moons for each year.

The Goddess became the primary image of culture and deity for nearly 20,000 years. She became the unifying symbol of the Heavens and the Earth; evident through the rhythms of the seasons and three phases of the Moon correlating with the three stages of women's life. Furthermore, the three lunar aspects eventually gave rise to the Christian doctrine, known as the Trinity; God the Father, God the Son, and God the Holy Spirit, derived from the sacred law of three of the Goddess.

The most important observation of the Moon and its powers was the disappearance of the moon thirteen days after its fullness in the sky. The cycle of the moon was observed, how it grew from the New moon to the Full moon and then waned altogether until it was completely gone. The drama of the life and death cycle of the Moon was revered with great honor, where even ritualistic dances were performed in order to assure the Moon to come back. After three days in darkness, the crescent Moon would show up again.

This ebb and flow of life was also symbolic to our lives, and how we grow from nothing and then continue to grow smaller until we disappear altogether. This cyclic process of birth, death, and rebirth could be seen in ourselves, and in all of Nature. This has been ancient wisdom for a long time and was only recently covered up with men's interpretation of written history in the omission of all other history in evidence. Nonetheless, the interdependency of the rhythm of life itself and that of the internal cycle of women, is an intricate part of healing our Feminine body, heart and soul.

RESTORING OUR RHYTHM

The physiological menses of our womb clearly show the interconnectedness of the cycles of the moon with our feminine body. In modern times, women menstruate during varying phases of the moon, yet in ancient times, they would usually begin their menstruation during the dark moon, reflective of the harmony that existed between the outer rhythm of our Universe and the inner response of our bodies. Nowadays, our bodies are out of sync with the greater rhythm of life itself. Although, in our present-day culture, there are actually a great deal of women that begin their menstruation on the full moon versus the dark moon, evident of a culture that is focused outwardly skewed towards the more yang, masculine qualities.

And as we all slowly activate the hidden aspects of our Feminine light codes, we also see the phenomenon of more full moon ceremonies popping up in our culture, which again, signifies an outward yang masculine celebration, versus the inner yin Feminine qualities. Nonetheless, the increased rituals in celebration of the moon depict the return of the Feminine, greatly desired in any form. Expanding our consciousness onto the return of moon rituals exposes us all to the inward recalibration of the Feminine, even if it's in her masculine predisposition.

During the time of women's monthly menses, her body produces DMT; Dimethyltryptamine, a compound that provides an expanded state of awareness. This DMT is found in the menstrual blood, which is an indication of the expanded consciousness that is inherent in the state of our menses every month. Women's bodies are designed to experience these expanded levels of awareness during her monthly cycle, enabling her to reach the expanded level of the unified consciousness field. DMT, also dubbed the spirit molecule, has been used for divinatory and healing purposes, as a brew made from specific plants, in shamanic rituals.

Many cultures in post-matriarchal societies have used hallucinogenic herbs to reach the same states that are produced in women's bodies naturally. Women release this hormone from the pineal gland during their monthly menses, which allows this time of the menses to be sacred and powerful. This is the time when they're closest to Divine Mother. As her consciousness innately expands in this sacred time, she can deeply purify the shadow wounds from herself, her family and her community and receive divinely inspired messages directly from Source.

Her cycles represent a time of death and rebirth that happens monthly. This death and rebirth, is not just physically, but happens at every level of her being; an opportunity for cleansing of old ideas, old patterns and negative old conditioning that no longer is needed. It's a time to dive into the deep altered states of the Divine dimension of Oneness and surrender all that is not useful, allowing it to be transformed and transmuted by the purity of Essence itself. This is a time of deep purification, innately designed.

During the second half of a women's cycle, at the time of ovulation, comes a rebirth of all new possibilities. The rebirth is a time of receiving new ideas, inspirations and messages from the Divine Source through the resonance of her body wombs. Throughout this time of expanded consciousness, women can easily communicate with the Divine consciousness and receive messages that not only help them evolve spiritually, but also help their chosen community and to be of greater service. It's an opportunity each month for divine guidance and evolution.

This sacred time of women's menses has been observed and respected throughout ancient cultures although to us in modern society, many secrets have been forgotten. Women generally feel disconnected from their bodies and from these deeper truths. Many women experience their cycle as something to tolerate, altering it with hormones for convenience, or taking medication to make it disappear altogether. Many women have severe pain and discomfort, resulting in many gynecological disorders which result in further assault of the body with invasive treatments. For women to physically heal their bodies and create health, the observation and restoration of the sacredness of these cycles is critical. As we return to the honoring of our bodies and what these cycles mean, we slowly restore our personal Feminine rhythm, as well as the rhythm inherent in all of nature.

It's women's disconnection from their innate mysterious oneness with Nature, that continues to contribute to our disharmonies on all levels. Slowing down and becoming present is the first key to restoring this internal rhythm. Allowing the time for reflection, meditation, and heart connection with Cosmic consciousness can allow women to experience quantum leaps in their own healing. The menses is the time of month, where she can return to be with herself and less with the world. If a woman continues her regular pace of interacting with outer life during her menses, she loses the opportunity to reconnect, to re-sync with the greater inner pulse of life, itself. She can observe this time by slowing down and turning inward, being gentle with herself, taking baths, nurturing and honoring the Feminine within. This begins the process of reconnection with the sacredness of her body and the mysteries therein contained.

It's this essential separation from our sacredness and disconnection with the rhythm in our bodies that adds to the distortion of the Feminine. I find that, for women, the dysfunctions we experience in our reproductive and endocrine systems are directly correlated with the degree that the Feminine archetype is distorted in her psyche. This often gives way to disorders involving the reproductive organs, immune issues, infertility, endometriosis, and many of the '1st world Feminine disorders' of our time.

In ancient cultures, women isolated themselves and would go into seclusion during their menses in order to maximize their experience of these powerful states of expanded Cosmic consciousness and healing. These retreats allowed space for transmutation and transcendence during their monthly cycle of death and rebirth. This powerful practice could be restored today, to provide sacred time during our sacred bleeding time of the month.

When women reject their periods, they essentially are
rejecting the Feminine within them…
They reject that aspect of themselves that creates Life itself…
The reject the Creative force within them.
We live in a culture that has hijacked women's Feminine power…
And made it, along with our periods a thing of
inconvenience, shame, disgust and detriment
and convinced most of the women… that they are
better off without it.
What better way for women to inherently feel disempowered…?
disenfranchised and inadequate…
by shaming the substance (blood) of the very source of
Creative power, Herself…
and the mystery that bears life to all!

~leonor murciano-luna

AS ABOVE SO BELOW

The moon is a body that reflects the light of the Divine, just like our body reflects the light of the Spirit Consciousness. During the 29 1/2-day cycle, the moon's body reflects varying degrees of light symbolized in three main phases; new moon, full moon and dark moon. Respectively, these moon phases relate to our body as new Moon with new creation, regeneration or birth, full moon with full expression, power or personal ovulation and dark moon with our menses process and time of death and release.

As the cycles move within us, our bodies are attuned to these cycles of nature mirroring birth, growth, death and regeneration. Our bodies are a part of nature and we've disconnected ourselves from this rhythmic cycle of nature. These cycles not only affect our menstrual cycle, but profoundly direct the greater rhythm of our bodies, mind and life.

The dark moon cycle is a time of letting go; a time where the old is released in order to make room for something new. Currently, we find ourselves metaphorically, at our most inward phase of connection with spirit, in the darkest space of the womb of Cosmic Mother. If we happen to align our bodies to menstruate at this time of the moon cycle, we receive the benefits of being energetically supported in the process of letting go, releasing and making room for a new creation within ourselves.

Secondly, from the dark moon (which lasts three days) the new moon is regenerated as a new creation. This is the time for something new to be created, outward motion from spirit into form. The new moon continues its growth through the waxing moon, when the light is growing and continuing the creation of something new, new hope, new ideas, new outward motion into the physical world, until we reach the full moon on day 14. This beginning phase of growth, Day 1-14, is the spring time in the greater cycles of nature representing a new birth and the growth period of a new creation.

The full moon occurs around day 14, midway during the cycle of the moon's 29 ½ day cycle. The full moon is related to our ovulation, a time of great expression on the outer. In the greater cycle of the seasons, it relates to the summer time, where spirit is in full expression on the physical plane. The body of the moon is in full expression of its light, dancing in the outward celebration of form; of creation. This is a time where we see our culture enjoying, dancing, and celebrating life with full moon ceremonies. And on the inner, it's related to our abundance, vitality and expression. It's a time to celebrate our unique light expression in the physical world.

The full moon quickly moves into the waning phase, between the full moon (day 14) and the (day 28-30) dark moon. This waning moon begins the process of moving from the outward focus of the physical world to the inward focus of the inner world of spirit.

This is a time of shifting gears, slowing down and reaping what we've sown. This phase correlates with the autumn energy and harvesting of the new creation. The waning moon phase is a preparation for the death phase of the dark moon, therefore not a time to start new projects or launch ideas in the physical realm, rather a time of gathering and completing.

Once again, the waning moon phase brings us to the dark moon phase, three days culminating in what we culturally know as 'new moon.' During this dark moon phase there is a portal in which the Universe offers us an opportunity to purify our illusions held in our minds, emotions, heart, and our soul; allowing dissolution of the veils that stand between us and Divine union. Every month, the dark moon offers us a time of death and rebirth, honored in ancient cultures as a sacred time to dive deeply into divinatory levels of consciousness and allow ourselves to be completely dissolved by the primordial force. This the winter time of the year where death takes over on the outer, and yet there's still an Essence of life, hidden deep within the seeds that continue to sprout the next season. Physiologically, it's a time of letting go as we shed our lining and release the imprints that stand in the way of greater union with our Essence.

The time of the dark moon is our acknowledgment of our spiritual nature, our time to commune with Divine, to honor ourselves and realize who we are. It's a time to honor the Feminine within us. As a culture, we're devoid of this reality, union, and acknowledgement of the sacredness of life; we've lost the connection with our dark moon phase. The dark moon phase is also when the moon is out of our vision. We cannot see Her, nor the light of her body; She has dissolved. Following in Her footsteps, it's a time for us to dissolve what we know in our heads and return to our Essence of No-Thing, the place of not knowing, just surrendering to primordial Essence.

Every month we have an opportunity to realign and return to the rhythm of our nature by honoring these cycles within us. Ancient cultures of the Wu Healers lived by the light of the moon, in sync with the cycles. We too, can restore this internal rhythm that we've severed in our constant outer quest and dependence. Acknowledging these lunar cycles of movement, while we slow down and focus internally during the dark moon time is essential in our restoration.

As a culture, we're used to the yang aspect of acting, doing, and constantly focusing on accomplishment. We're dependent on these outer forms of gratification for satisfaction within ourselves. And yet, we live exhausted, stressed out, and completely unhappy, too quick to turn to stimulants when we fall short of this continuous expectation of moving. Making time to return ourselves to the cycles of nature, the nature of who we really are, is key to restoring our health, our wellness, and more importantly, reaching that deep yearning of happiness in our soul. Shifting our focus to slow down, creating boundaries that honor the cycles, turning inward during our menses or during the dark moon time are all ways in which to balance the missing yin aspects of our states.

What we truly yearn is a deep satisfaction and joy that only comes through the union of our inner levels of consciousness. Most of us are somewhat aware that our outer accumulation of monies, accomplishments and successes will not meet this inner yearning of our heart. Yet we're still caught in the disconnected rhythms of our western culture. A rhythm that denies the reality of spirit and our deeper dimension, and further denies that there's a balance needed between these two realities of yin and yang, light and dark, action and rest, inhale and exhale. These are the cycles of life; we can deny them only for a little while, until we start seeing the destruction of our own dysfunction. Our collective dependence on the outer form for survival and wellness has also made us lose our internal rhythm and connection to that which nurtures us, GAIA, Mother EARTH. We are living out of tune with Her cycles, Her environment, the sun and the cycles of light and dark.

In our taxation, we don't allow recovery time, therefore, our system doesn't have time to receive, and shift gears. We're functioning from one sided doing. It's obvious that no system can constantly be on the go without recovery time and yet as a society, we expect to function like this. You may say we get rest during sleep, but in actuality, we don't sleep enough in this culture to afford our daily regeneration. Most westerners have trouble sleeping and when they do fall asleep, it's very superficial with their minds staying active and not deeply rooting.

Physically, this taxation causes dysregulation in our systems and we begin to see the affects in the first world Feminine disorders; infertility (reproductive issues), anxiety (nervous system), thyroid issues, immune system disharmonies (autoimmune issues), depression, and so on. Our whole body is constantly attempting to restore this rhythm within and yet we continue this viscous cycle not just with our mindset of 'more' but also stimulants, medication, and hormones to try to 'fix' the dysregulations. We add to the dysfunction even more, because what is needed is a deep restoration of our rhythm, not a quick fix.

As a culture, we're stuck on the inhale, and don't' know how to exhale. Life has rhythm, and yes, we can pretend and continue to focus on one aspect of functioning, denying the other, but with the deep consequences we've already discussed. The aspect we're denying is the exhale, the emptiness, the unseen, and our spiritual nature; all related to the Feminine. And part of the reason why we continue to be caught in this vicious cycle is that we have bought into the collective conditioning of judging our own bodies and belittling ourselves and our feminine nature. We've allowed the shame and doubt to creep in and subtly manipulate us. This manipulation is a result of our experience of living in survival fear, not feeling safe enough to be ourselves, therefore, sacrificing ourselves, our needs, expression and our authenticity, in an attempt to stay safe and alive.

In moving forward from the pain, we must ask ourselves, why do 85% of women experience pain during their monthly cycle? It's such a high number in our society, and women's bodies aren't designed to innately be in pain, month after month. This pain is an outward sign of our inner energetic dysfunction. Our cycle is symbolically our personal dark moon phase, it's a time to go inward, dissolve and come into union with Source; but do we? With the fast pace of work, school and other demands, do we have the support of our culture to slow down for a few days? Can we miss work and is it acceptable to say we can't work today because we are on our menses?

Of course not, there's no permission in our society to allow us, to take care of our physical, emotional, or even spiritual needs. With attention to our physical or emotional needs, the attitude is one of disfavor, and in our culture, it sets us up for the criticism and stereo type that women are inadequate, weaker and cannot be trusted, compared to men's work ethic. Furthermore, in a patriarchal society where the rules are created around what's needed for men, instead of women, it's impossible to say these things and not be shamed, judged and culturally punished in some way. This is how the patriarchal collective continues to control the psyche of women into compliance.

The obvious medicine for returning to our rhythm begins with the slowing down to tune into the unknown dimension of being, rather than continue our outer doing. We may not have the luxury of calling out of work when we have our menses, but we may be able take account of what's happening, shift our focus and attention, and give ourselves space during this time of the month. On a greater scale, it's about including the Yin aspect of the cycle, the dark moon cycle in all areas of our life. Taking time to rest is as critical as time for action. Time for rest is really time for being, feeling with no agenda. This is when creativity can come through because, mentally and energetically, we generate enough space for something new to be born. One of the secrets of the dark moon phase is to allow us a time to die, as well as time of letting go and a time of emptiness. It is this very dying process that creates the space for new birth, for new creativity, for new life and for regeneration. If we don't let ourselves be, and don't take time to exhale, we can never be empty enough to expand into our true creative fullness.

Our breath is the foundation that preserves this innate rhythm within us. Focusing on our breath is elemental in restoring our rhythm. Our breath is symbolic of the duality of yin and yang; two opposites coming from oneness. Our breath expresses this duality of physical reality. The inhale fills us up with oxygen, symbolic of filling us up with what we need, and the exhale releases the carbon dioxide and releases what we no longer need. At the end of the exhale is the emptiness, the union with our Essential Self. The inhale is our Yang phase; it's the movement, doing, expressive nature of us relating to the first cycle of the moon, from new moon to full moon; the first 14 days. Our exhale is the dissolving phase, the letting go, the death cycle, or the last half of the moon's cycle, from full moon to dark moon of complete emptiness. This is the Yin cycle of the moon, the time when we dissolve into Divine Essence.

Below we can observe the 29 ½ day rhythm of the moon, from which she grows from empty in the dark moon to full moon of fullness and then waning back down to dark moon. The moon reflects our own internal rhythm as well as the greater rhythm of the Universe.

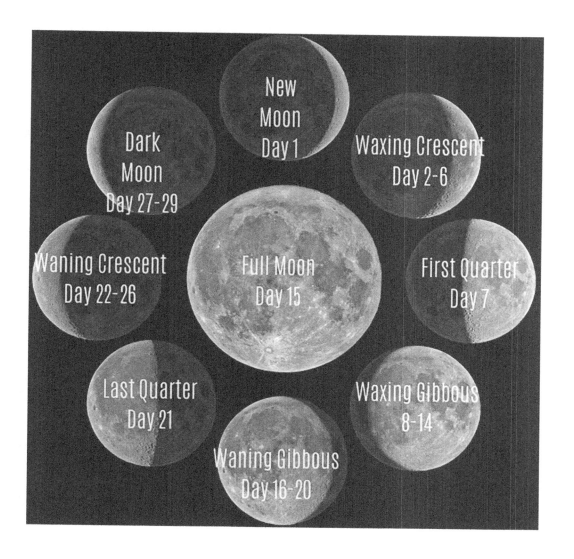

RETURNING TO THE RHYTHM OF OUR WOMB — 9 DAY JOURNEY

There's a sacred window of time which spans during the three days before, during, and after the period. These are the nine sacred days of creation, Herself. These days, whether you're menstruating or already in menopause, hold great healing and great secrets to the mystery that we are.

During this monthly nine-day journey, you're able to create health and healing in your body. Engaging in these nine days every month will help to restore the rhythm of the cycles within you. As we shift the balance from go, go, go to presence and stillness, we begin to restore the long-lost rhythm in our bodies and establish a new relationship with our own wombs. Along with the healing benefits and restoration of our rhythm, it also offers us the opportunity to merge with the primordial essence of the Cosmos, with the Essence of the Great Cosmic Womb and receive the wisdom.

You may follow this nine day cycle if you're bleeding, menstruating or if you've already entered into menopause. If you're no longer bleeding, the opportunity is still there as you enter into the Cosmic moon cycle consciousness, working on the collective level. This is the dark moon time.

You should begin this process ideally three days before the onset of your menses, or if you're no longer bleeding, then you'll begin on Day 27 of the waning crescent moon cycle (Day 1 being the New Moon), to be in sync with the moon cycle.

Each day dedicate 15-30 minutes to reflect on the significance of each of the 9-Day Journey processes below; reflecting, journaling and engaging in the 'Rhythm of the Womb' practice.

RETURNING TO THE RHYTHM OF THE WOMB
ACTIVATION

Each day of the nine-day journey contains a vision and theme. However, first read the steps below and engage this 5-step process, with each of the nine days of the journey, one day at a time.

1. HEART CONSCIOUSNESS - To begin, you want to place your hands on your Heart and breathe into your Heart center space (Heart gateway) for at least five cycles of breath. Let yourself feel the Divine presence in your breath and in your Heart.

2. WOMB CONSCIOUSNESS - Place your hands on your Womb and breathe into it at least 5-10 cycles of breath, feeling the Divine presence expanding into your Womb.

3. SOMATIC CONSCIOUSNESS - As you do this, notice what you're experiencing physically, emotionally and mentally. Whatever it is, let yourself breathe into it, slowly and gently. Let yourself become aware and continue to breathe through these waves of pain, emotions or stillness until you feel your system quieting down.

4. ENVISION VISCERALLY - Envision the words from the day you're on and brings these into your womb. Sit in awareness and **LISTEN** as you breathe into your womb 5-10 more cycles during this visceral envisioning.

5. RECEIVING WISDOM – Ask your body what it may want to communicate with you, what wisdom, guidance, thoughts or inspirations does it need you to know. Write down any thoughts, inspirations and guidance that you may have become aware of. Let yourself bow in gratitude for the connection with your body, and for what you have received. Your session has completed.

DAY 1 - INWARD SHIFT - DAY 27 OF THE MOON CYCLE.
(DARK MOON)

Day 1 is day 27th of the moon cycle or 3 days before your menses. It's a time to slow down, to shift your focus inward and reconnect with your body. Allow yourself to slow down during this time of the month, as you start to pay attention to your emotional body, your mental body, and essentially your sacral womb. Take a few minutes to notice what challenges you've been experiencing in the last few days or since your last menses (or the last dark moon). Jot down the challenges you're facing and allow yourself to be with these emotions, as you invite your vulnerability to come to the forefront. Take at least 5-20 minutes of breathing through these emotions or challenges that you're facing this month, welcoming them to come to the surface where they can be dissolved, as you return to your breath, time and time again.

DAY 2 - ENTERING THE DISSOLUTION - DAY 28 OF THE
MOON CYCLE.
(DARK MOON)

Day 2 is all about becoming aware of what needs to be released at this time. Perhaps your emotional body is becoming agitated, irritable, or you're aware of sadness, grief or sensitivity. Regardless of whether you're aware of the root of your emotions or not, allow yourself to feel them, be with them, and notice where in your body you're experiencing them. At this time, we may become aware of something that we're ready to release which could be our sense of insignificance, or our anger. Let yourself journal and write what it is you're ready to let go of and surrender. Continue with your breathing cycles.

DAY 3 - SURRENDER - DAY 29 OF THE MOON CYCLE.
(DARK MOON)

Day 3 is a surrender to the primordial essence that courses through us and is us. Become aware of your womb and how it feels physically and emotionally. Are you holding a lot still in your womb? What is ready to be released? Is their pain and contraction? Is there fear? Let it all arise as you let yourself move through the unknown territory of your Womb and all the emotions that might arise from entering the unknown great mystery. Let yourself release all the thoughts, feelings and physical sensations that have brought you here, up to this moment, especially anything that you are struggling with. This is the time of total submergence into the Cosmic womb of the Mother. Let yourself surrender fully into Her arms for something new to be born through you.

DAY 4 - EMPTINESS - DAY 1 OF THE MOON CYCLE.
(DARK MOON-NEW MOON)

Day 4 is the day you begin to bleed. This is a complete release on all levels as we become one with our primordial Essence and turn completely inward. This is the time to just Be completely in sync with the releasing lining in our womb and the stillness of the Essence within. As you allow yourself time and space to be in the stillness, let yourself be open to receive. Let all the structures and struggles release, moving from trying to solve anything in your mind, to completely bowing to the sacredness in your womb. This is the time to be in union with the Womb of the Cosmic Mother. Let yourself just be in this sacred time in your being.

DAY 5 - NEW LIGHT - DAY 2 OF THE MOON CYCLE
(WAXING CRESCENT)

In Day 5 you continue to merge into the deep surrendered space of the Cosmic Womb Mother as you begin to feel her new light coming in to you, nurturing you, loving you, and healing you. While your body may still be releasing and shedding the lining, your being is in a receptive mode. Let yourself be internally focused throughout your day, paying attention to your womb, your needs, and your inner world. In this profound place, you can receive the nurturing you've been longing for, by tuning in and breathing with your womb.

DAY 6 - FILLING YOUR WELL - DAY 3 OF THE MOON CYCLE
(WAXING CRESCENT)

Day 6 continues this inward focus as you begin to receive even more. There's a lot of light coming into your being; you can envision the light of the heavens (Yang-masculine) coming in through your head and the light of the Earth (Yin-feminine) coming in through your base root center. It's this Light from Source that brings you the wisdom through your own being. Take time to be with this Light of Divine presence in your womb and receive the wisdom that it offers you. Bring the questions in your heart down to your womb and listen deeply for the answers as they arise from Divine presence. Let yourself feel the flow of the Light of Love and compassion surrounding you and loving you as you receive the wisdom.

DAY 7 - INSPIRATION - DAY 4 OF THE MOON CYCLE
(WAXING CRESCENT)

In Day 7 the light of the Moon is just a crescent and we still need deep communion with our heart and womb to listen to the inspiration that is coming through. It's time to begin to gather the light in your womb and allow it to be the beginning of something new in your life. What is it that you'd like to receive this month? Would you like more peace in relationships, abundance, security, joy? This is the day to begin envisioning these qualities and begin to be open to these qualities in your life.

DAY 8 - DIRECTION - DAY 5 OF THE MOON CYCLE
(WAXING CRESCENT)

In Day 8, the wisdom and the gathered energy become direction. You can perceive the direction it may be offering you this month. Is there something you need to do to be in alignment with this new direction in your life? Perhaps your mindset needs to be focused on the possibilities instead of the negation of these possibilities. Be open to the direction that is coming from within and see what your role in following that direction is. What is that asking of you in your life?

DAY 9 - NEW CREATION - DAY 6 OF THE MOON CYCLE
(WAXING CRESCENT)

In Day 9, you're ready to come out into the world as a new creation. Something has been released from your being, and in many ways, you're a new creation. Your focus shifts from a complete inward listening to gently moving outward into the world. Your new creation is fragile and needs plenty of watering and loving attention at this stage, so continue to dedicate time to your inner world through your heart and womb. As you move into the quarter moon phase in the next couple of days, you'll be balancing your inward knowing with the outer world. This is a time of discovery of how to be in the world in a way that still honors your sacredness, knowing and wisdom. What needs to change and shift in your world, for you to honor your Truth?

Embodiment of the 5 Elements of the Feminine

Earth relates to our physical body…
and roots us deep with the gravity of Love.

Air relates to our mental body…
as it invigorates us with creative thoughts.

Water relates to emotional body…
as it purifies and soothes our being.

Fire relates to our soul body….
as it invigorates our life essence.

Ether relates to our Consciousness & Space…
as it contains us in the reality of Love.

~ leonor murciano-luna

RECLAIMING THE FIVE UNIVERSAL MOTHERS

We've separated from our Mothers, not only from the Feminine face of the Source, but from the nurturing, nourishing aspect of the Source we refer to as the Mother. These five archetypes of the mothers are necessary for our full integration with the Feminine, in all her forms. The Five Mothers live within us, as well as in our outer world. They represent themselves in the elements that all material form is comprised of, including our physical bodies. They're the energetic and material aspect of our being and bodies. The embodiment of the five elements and full integration of the Five Universal Mothers allows us to come into integrity with the great Mother energy in the Universe.

Without the integration of the Five Universal Mothers we may feel un-nurtured, lost, insecure, empty, weak, unrooted, and essentially disconnected from at least half of ourselves. While many spiritual paths have integrated the masculine transcendent aspect of our being in the ethereal realms, we've forgotten the embodied aspects of the Divine. We're living in a body, and this body is part of that sacredness divine Essence. We need to shift our thinking from one of thinking the body is separate from Spirit, to one of realizing that our body is an extension of Spirit and essentially, as such, sacred.

The five elements that create the Five Universal Mothers, nurtures, strengthens, feeds, sustains, transforms and invigorates us on every level.

We invite you to take the journey through the subtle archetypes of the five Mothers that have been waiting for your arrival and remembrance of them within you. This is a journey of transformation, thus invoking each Mother to retrieve the aspect of your Feminine soul that has been lost and allow the mental constructs that aren't in alignment with this truth, to be dissolved. As you invoke these energetics blueprints of the Mothers within you, they'll guide you individually, activating these blueprint light codes within you, allowing you to awaken and embody them for yourself.

After you read each archetype, take some time to become present with what you are feeling in your body, what is arising from within and how She is moving within you. Spend some time every evening with the Universal Mother that calls you the most. Journal the wisdom you receive from being with this image of Her and take some time to dialogue with these new levels of consciousness within that you are awakening to.

We bow to the COSMIC WOMB MOTHER
and ask Her to merge us into Her Mystery through our Breath,
as we allow our hearts and souls to deeply rest in Her Womb…
And feel the nourishment and containment
of the Cosmos.

Cosmic Womb MOTHER – AIR

The Cosmic Womb Mother of Air breathes life into us, sustaining us as we travel in between the worlds, from unmanifested consciousness to manifested life on this realm.

In Her Womb, we are in Oneness and Unity consciousness, where NO separation exists. Resting in Her breath recharges us and restores our Essence, allowing ourselves to merge once again with the state of Oneness.

She sustains us through the oxygen we breath, she creates through our thoughts, and inspires us with Her Essence.

In Her Cosmic Womb, we can let go, receive and return to the core of pre-eternity. She holds the Birth mysteries in Her womb and we're each birthed in Her image, carrying the blueprint of creation within our own wombs.

Through our sacred Breath, we enter the alchemical process of being purified, distilled, returned and ultimately, sustained by our core Essence of being.

We bow to the EARTH MOTHER
and ask Her to root our souls deep into Her Body…
as we feel Her strength anchoring through us…
clearing the veils of shame and unworthiness that have lived
in our beautiful Feminine Form.

Earth MOTHER

Earth Mother gives us the structure to move with, empowering us through the material necessities of form. She lives in our bones and our material form.

She's the sacred ground that we walk on, keeping us close through Her force of gravity. As a Mother, She provides all the nourishment we need, continuously giving of Herself.

She's created us in her liking; our bodies are Matter, made from Her Matter. She feeds us, and even though we've forgotten Her, She hasn't forgotten us.

Through our root gateway She anchors us, holding us, nurturing us, strengthening us and creating the safety we need to flourish. She is our rock.

She is the great Mother, mother to all on the planet. She is the ground for us, and we are Her strength. She is completely committed, no matter how far you have strayed. She welcomes you back with open arms, ready to infuse you with stability, sacredness and strength by reconnecting with Her

We bow to the DARK MOON MOTHER
and ask HER to annihilate us into Primordial Essence…
as we dissolve who we think we are into the
ESSENCE of our BEING…
and release all the constricting patterns of fear and illusion of separation.

Dark Moon MOTHER - Ether

Dark Moon Mother lives in between the worlds of seen and unseen. She plays in the playground of consciousness, dissolving the you of existence, in the hidden depths of the underworld.

Through the eyes of the outer, She is misunderstood. And yet, through the eye of the Eternal, She's the primordial force, committed to our evolutionary impulse of purification and transcendence.

In Her world, She unveils your forgotten shadow as a gift of transformation and transmutation. She opens the doors of alchemy where existence dissolves into no-thing and where the gates of separation merge with the heavens of eternity.

She welcomes you into your Dark night of the soul where Her devouring Love forces you to let go of the known in exchange for the unknown. She guides you through the dark watery realm of illusions, with no judgment, nor discrimination, knowing all of existence eventually dissolves into Her realm of our Primordial Truth.

*We bow to the DRAGON MOTHER
and ask Her to awaken Her Life force within us…
as Her dance of joy enlivens our very being,
we learn to listen to the deep voice of our soul's pleasure, joy and bliss
as our guiding force.*

Dragon MOTHER - Fire

Dragon Mother pulses deep within us, igniting the very essence of life. If we're still enough, we can feel her presence activating our existence within the depths of our 'body temple' cave. There, as primal essence Herself, the Dragon Mother pulses, as she lets Herself be known.

She is the life force of our Being, the spark of creation, continuously infusing vibratory spiral light of Life into our form; from the chakras of our subtle bodies to our material form.

She infuses passion, excitement, sensuality and pleasure. She's the catalyst for new creation, in the Cosmos and our bodies, reverberating Her fiery magnetism of ecstasy throughout our Being.

Dragon Mother is always present, infusing life force, energy and drive into our experience. She's the fire of transformation that burns through the veils of our illusions and stagnation, opening us onto the rich visceral embodiment of our ecstatic wholeness.

She's the catalyst, bridging non-existence into existence. She fuels us into the hidden excitement, pleasure, and enjoyment of our Being. She's the dance of life Herself, quietly pulsing stillness in the movement of our Being.

Dragon Mother of Fire is our activating force, igniting us with the ecstatic magnetism of Creation, Herself.

We bow to the OCEAN MOTHER
and ask Her to immerse us into Her unconditional OCEAN of LOVE…
as we replenish our own thirst and recognize ourselves as this very
OCEAN of LOVE,
transmitting the UNITY consciousness of LOVE to all others.

Ocean MOTHER of LOVE - Water

Ocean Mother of Love lives in the depth of our hearts and provides us with the essential love that our hearts and souls yearn for. She's the Water of compassion, mercy and love that nourishes our existential separation pain and softens the harshness of our egoic existence in the illusion of separation.

Her essence permeates our human suffering and seeps through our filters of calcified judgements and illusion. She waters our hearts when we feel broken and continues to wash away the illusions of perceptual reality.

She continually contains us in Her ocean of mercy as we awaken into deeper levels of Truth. Her ocean softly guiding us and nurturing us along the way, as we find the depths of Truth in Her Love.

Her Ocean is our existence, as She sustains us physically in our form. She is 70% of the fluids that continuously imbibe our Being with Her frequency of Love, continuously returning us to the Essence of our Being.

"You are not just worthy of Love my child... You are My OCEAN of LOVE! You are the Love of Creation Herself, the Love that births everything into existence... this is the Love Consciousness that You are... and that forms you, even in form! "

We've come to the turning point of the book in which we've laid out the terrain in the previous chapters, of what, when, where and how. Now, we're ready to begin the transformation process through the Sacred Initiations of the Feminine that were downloaded to me through the last few years, since 2012. As I worked with hundreds of women, transforming their inner wounds and places of suffering, these sacred initiations continued to show up and reveal the complex physical, metaphysical and esoteric nature. The sacred initiations are happening within all of us that are asking for this greater knowledge and are ready to enter the transformation of our Feminine soul.

The next few chapters gracefully move us through the healing of our Feminine Soul step by step and we can choose to engage in the practices that really call to us. At the end of each chapter are the practices that will ignite, activate and transform those themes in that corresponding sacred initiation. Like many of us, you might feel that you have a lot more work to do in one specific area. Therefore, pay attention to what feels right in your body and stay with the practices that resonate. Sometimes, we continue to work with a transformation for months and even years, as we continue our evolutionary process. Even though this is presented in a linear process, once you're familiar with all the initiations, then you can spend more time with the ones that you're really needing.

What you will see are embodied practices that are designed to allow the light of the Feminine Spirit to fill you in places that have been blocked up to now. This is what offers us the transformation and healing. This is where we move deep into our body and start to shift the consciousness of our being. This process isn't an intellectual one, even though it begins with awareness and understanding in the mind. However, we then must move it into the body realm, of embodied experience and then merge into Oneness consciousness, but not despite the body, through the body. We won't continue to commit the same mistake thousands of the spiritual paths have led us through, the absence of the body.

Dissolving ~ Return ~ Resurrection

As I sit in contemplation,
I travel into the Gates of the Unknown.
Inquisitively, I explore the prohibitive dark path of the Hidden.
I stumble upon the Light of my existence.
Here, I enter the Womb of Dissolution and find the birth place of Separation.
I enter cautiously and I am pleasantly greeted by the
Queendom of Heaven, within.
I find the light of my existence dissolving into the Ocean of Pre-existence.
Here, my Soul rests, expands and renews and there is No-Separation.
My Soul is Her Soul,
where manifested consciousness merges with unmanifested consciousness.
I have been absorbed into the Essence of my Being, becoming No-Thing.
I rest, I expand, and I dissolve and there is No-I.
Then it is time and She returns me…
Breathing Life in the Me of full existence,
once again, I am resurrected into a new creation,
Birthing through me the lost wisdom of Her Mystery.

~leonor murciano-luna

6
1ˢᵗ *Sacred Initiation of*
Conscious Feminine Essence

AWAKENING TO YOUR CONSCIOUS FEMININE ESSENCE

As we awaken to the evolution of the Feminine, we begin our journey with the first Sacred Initiation of the Feminine, *Conscious Feminine Essence,* which allows us to anchor our awareness in our sacred essence of light; our Essential Self. Through this Initiation of Conscious Feminine Essence, we begin our dissolving process into the unknown, moving from our minds to our hearts. Through the specific cultivating practices in this initiation, we'll discover how our body begins the transformation of re-wiring itself to align with the greater truth of our Essence, hiding within us. It's important to note that while our work is to establish ourselves in our Essential Self, we will be traveling through the Conscious Feminine Essence. It's the opening of our Feminine Essence that provides a map to arrive at our Essential nature of wholeness within. Our Feminine Essence has been blocked, repressed, rejected, excluded and wounded. Reclaiming our Feminine Essence from all places of our consciousness where She has been casted away, is truly the retrieval our Feminine Soul. This is the journey that allows us to awaken, realize and establish our self in our Essential Self. Here, in this first initiation of *Conscious Feminine Essence,* we begin the process of being, feeling, and communing directly with the Essence dimension of our Being.

In these processes of the Sacred Initiations, our Conditioned Self, which is our egoic nature that experiences itself as a separate entity, becomes aware of the unconscious conditioning patterns that have been dictating our reactions and responses to life itself. As we walk through these sacred initiations, we create space between our conditioned reactions, wounds, and our sense of true self. This process allows these 'conditions' that we've erroneously identified with ourselves to dissolve into the Ocean of the Mother.

The road back home to our Essential Self is paved with all the places of unresolved pain and suffering in our being. We have created a functioning pattern to protect ourselves, that overlay these unresolved memories of pain and create our conditioning. And as we bring in the light through these transformational practices, these wounds come up, one by one to be healed by receiving the unconditional love that it never received. So, you're the map, and the light enters the places that has been cracked and holds the unresolved trauma of the past.

These Sacred Initiations also break through the collective conditioning patterns that have been caused by the collective wounding of the Feminine, because every woman is also carrying the place of oneness where there's no separation. Our wound has been experienced by many other women. And so, when we heal our wounds, we simultaneously heal the wounds of many other women on the planet; seven generations forward and seven generations backwards. This is sacred work, not only personal, but also global.

You Are A Hidden treasure

We carry the secret, the unknown and the Oneness within. It's the breath of the Divine within us... it (we) are consciousness itself. We're created in the image of our maker. There is nowhere to go, enlightment is not a destination. All the levels of consciousness, as well as all the aspects of the Universal Mother exist within us and are ready to be explored and experienced. The Sacred Initiations of the Feminine unfolds these levels of consciousness for us to experience and witness life from other perspectives, untangled from our limited, wounded Self. As we cultivate and unravel our Soul's Truth within, we free ourselves from our preconceived perspective of separation allowing our witnessing (where we experience life from) to become open to subtler and subtler levels of consciousness that have been veiled to us. But contrary to popular belief, these levels of consciousness aren't outside of ourselves; they are within, they are us.

It's hard for our minds to grasp the fact that there is no destination and that all levels of consciousness exist right now, in the present. It's challenging to the mind because the mind experiences it's thoughts in linear time; past and future. And yet, when we experience these deeper levels of consciousness, we experience no-time, only presence. And that presence that we experience is our Essence. Thinking often blocks us from experiencing the now, and catches us in the mind of past and future thoughts.

Furthermore, we're constantly experiencing these varying states of consciousness through our awareness and consequently mistaken who we are with the states that we're experiencing. Therefore, we mistaken ourselves for our sadness, anger, suffering, or however we may "think" of ourselves, perhaps through definitions of our roles and accomplishments. Yet the deeper truth is that we're presence, truly the Essence of primordial consciousness; that which experiences those levels of consciousness itself.

In the CFM model, the initiation begins with the realization of our Essence, and Feminine Essence, because we have been disconnected from Her for so long. We become aware that we are Feminine Essence in a physical body, explore all the ways we can embody and realize Her in our Being. We recognize the feelings of inadequacy that we've been feeling for so many years are reflective of our survival conditioning rather than on the true Feminine Essence that we are. These include the parts of ourselves that haven't quite fit into the prescribed patriarchal cultural mold and that we have made 'wrong.' The initiation begins our evolutionary process of experiencing ourselves as the canvas behind our preconceived ideas of Self and, more importantly, as the continuous expression of Oneness, but not as a concept, rather an embodied truth.

The wound is the place where the Light enters you.

~ Rumi

AWAKENING TRUTH

How do I experience Feminine Essence, you might be asking? Essentially, it begins (or perhaps continues) with our willingness to let go of the things we think we are face the places where we have rejected the Feminine. On one level, we don't want to deny our roles; we're still mothers, daughters, teachers, sisters, lawyers, writers, etc., but we begin to recognize that it's our persona, aspects of our personality and what we do. Those are all based on separation, the egoic aspect of yourself that thinks of you as separate. From the humanistic perspective of duality we are separate; we function with individual minds, individual emotions, individual dreams and visions. The problem comes in when we think that it's all that we are and lose the connection to the unseen aspect of ourselves, living in denial of our eternal wholeness. Losing this unseen aspect of ourselves is losing the foundation of our Being.

Acknowledging our Essence of Divine light within means we no longer have to continue the collective story of victimization rooted in fear. Awakening to this truth, allows us to own our power in connection with Source, as well as become completely responsible for ourselves; emotionally, mentally, physically and spiritually. No more blaming. No more excuses. No more denial. While this may seem challenging, it offers us the opportunity to stand in our strength and sovereignty rather than on dependence and disconnection.

By embodying our innate Feminine Essence, we no longer need to give away our power to someone else by believing that others are our authority. Deep in our being, through our visceral embodiment of Feminine Essence, we can access direct wisdom and guidance. Through this awakening, we realize that the source of wisdom is within, not necessarily in someone else. The right action is available to us because it stems from us, it is us, and we have access to the deeper dimensions of our Self.

For me this journey has resulted in the realization that the Light lives within me and that the source of guidance that I have been searching for all my life, was within me all along. Spirit truly is speaking to each one of us, always, through our thoughts, through our emotions, through our Essence and yet we realize we are not separate from Spirit, but an aspect of Spirit. Developing the ability to trust this truth about ourselves is an important key in experiencing ourselves as Essence.

"Know thyself" is an old ancient Greek adage that was inscribed on the temple known as the Oracle of Delphi. This adage speaks volumes, our evolution is to know ourselves, know our Truth and to know who we really are. Experiencing our Essence, which is at the core of everything else we experience in life, is the first initiatory process that begins the unraveling of our false identity and opens us up to the embodiment of the Feminine within.

Awakening to our Essence is always a choice. As human beings we have choice and thus we choose every minute of the day; do we want to move from Love or from other? Choosing the Love is synonymous with choosing our Essence. This is a conscious challenge we face moment to moment, which determines our responses and reactions to incoming life itself.

Choosing to experience life from our Essence and foundation of Love is sometimes challenging. We may be challenged by our emotions, our circumstances and the meanings we give those things outside ourselves. Nonetheless, every opportunity offers us an experience in which we either experience it from an egoic (sense of separate self) wounded, conditioned, limited sense of self, or from our whole Self. Our reactions from our egoic wounded sense of Self aren't the problem, we all have conditioned wounded patterns that we react from, the problem is when we confuse these reactions of ourselves for the whole of ourselves. In other words, when we believe the limited wounded meaning that we are giving these experiences; believing the shame, the inadequacy, the failures; believing that we are our 'emotional' states and thoughts, rather than knowing that we are true Essence.

In our Feminine Essence we experience the deep love that is us. The Love isn't separate from us, it's who we are. However, many women have lived in fear and terror for a long time, unable to safely express the unconditional love of their Feminine Essence. And so, we have forgotten the Love and being in our truth of Love terrifies us, does not feel safe. Instead of knowing ourselves as love, we've believed the story of thinking that we're inadequate because we feel inadequate, or because our minds are comparing ourselves with something that we haven't accomplished yet and thus concluding we are inadequate. The truth is these are just thoughts and emotions and we are mistaken ourselves for these experiences rather than for the truth of who we are. When we decide that we are Love, over and above whatever we may feel or tell ourselves, then we are choosing Love, then we can continue to work through our patterns of separation and illusion, our wounded conditioned defenses of the past and connect with the underlying truth of our Feminine Essence. This is how we choose Love over other.

The world in this moment hasn't chosen to function from Love, it's stuck in the ignorance of believing that we're our limitations, our woundedness and our inadequacies, which is why the Feminine is rising. Most humans haven't awakened to the love yet, they're still slaves to the fear, which manipulates and creates more pain and suffering. We have to choose Love, we have claim it, we have to awaken to it. In our Feminine Essence, we can face the unknown straight on and be willing to go against the monumental tide of cultural patriarchal conditioning. We have to believe in goodness, primarily goodness of our own Being. We have to be willing to give our lives for it, regardless of the whisperings of the fear within.

For me, taking that risk and facing the fear head on and challenging it, has been the most liberating thing I have ever done. Facing the fear and diving into the unknown with it did not result in more fear and devastation as my mind thought it would, it resulted in the dissolving of the fear and a deep, fierce expansion of my Feminine Essence. For most of us, the fear keeps us from venturing off too far into the unknown and yet that is exactly what the Conscious Feminine is asking us to do now. Can we trust the whispers in our heart rather than the fears of our mind? Do we dare to take a stand? Do we have the courage to invoke the wild, unpredictable radical Love of the Feminine, the one that burns through the conditions that have held us back for so long? This is what She is asking of us now!

Your task is not to seek for love, but merely to seek and find all the barriers within yourself that you have built against it.

~ Rumi

SACRED SOUND AND LIGHT SOURCE CODES

In the beginning was the "word", and the word was sound. All of creation is created by sound. Sound creates patterns through the vibration that it creates. Everything in the universe is in a constant state of vibration. And the most elemental state of vibration is sound. The earth's botanical world of nature vibrates to the frequency from the sun's energy and then transforms this frequency into oxygen that we breathe, to keep us alive.

Every organ, every cell, every aspect of our body resonates to a particular frequency and is receiving and emitting sound at all times. When we become stressed, we affect that frequency, creating disruption among its harmonious waves. Our human body is created through sound resonance. And sound creates form, from the galaxies all the way down to every single cell in our body. At every moment, we are receiving the sound and light vibrational frequencies coming in from the sun, and breathing it into our lungs.

When we laugh, we automatically sound the letters of AH-HA which vibrates at the same frequency as nature, Herself. Words are sound codes and frequencies which are creative in nature. Sacred sound is inherent particularly in the sounding of vowels, A-E-I-O-U. These sounds have been used by all spiritual traditions to tap into mystical, non-dual dimensions.

Mantras are an example of these sound and light codes. These words have been used for healing ourselves and our planet through the resonance it creates with varying states of consciousnesses. These resonant states also correlate with the vibrational frequencies of specific attributes of divine energy fields. These mantras also correlate with the gateways in our subtle field, that was discussed in chapter three. However, it's important to realize the connection between sound, light and creation Herself, which was codified in the statement, "let there be light", is one of the secrets of how creation continues to be manifested on the physical realm.

Of the many sounds of sacred mantras, you have a few that are regarded as having powerful resonance with our planet. The first of these is: OM, this is the oldest chanted name in existence and considered to be the original, primordial sound. The sound OM is a Sanskrit word said to be the origin of all creation and other sounds. It's also known as the name of GOD. OM has also been used in the transformational paths as AUM, pronounced AH-OH-MMM, resonating heart, throat and crown chakras. OM is a powerful mantra to activate all the Chakra gateways for greater transformation and resonance with higher frequencies of Oneness.

The second sacred sound I want to mention is the AH sound. The AH sound used in AUM is very powerful in its ability to open the heart, generate compassion, and purify the conditioned layers of one's egoic nature through (what the Sufi's call) alchemy of the layers of the Heart gateway. The AH sound is a profoundly transformative sound found throughout Hebrew Kabbalah, Tibetan Buddhism, Sufi's and other mystical traditions.

The AH sound is further used in sacred names or words relating to the Divine; Buddha, Krishna, Amen, Allah. The AH sound is also believed to be the primary sound that is created in our first breath, through our inhalation and exhalation. And it's said that two people can entrain their heart beat, respiration and brain waves through their breathing and chanting of the sound "AH" together.

The third sacred sound that is is the HU sound. The Sufi mystical path regards it as the highest vibratory name of GOD, leading to transcendence and enlightenment. It's said to be present in all of creation, from the bees to the wind, to the trees and in the water, bringing extraordinary shifts in consciousness.

The OM or AUM, AH and HU sounds are regarded as key sounds in transforming our consciousness and accessing the transcendent states of the Conscious Feminine. As we chant these names, we activate our subtle body gateways, transform our egoic nature of separation, access quantum field frequencies and access our Feminine body of light. These sacred codes are used to raise and shift our personal and collective vibration in our body, heart, mind, and soul.

These sacred light codes aren't separate from the sound codes. They're encoded in the vibrational frequencies of the sound codes. In the Sufi tradition, there are 99 names for God (Allah-the name of God in Arabic) which is said to activate a particular light frequency, that corresponds with all of creation. In other words, everything that we see with our eyes, is created from light vibration and sound frequencies, and these sound and light codes are the corresponding activation codes for all of creation.

These 99 names are also referred to as the Universal qualities. In reality, these Universal qualities are all around us as the underlining light that manifests everything in the world. When we chant and recite the Universal qualities, we ignite their unique light frequency from the Oneness consciousness all around us, but more importantly, it also activates these frequencies within ourselves. According to the Sufi tradition, our Essence is composed of these Universal qualities, unique to each of us, and the sound qualities of these names begins to resonant and activate within us and allows that particular light within to expand. As part of cultivation, reciting these qualities expands the particular quality of light within and dissolves the conditioning restrictive patterns within us. This is the process of awakening the Universal qualities within us by our conscious awareness and igniting these qualities within our DNA.

Transforming ourselves with these Universal qualities is the process by which the Sufi's reach enlightment and self-realization and additionally, is the process where we experience divine union with our beloved, in our physical body. Moreover, there are qualities that correspond with each of the seven subtle gateways, which can be used to awaken and transform our conditioning and wounding in these areas. We will explore these in our 1ˢᵗ sacred initiation at the end of this chapter.

Therefore, the integration of these Universal qualities is what we're seeking to unfold in this evolution of consciousness towards the perfected human being; the Anthropos. The beauty is that we aren't changing anything necessarily, we're creating consciousness, awareness to who we are first, and detaching from everything that we aren't. And specifically, we're creating consciousness of the Feminine aspects of ourselves, which have been repressed and suppressed and allowing the spiritual alchemy of the frequencies themselves to dissolve the layers of erroneous conditioning that we've accumulated in our being. Allowing ourselves to rest in our divine nature of Light Essence allows us to let go of the attachments to all these other perceptions that in many ways have served to keep us feeling safe.

We've created our toughness and repressed our emotions, to stay safe. We've become more aggressive and assertive to survive in a world that only accepts exaggerated forms of masculine traits. As women, we've drowned our own female babies, because our culture insisted for us to stay alive to feed the rest of the family. As women, we have bought into this consciousness, along with the men and cannot afford to continue to blame anyone else for what we have all created on this planet. And while there may be anger and rage at the price that we have all paid for our survival, most importantly, there's responsibility of acknowledging where our consciousness has been and what we need to shift within us to play the crucial role of creating that evolutionary consciousness on the planet.

There are two important distinctions I would like to make before we move into the physical process of activating the Sacred Initiations. First of all, we're now aware of our Essence and secondly, there's this other aspect of ourselves that we may call our egoic nature (the aspect of ourselves that experiences life in separation).

The 1ˢᵗ Sacred Initiation is the process of opening up to our Conscious Feminine Essence and establishing our consciousness in this frequency. As we establish our consciousness in this frequency, we also may say that we are awakening to this frequency.

In doing so, various things happen on the physical, emotional and mental and consciousness levels.

On the physical level, our body processes, our chemical processes, our hormones, our organ systems, etc. start to shift according to the frequency that your consciousness is focused on. In other words, it's important to note that these frequencies are always there, the unity levels of consciousness are always there, but we aren't witnessing that level of frequency, therefore, our consciousness does not realize that that levels are there. When we expand our consciousness to become aware of our light, of our Essential Self, then there are various other bodily, mental, emotional shifts that happen simultaneously, because there is a shift in energetic frequency.

For example, lets imagine that we're in fear. When we experience fear, our muscles tighten, and when we feel peace or safety, our muscles relax. In the same way (just a bit more complex), there are correspondences that happen when we begin to experience greater levels of expansion into our Essential Self. There is, of course, the emotional levels of safety, love, peace, truth, etc. that we may feel, but along with these, there are physiological shifts that take please depending on the level of consciousness that we're experiencing. If our physical body relaxes and engages the parasympathetic nervous system, for example, we stop producing stress hormones, our immune system doesn't feel under psychic or physical attack anymore, and stops reacting with excess antibodies, etc. and there is a healing response that occurs, simultaneously.

Therefore, by shifting our focus to our light, and discovering the limitless dimension of Love that exists within us, we begin the cascade of healing process in our body. This is the power of the 1st sacred initiation of Conscious Feminine Essence. Let's explore a few more ingredients that will contribute to our 1st Sacred Initiation before we dive in.

"If you wish to understand the Universe, think of energy as frequency and vibration"

~ Nikola Tesla

Holy Anointing

Holy anointing is a ceremonial practice designed to restore your sense of being fully alive as a soul in a physical body. This ceremony frees you from feeling stuck in an energy grid produced by repetitive tasks and programmed reactions into a new expanded matrix which accesses the greater web of life force energy.

Holy anointing by the laying on of hands ceremonies are found in all of the planet's earths' major religions.

When these elements of earth, water, fire and air are in balance, we enjoy great health and vitality. When any one of these elements is lacking, our health suffers, leaving us disconnected from life.

The old testament teaches us to anoint to heal the sick and also as ritual to dedicate the body, place or object towards the divine purpose.

The human body is a five-pointed star which reflects our soul's heavenly home. Your head and face are the top point of the star with arms and legs outstretched completing the celestial star body.

Using all four elements to help us feel more whole at the cellular level. Incense sage and sweet grass are burned to carry our intentions upwards to the father… sacred waters in fountains or ceremonial bowls candles flicker with the illuminating power of fire and light and living plants, stones, crystal and herbs help ground the body to the earth plane of existence. You are Self-sovereign powerful and loving.

~ Tracy Elise

Oklevueha Native American Church Medicine Woman and Elder Medicine Woman for Onac Mother Medicine Wheel

ANOINTING AS A RITUAL

Anointing, as so beautifully iterated from Tracy Elise, is a process where we touch the body with essential oils and allow the vibratory frequency of the oils to shift the frequency of the body, initiating an innate healing response through vibratory resonance. Using essential oils in this way, can uplift the overall energetic resonance to the living consciousness of Nature, through the frequencies of the plants, themselves.

In the great cultures of Sumer, Babylon and Canaan there were Temples that were the home to priestesses that were very well schooled in the sacred practice of using essential oils for healing. Many of these included ancient rights that ritual, prayer, divinatory messages and healing through anointing of the body. Essential oils and anointing have been used as sacred practices for union with the Divine, mystical practices of awakening, and spiritual union throughout civilizations and cultures.

Essential oils vibrate at a particular frequency that helps elevate our consciousness to that of the higher divinatory levels of union, thus very often being used, not just in anointing, but also in meditation and other mystical practices. The oils are said to represent the Spirit and the scent, to be the fragrance gateway to connecting to higher levels of consciousness.

The Egyptians used anointing and essential oils for thousands of years. This knowledge of anointing was handed down by the priest initiates, for over 5000 years, as recorded on the walls of Dendera temple. Some people believe that Jesus and Mary Magdalene participated in the mystery school as taught at the Dendera and learned the magic of the esoteric anointing oils. Isis priestesses were proficient at healing with anointing as well as delivering and birthing the next generations. Essential oils were honored for being part of the transformational alchemy secret practices they practice. These healing substances were revered as medicine for not just the physical, but also the spirit on all levels of manifestations, it is a direct healing force of Mother Nature, Herself, in physical form.

Essential oils in nature are powerful antioxidants, anti-bacterial, anti-fungal, anti-viral, and antiseptic. Through inhalation or absorption by our skin, they affect the limbic system of our brain, quickly shifting the chemical balance within our biology. Used on our skin, these oils have the ability to penetrate directly through the blood barrier, quickly being absorbed into our system for powerful changes in our physiology, and also our subtle energetic bodies. Part of their power is that their chemical compounds affect us physically through the effects on our brain, but their energetic vibrational frequency also creates transformational alchemy within our subtle bodies. And as we enter this initiation with the Feminine, essential oils and anointing prove to be a direct powerful healing method to incorporate in our activations. It's one of many healing gifts our Mother has provided us; human kind, with, reminding us to remember our true Essential Self through Her creation.

In my practice, and in *Conscious Feminine Medicine*™, I work with a specific number of healing oils listed on the next page. There are many healing oils that are wonderful to work with, however, I find that these are the subtlest and produce the finest frequencies to affect the body and consciousness, simultaneously. It's important to make sure that your essential oils are organic and sustainably sourced from all around the world.

Anointing is incorporated in the *Conscious Feminine Medicine*™ Activation and in most of the practices of *Conscious Feminine Medicine*™. Below, I have associated a couple of words of the healing potential of each of the eleven essential oils, but by no means is this a complete list of their ability. Furthermore, I suggest you choose these oils, not by your intellectual knowledge of what they do, but rather through letting yourself blindly choose three essential oils to work with or by smelling them and seeing which ones resonate with you on any particular day. Dropping into your body and allowing your embodied wisdom to communicate what to use, by choosing the one that 'feels good' in your body senses, will direct you to the greatest harmony within

My Favorite 11 Sacred Essential Oils

Frankincense

Spiritual awakener & wisdom oil.

Myrrh

Sacred transcendence, purification, mothering oil.

Spikenard

Transformational & purification oil.

Helichyrysum

Oil of Healing & Hope.

Neroli

Inner peace, love of the Beloved, clears mental confusion oil.

Rose

Unconditional love, compassion, inner peace oil.

Jasmine

Sensuality & blissful oil.

Vetiver

Grounding, prosperity consciousness oil.

Sandalwood

Sacred devotion, inner peace, transcendence.

Cardamom

Clearing & clarifying on all levels.

Chamomile Blue

Gentle, nourishing, inducing healthy inflammatory response.

CONSCIOUS FEMININE MEDITATION

I would like to take the opportunity to introduce another concept of practice that we will be using throughout the Sacred Initiations, which is *Conscious Feminine Meditation*. As the name implies, this is a method of meditating that actually focuses on becoming conscious of what you're experiencing in various levels of your subtle body. Throughout the practices that I will be introducing you in this book, this form of meditation will be applied constantly.

Conscious Feminine Meditation also carries the name of the Feminine, because it's the very feminine essence that is connected with the acknowledgement and inclusion of the physical body and spirituality. In other words, we're entering these spiritual states of Essence and light, through our physical body, not in lieu of it. It's the Feminine that lives in the body, and that recognizes the sacredness of the physical realm. Thus, using the very name in the method itself, Conscious Feminine Meditation.

In Conscious Feminine Meditation, we're allowing ourselves to slow down enough to enter (become aware of) varying levels of consciousness that are co-existing at all times, through the map of our inner body. These techniques, of course, are pointers to a particular state, rather than the state themselves. They are things we can do to prepare ourselves and set ourselves up to experience these levels of consciousness in our being.

As we slowdown the process of *Conscious Feminine Meditation*, we also allow ourselves to become present, or bring presence to the moment, this moment, rather than being in our minds (in the past or future). And through our presence we can begin to feel the level of consciousness that we associate with our Essential Self.

Furthermore, through *Conscious Feminine Meditation*, we can also experience our emotional body in its fullness, along with all the unresolved traumas that we may still hold within; anger, grief, sadness or fear. It's important that we release any judgments that might arise as we become present to what unresolved emotions may be in our heart or field. It's important to the Feminine to feel our selves fully and be willing to express our emotional body that has been shamed and repressed for such a long time.

Through *Conscious Feminine Meditation* we allow ourselves to be awakened to everything that we have been holding within, realizing that it's all sacred. It includes the process of meditating consciously on your being through the sacred container of your body; including all sensations, emotions and thoughts to arise, allowing presence to penetrate, transform and be embodied in the greatest way possible. When we have a judgment or expectation of how we should be, what we should feel, or make any aspect of our experience wrong, we don't allow ourselves to resolve the underlying shadows, fears and other vulnerabilities that have previously been met with judgment. One of the reasons we have these conditioned patterns within us in the first place is because we've created defenses against those very same judgments of expressing ourselves to survive in a hostile environment. Judging ourselves, our reactions, our responses and our Conditioned Self only perpetuates the conditioning and prevents us from truly opening ourselves to the limitless Love of our primordial Essence.

As we move into the *1ˢᵗ Sacred Initiation of the Feminine*, I highly suggest you record your own voice and guide yourself through the steps of these processes and all that follow. Then you can relax and play the recording without having to look at the steps or book.

The *1ˢᵗ Sacred Initiation* will begin with a writing reflection, awakening your relationship with your *Conscious Feminine Essence*, followed by *Conscious Feminine Trinity Womb Activation* and ending with a comprehensive *Conscious Feminine Medicine*™ *Activation*, which will allow you to embody all of the concepts we have explored in this chapter.

1ST SACRED INITIATION: CONSCIOUS FEMININE ESSENCE
WRITING REFLECTION:

To begin your 1st Sacred Initiation of Conscious Feminine Essence, I invite you to take a few minutes of reflection time and begin with reading some of the qualities below of the Feminine, and perhaps reflect and write about your relationship with your Feminine Essence.

Remember that the qualities below are not a complete list, but rather a reflection of some of Her qualities within us. Reflect upon these questions:

1. What is my relationship with expressing emotions?

2. How comfortable do I feel with expressing my truth, even if it goes against what everyone else is saying?

3. How do I feel about tears in public, about showing affection and following my intuition?

4. How do I feel about my wild, untamable passions, being vulnerable?

Look at this list below and reflect upon how much you allow yourself to experience these Feminine qualities and/ or how much you may be judging yourself or rejecting yourself because you experience these qualities.

FEMININE Light Codes

Experience Oriented	Sensitivity	Nurturing	Inward	Nourishing	Surrender
That which holds all potential		Receptive	Affection	Emotional	Sensual
That which all is birthed from		Empathic	Hidden	Darkness	Creative
Slow Moving	Unseen	Restful	Retreating	Transformational	
Cooperative	Being	Allowing			

REFLECTION JOURNAL

_____

_____

_____

_____

_____

_____

_____

_____

_____

_____

_____

_____

_____

_____

_____

_____

_____

_____

_____

CONSCIOUS FEMININE TRINITY WOMB ACTIVATION
USE DIAGRAM ON THE NEXT PAGE

1. Become aware of the three wombs spaces in the above diagram.

2. Sit quietly preferably with your back straight in meditation lotus pose.

3. Bring your hands over the one of the wombs, beginning with your Sacral Womb and breath into it for a few minutes, becoming aware of what your sensations, feelings, and thoughts may be in this area. Breathe acceptance and love into any and everything that may arise here, knowing that we store and carry a lot of old conditioning filters in these womb spaces. Just continue to breathe and notice, bringing presence into these areas.

4. Next say these three statements into the womb, slowly and allowing yourself to integrate each truth into this space.

   I Trust My Body

   I Trust Myself

   I Trust the Ever-Flowing Feminine Essence that moves through me and is me.

5. Now listen and here what any messages that Consciousness may be communicating with you. Jot them down if you need to.

6. Now repeat steps 3-5 for each of the other two Womb centers. Take your time, jotting down any messages to remember and honor after your process.

7. When you have completed all three, feel a tunnel of light moving from the lowest sacral womb center to the center... to the upper womb. Feel the light moving through each... connecting them and flowing right through you. Let this light expand through your whole being, until you are only aware of your light body. Trust your body, trust your light.

   Bow in gratitude.

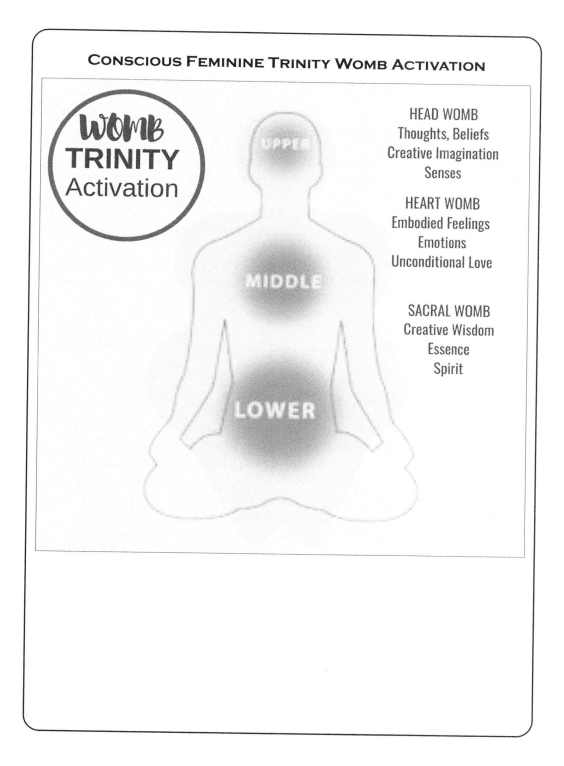

1ST SACRED INITIATION OF CONSCIOUS FEMININE MEDICINE™ ACTIVATION

Conscious Feminine Medicine™ Activation Preparation

This is a process of activating the sacred medicine of the Feminine, that's hidden within you. Through the activation of the Feminine, we awaken our consciousness of Her and open up to the powerful medicine that we carry as women. This is the medicine that heals our Body ~ Heart ~ Soul, and activates the return of the lost, rejected and abandoned aspects of ourselves back into wholeness.

These are the preparation steps to activate the *Conscious Feminine Medicine*™ within you. My suggestion is that you read it through and then record it with your own voice and with the particulars of each of the Gateway steps. Then listen to the recording and allow yourself to feel into your body and connect with your visceral experience of the practice. Make the practice your own by actually tuning in and feeling the Practice this protocol every day, at any time, and see what resonates with you.

Choose your Essential Oils

Prepare your essential oils of choice before you start your activation, so that they will be available to you. I prefer to use three that resonate with me that day. I usually allow myself to pick them out, setting the intention for the Divine to choose for my highest good. Inhale them, taking it in through the whole body and then throughout the process gently touch your body in the varying places of the openings.

Invocation

Below I have offered some invocations that you can use for the *Conscious Feminine Medicine*™ Activation. Please choose these in advance and include them in your recording. Invocations help to create sacred space and invite particular frequencies that contribute to the alchemical transformation process. Choose one of these listed below or choose your own invocation or prayer.

A word about Breath

Breath is a key to our transcendence and union with the subtler levels of consciousness. When you think of breath and breathing, think of the breath as the substance that unites you to the spirit of Oneness that brings in the Universal qualities into your physical vessel. Your breath allows the in breath of Oneness, supporting you completely. Remember this as you are breathing and allowing.

"There is one way of breathing that is shameful and constricted. Then there's another way; a breath of love that takes you all the way to infinity."

~Rumi

Light Invocation

Divine Mother, Father, Birther.
May you grant light in my heart,
Light in my mind,
Light in my emotions,
Light in my body,
Light in my blood.
Grant Light in my soul,
Light in my secret,
Light in my being,
Grant Light above me,
Light below me,
Light to my left,
Light to my right,
Light in front of me,
Light behind me,
All around me, grant me light, make light abundant for me
Make me Light.

Lord's Prayer

O Birther! Father- Mother of the Cosmos
Focus your light within us - make it useful.
Create your reign of unity now-
through our fiery hearts and willing hands
Help us love beyond our ideals
and sprout acts of compassion for all creatures.
Animate the earth within us: we then
feel the Wisdom underneath supporting all.
Untangle the knots within
so that we can mend our hearts' simple ties to each other.
Don't let surface things delude us,
But free us from what holds us back from our true purpose.
Out of you, the astonishing fire,
Returning light and sound to the cosmos.
Amen.

~translation by Neil Douglas-Klotz in prayers of the Cosmos

The Prayer To Our Father

Abwûn
"Oh Thou, from whom the breath of life comes

d'bwaschmâja
who fills all realms of sound, light and vibration.

Nethkâdasch schmach
May Your light be experienced in my utmost holiest.

Têtê malkuthach.
Your Heavenly Domain approaches.

Nehwê tzevjânach aikâna d'bwaschmâja af b'arha.
Let Your will come true – in the universe (all that vibrates)
just as on earth (that is material and dense).

Hawvlân lachma d'sûnkanân jaomâna.
Give us wisdom (understanding, assistance) for our daily need,

Waschboklân chaubên wachtahên aikâna
daf chnân schwoken l'chaijabên.
detach the fetters of faults that bind us, (karma)
like we let go the guilt of others.

Wela tachlân l'nesjuna
Let us not be lost in superficial things (materialism, common temptations),

ela patzân min bischa.
but let us be freed from that what keeps us off from our true purpose.

Metol dilachie malkutha wahaila wateschbuchta l'ahlâm almîn.
From You comes the all-working will, the lively strength to act,
the song that beautifies all and renews itself from age to age.

Amên.
Sealed in trust, faith and truth.
(I confirm with my entire being) [6]

1ST SACRED INITIATION OF
CONSCIOUS FEMININE MEDICINE™ ACTIVATION

Sit comfortably and allow yourself to be undisturbed for at least 10-30 minutes, if not longer.

A. Become Present to your Physical Body

Start to slow down and breathe into your body. Become aware of your breath. Notice the expansion and the contraction of your body. Notice the sensations when you breathe. Become aware that you are in this body and that this body is a vessel and expression of the Oneness. Notice that there are many layers of consciousness in this form of your body. Become open and willing to explore these layers of consciousness and how they manifest in you.

Realize the portal to this inner world of consciousness can be accessed through the heart. Breathe and become aware (present) with your physical sensations, without any desire to change, alter or judge anything at all just experience the sensations in the moment.

B. Set your Intention

Align your heart, soul, mind, emotions, and thoughts with this statement or something similar. You can also add a particular request for something that you'd like to receive; i.e.; compassion, love, health, specific healing of some sort.

"I allow my being to become a complete vessel for Divine Consciousness of Oneness to flow through me and I surrender all aspects of my being in my mental, emotional and physical body, my heart and my soul that may be in the way of experience complete union with the Divine Essence of Oneness."

C. Use an Invocation of Choice

"I ask the Divine Oneness to allow my heart, soul, physical, mental and emotional body to heal on all levels."

D. Open the 7 Gateway Chakras

The seven Gateway Chakras act as intermediary between the seen and unseen levels of consciousness in your body and tune in with the specific breath & Elemental MOTHER for each Gate Chakra.

Root Gateway

~Bring your awareness into your **Root Gateway**-located at the base of your spine, the perineum and pelvic floor. **BREATH-EARTH:** In through the NOSE, out through the NOSE. HANDS **over ROOT GATE,** breathe three times with **EARTH breath**.

~Bring your awareness to the **Elemental Earth MOTHER** awakening in your tissues, organs, bones, muscles and all other forms creating your body. Feel her support, stability, strength and solidity outside as the **Elemental Earth MOTHER** in the plants, the trees, the abundant supply of food and inside as the gravity that sustains you.

~Bring your awareness and your breath into this area and allow yourself feel the safety, rootedness, and **Earth** beneath you, holding you, supporting you, stabilizing you, and strengthening you.

~Continue the **Earth Breath** in and out through the **Root Gateway,** add the sound AHHH to activate this gateway chakra with at least seven exhales, (AHHH, AHHH, AHHH, AHHH, AHHH, AHHH, AHHH). Allow yourself to feel the opening and activation of this **Root** gateway with the Earth.

Sacral Gateway

~Bring your awareness into your **Sacral Gateway** located on the lower abdomen, right below your umbilicus (belly button). **BREATH-WATER:** In through the NOSE, out through the MOUTH. **HANDS over SACRAL GATE,** breathe three times with **WATER breath**.

~Bring your awareness to the **Elemental Ocean Of Love MOTHER** awakening in your blood, lymphatic system, and all other fluids in your body. Feel the waves of love outside yourself through the **Elemental Ocean of Love MOTHER** and inside yourself, as waves of LOVE.

~Bring your awareness and your breath into this area and let yourself feel the creative force of life itself, dancing into your relationships inside and outside yourself. Let the LOVE Essence of spirit move through you as a creative force, igniting passion and love as the foundation of all your relationships.

~Realize that all your relationships are a mirror of your relationship with Oneness itself, manifesting through you as others.

~Continue the **Water Breath** in the **Sacral Gateway** and add the sound AHHH to at least seven exhales, (AHHH, AHHH, AHHH, AHHH, AHHH, AHHH, AHHH). Let yourself feel the opening and activation of this **Sacral** gateway. Feel the sound and breath move in through the front of your body and out through the back of your body, at the level of this gate center.

Solar Plexus Gateway

~Bring your awareness into your SOLAR PLEXUS GATE center located half way between your umbilicus and the center of your chest. (HEART center). **BREATH-FIRE:** In through the MOUTH out through the MOUTH. **HANDS over SOLAR PLEXUS GATE** breathe three times with **FIRE breath**.

~Bring your awareness to the **Elemental Dragon MOTHER of Fire** awakening the **Fire element** within you, in your endocrine system, nervous system, digestive system and initiating all the necessary processes in your body. Feel her spark of life, the life force within you, bringing you life and movement, and outside as the **Elemental Dragon MOTHER of Fire**, rising through the Kundalini life force and Fire element.

~Bring your awareness and your breath into this area and let yourself feel the beauty and sacredness in your being... as it manifests as your individuality, connected to greater source.

~Continue the **Fire** Breath, in the **Solar Gateway** and add the sound AHHH to at least seven exhales, (AHHH, AHHH, AHHH, AHHH, AHHH, AHHH, AHHH). Let yourself feel the opening and activation of this **Solar** gateway. Feel the sound and breath move in through the front of your body and out through the back of your body, at the level of this gate center.

Heart Gateway

~Bring your awareness into your HEART GATE center located at the center of your chest. **BREATH-AIR:** In through the NOSE, out through the MOUTH. **HANDS over HEART GATE** breathe 3 times with **AIR breath**.

~Bring your awareness to the **Elemental Cosmic Womb MOTHER** awakening in your breath, oxygenating all the cells in your body... sustaining you, breathing you. Feel her holding and comfort

as you breathe, providing you with the air element within and outside. Let yourself fall into her **Cosmic Womb** as you allow the Universe to sustain your every breath.

~Bring your awareness and your breath into this area and let yourself feel the depth, beauty, compassion and unconditional love that is the very core of the existence of you and everything in the Universe. Let this truth awaken in your whole being and radiate outward like ripples into the world.

Continue the **Air Breath** in the **Heart Gateway** and add the sound AHHH to at least seven exhales, (AHHH, AHHH, AHHH, AHHH, AHHH, AHHH, AHHH). Let yourself feel the opening and activation of this **Heart** gateway. Feel the sound and breath move in through the front of your body and out through the back of your body, at the level of this gate center.

Throat Gateway

~Bring your awareness into your Throat Gateway located at the center of your throat. BREATH- ETHER: GENTLY...In through the NOSE, out through the NOSE. HANDS over THROAT GATE front and back of neck, if possible. Breathe three times with ETHER breath.

~Bring your awareness to the **Elemental Dark Moon MOTHER** awakening in your consciousness as she holds the transformational alchemy of purification and entering into greater levels of consciousness through the element of ETHER. Ether is consciousness, awareness; it is the water that you swim in. Let yourself feel her presence as you open to greater levels of HER expression (of consciousness) through this **THROAT GATE**. She is the **Elemental Dark Moon MOTHER** of ETHER... the consciousness that we swim in.

~Bring your awareness and your breath into this area and let yourself feel your creative expression in the world... how you bring out your unique expression of Oneness consciousness. Do you let yourself express the beauty of Oneness through your body, your mind, your unique thoughts, your actions in the world? Know that all your actions are an expression of Divine consciousness moving through you.

~Continue the ETHER Breath in the **Throat Gateway** and add the sound **AHHH,** to at least seven exhales, (AHHH, AHHH, AHHH, AHHH, AHHH, AHHH, AHHH). Let yourself feel the opening and activation of this **Throat** gateway. Feel the sound and breath move in through the front of your body and out through the back of your body, at the level of this gate center.

Third Eye Gateway

~Bring your awareness into your THIRD EYE GATE center located at the center of your eyes. **BREATH-ETHER: GENTLY** In through the NOSE, out through the NOSE. **HANDS over THIRD EYE GATE** breathe three times with **ETHER breath.**

~Bring your awareness and your breath into this area and let yourself see beyond what your eyes can see, feel the Subtle levels of the Divine love behind all manifested form; feel the continuation of the unseen levels of consciousness into all that you see. Let yourself be open to seeing through the inner levels of your being, open to the inner worlds of realty where you can find truth, love, joy and all the Universal qualities.

Let your Inner vision open and begin to trust inner realms.

~Continue the ETHER Breath in the **Third Eye Gateway** and add the sound AHHH to at least seven exhales, (AHHH, AHHH, AHHH, AHHH, AHHH, AHHH, AHHH). Let yourself feel the opening and activation of this **Third Eye** gateway. Feel the sound and breath move in through the front of your body and out through the back of your body, at the level of this gate center.

Crown Gateway

~Bring your awareness into your CROWN GATE center located at the top of your head. **BREATH-ETHER: GENTLY,** in through the NOSE, out through the NOSE. **HANDS over CROWN GATE** breathe three times with **ETHER breath**.

~Bring your awareness and your breath into your CROWN and let yourself feel the pouring in of Divine Essence through your own opening, where all the yang forces of the Divine Oneness come through into your vessel, igniting your being on all levels, at all times. Feel it illuminating your brain and rewiring you completely to the new levels of consciousness that are opening at this very minute. Let your being be awakened to even greater levels of consciousness. Every moment is a moment to open into greater LOVE and beauty of union with Divine Oneness.

~Continue the ETHER Breath in the **Crown Gateway** and add the sound AHHH to at least seven exhales, (AHHH, AHHH, AHHH, AHHH, AHHH, AHHH, AHHH). Let yourself feel the opening and activation of this **Crown** gateway. Feel the sound and breath move in through the front of your body and out through the back of your body, at the level of this gate center.

Integration

Let your body integrate the Activation of these higher frequencies by sitting in meditation as long as possible. Letting yourself just absorb all the frequencies that have been given to you by GRACE.

Journal

After your integration process feels complete, let yourself take notes of any awareness, feelings, inspirations that may have surfaced during your *Conscious Feminine Medicine™ Activation*. Making sure you just allow to be with whatever shows up without any expectation or criticism for yourself. Enjoy the opening and make some notes. Sometimes the energy is quiet, sometimes it's louder, sometimes it's very emotional, and at other times it's ecstatic. Allow yourself to be in an accepting space in order to dance with what the Divine Oneness is showing you at every minute.

Gratitude

Always close with GRATITUDE through a bowing of your heart to the DIVINE ONE-NESS and expressing gratitude for whatever your experience was. There is blessing in all of it... even if you don't know it at the time!

7
2ⁿᵈ Sacred Initiation of Conscious Feminine Power

TRANSFORMING THE SHADOW OF POWERLESSNESS

The second sacred initiation of *Conscious Feminine Sacred Power* is where we begin to work with the first collective wound of the Feminine: Powerlessness. The collective oppression of the Feminine has created deep conditioning patterns that have stripped away our sense of power. Our sense of power is related to our sense of self, and as women, we have a very weak sense of self because it hasn't been safe to be ourselves.

Nonetheless, transforming this collective wound of powerlessness, initiates us into the freedom and safety of being part of a greater consciousness, thus activating our sacred power that has been there all along. This initiation gifts us with the medicine of True power, which is sourced from the source Herself and is experienced in our Selves as our Essential Self. True power isn't a force outside us, but rather the force of consciousness Herself, that births all of existence into Being. Our ability to genuinely trust, connect and access this dimension of ourselves; our Essential Self, is True Power.

Power is a loaded word and action. Historically, we find ourselves intertwined between unconsciously giving our power away to others due to fear, attempting to attain power through outer forces such as social position, careers, or money, and/or unconsciously rejecting power either because it isn't safe to have, or because we may feel unconsciously unworthy. We may also have rejected power due to underlying feelings of injustice and/ or shame and blame, because power has been abused for so long. It's no surprise that we may unknowingly keep our own sense of power hidden, due to our own unprocessed fears about being too much 'like them', those that have caused the suffering. On the other hand, feeling powerless and voiceless and identifying as a victim doesn't serve us, in any way. Nonetheless, this isn't the power that we're talking about, it's actually abusive power, rooted in a lack of power altogether. This sacred power is power that returns us to our sovereignty and frees us from false sense of safety from pleasing others. Sacred power demands that we take full responsibility over ourselves, and requests us to discontinue the dance of blaming others for our suffering. However, this doesn't dismiss the fact that there are many that abuse their power and have caused humanity great suffering throughout history. We do acknowledge that this is a fact, and this is the world that we live in. But for the rest of us that are still caught in the past and the powerlessness of our challenges, sacred power changes the relationship we have with ourselves and with how we think of ourselves. In so doing, it allows us to take control and responsibility for those things that we're are able to and surrender to those things that are beyond us. It helps us navigate through the gates of our destiny and our fate and helps us to discern accordingly.

Culturally, women have been conditioned that power is a man's thing. As a woman, wanting to have power is usually met with suspicion or judgment as a "bad" thing, in the category of bitchiness or power tripping. However, for most men power it's not questioned; it's a sign of their success. Often, the qualities of kindness, love, and compassion are seen to be at the opposite end of 'power', and so how can one be spiritual and loving if they want to feel powerful? Isn't that a contradiction? Well, my answer is - it's is absolutely not a contradiction.

To clarify even more, sacred power isn't the power to use over someone else, it's completely a state of being within ourselves. This is the type of power that you feel when you know that your desires, needs and opinions matter as much as the next persons. It's the power to feel respected, to feel like you count, to feel part of the bigger picture. It's the power to know that your life matters and that you aren't dispensable, that there is purpose, and that you affect things and people around you.

Sacred power is tied in with self-confidence and self-worth. To have a conversation of power, we have to include our value, or at least our perception of our value. The relationship we have with power is greatly determined with the value we feel we have (our self-worth). Most people that abuse their powers on the outer are clearly compensating for a lack of self-worth and engage in a display of "showing" the outer world how much power they actually have.

Therefore, to connect with our power, we have to first unwind the layers of self- blame, self-judgment, self- criticism that cloud our true sense of Self, both divine and human. Without due diligence here, we cannot reclaim our sense of Self, nor our sense of power. In the body, this sense of Self and empowerment is reflected in our Solar Plexus. Here is where most women, and some men, contain the fears, judgements, blame and other unresolved layers that make us forget who we are. And of course, the added 5000 years of living in a culture that has outwardly rejected our Feminine nature, along with our Feminine gender, has created a substantial separation from the truth of Self.

But here is the good news; we already have the power to correct this. We don't have to wait on anything to happen; we have everything that we need to reclaim our power and move out from under the cloud that keeps us feeling powerless. Our sacred power has never left us, although we've been living as if we didn't have it, and because of this, it's been obscured from our awareness. Reclaiming and finding the way to access this dimension within us doesn't mean that the world changes automatically. However, it does make you realize that you've been living a lie all this time and it changes your whole experience of living in the world. This sacred initiation allows you to burst the bubble of illusion and reclaim your divinity.

POWERLESSNESS AND OUR DNA

In chapter one, we talked a lot about our DNA and how, through our attitudes and our beliefs, we are actually, subconsciously, choosing the DNA that gets activated in our genes. This is what the study of Epigenetics informs us. And even more fascinating is what we are seeing in the studies of neuroplasticity, which shows us how are brain is capable of changing itself and creating new neuropathways that support new patterns of behavior and thought processes, as we evolve. Therefore, it's clear to me, and many physicians, that we're capable of evolving our mind set, and that our body is continuously supporting this growth in more ways than we even know.

So how do we choose ourselves? How do we change our sense of worth, our value and reconnect with the inherent sacred power that we have/are? We've already established that our power lies in our ability to experience our divine consciousness, our Essential Self. It's really our presence with this dimension of our Self, that returns the power to us. Instead, we've buried our sense of self under all the personal conditioned stories in our psyche, plus those of the collective that we may have unconsciously enmeshed with. This is what we've learned the norm to be and what your ego has defined as 'yourself'. The truth is, what we think of as 'normal' is just a list of beliefs and stories that you have bought into, and in reality, it is not normal, albeit the majority of what our culture believes. The reason I say it's not normal is because it isn't really representative of the wholeness of who we are, yet it is 'normal' to our dysfunctional society that is limited in their acceptance and expression of their wholeness. This is a path of awakening, awakening to subtler and subtler levels of consciousness that have remained hidden within us, that which we call divinity.

In order to unlock our power, we must understand our relationship with power and how it is intertwined with our powerlessness. We often feel that life and events have power over us. We attribute our feelings to events and situations that are happening outside ourselves, and allow them to determine whether we're happy or not. We may feel that our happiness is at the mercy of ongoing occurrences that continuously come at us, but as we will discover, power resides within, first through the personalized meaning we assign to things and secondly through our internalized and unconscious dependence.

Our power begins with the meaning that we give events and experiences that are coming at us, determined by our relationship with life itself. If you feel the Universe is a 'loving' Universe that is watching out for you, and you acknowledge that this force of Love is coursing through you at all times, then you can surrender into your powerlessness, releasing any negative outlook or resistance you may have about your life looking a certain way, because ultimately, you trust in the inherent, limitless love of the Universe. However, for most of us, this isn't the case. Women in general don't find the outer world to be particularly loving and unfortunately have many generations of being unsafe in the outer world because of their gender. This lack of trust that has been developed from years of pain and suffering, will influence and to a great extent determine the meaning we give our experiences in life. While we may be powerless with what happens to us in life, we are not powerless in how we interpret it, or the meaning that we give it.

Therefore, one of the greatest gifts we can give ourselves is to rewire the relationship we have with life itself, and with the Universe. Understanding the Universe is within us, and developing trust, so that we can understand that we are held in that Feminine love of the Universal Mother is key in shifting our meaning of what is happening in our world. Our bond with the Universal Mother, the Feminine aspect of Divine Oneness, has to be restored within us to trust in the Universe. We have to be willing to let Her in to hold our hearts, to love us with Her limitless love and to nurture our soul. We have to allow ourselves to turn to Her, to trust Her and to depend on Her to heal our wounds, and ultimately realize that She is us and that we are birthed from Her.

And so, when we realize that there's a Feminine aspect of the Divine field that creates all from limitless love, and that everything in this world is created from love, then we can begin to experience and surrender to it, even when challenging things happen to us. We can begin to trust in love and that She is ultimately awakening us and breaking a pattern of limitation within us, through our challenges. We can only begin to have this experience once we begin to restore our relationship with the Universal Mother.

Nonetheless, it's important to realize the ways in which we give our power away to things outside ourselves, by letting them influence the meanings. If something happens that we don't like, we immediately resist it, try to change it, control it, or allow our emotions to be controlled by it. When we experience something happening to us that is unpleasant, many times we also judge it as "bad" and wrong, with an underlying narrative of "this shouldn't be happening to me". Again, this is an example of not truly believing in the inherent underlying fabric of goodness of the Feminine, and buying into a world that is governed by a punishing, merciless, harsh Source instead. In this way, we are giving our power away to outside events, blaming our unhappiness on the outside world.

However, if we live in a world that completely supports us and the impulse of life itself is to evolve from our limited experience of separation into the greater Essence of Love, then perhaps we can assert that we might be wrong in our interpretation. Perhaps we're wrong in our judgment of the event; perhaps we're wrong in thinking 'this should not be happening to me'; perhaps we're wrong in only expecting pleasant things to happen to us; perhaps what we experience as unpleasant is the exact experience our soul needs to open up to a greater reality of ourselves. And yes many things may happen that we don't like, but that doesn't mean that they are intrinsically bad, perhaps they challenge our way of thinking to pressure us into awakening to hidden realities within ourselves?

Our perceptual reality matters here because that is what our true happiness is based on. In other words, we can be homeless and still be happy, even though it may be challenging to your mind. The story we tell ourselves about what is happening is truly what determines our ultimate satisfaction. However, we aren't ignoring, nor excusing any of the horrific events that happen in our world; these do happen, and we have emotions about them, rightly so. But ultimately, what I'm addressing is the inherent power that we each have access to. This being the dimension within us that gives definition to what is happening outside of us, which ultimately positions us as victims or participants with Life itself. Evidently, we have choice through our interpretation, and that choice is reflected in our DNA, as well as in the neuropathways created by our brain. In reality, our whole system is constantly responding to whichever interpretation we choose to make about our lives. We choose, consciously or unconsciously, and our body reflects those choices.

RADICAL UNIVERSAL ACCEPTANCE

In the previous chapter I wrote about suffering as an evolutionary force and now we want to take that concept one step further into embodiment, which leads us to 'radical universal acceptance'. Our next logical step would be to shift our viewpoint so that we can actually accept and use everything that is happening to us, in our lives and around us, to be of service to us.

To do so, we first must contemplate trust. Can we trust something that might induce feelings of pain and or suffering, or that makes us feel 'bad'? This is not an easy task. Our trust is dependent on our experience of Source or what we may think of as the Divine, or Creator. Therefore, if we already established a source of goodness within ourselves by opening up to our own divine Essential nature, as suggested in the first sacred Initiation, then we can continue to extend that experience of love within, a field of Love, that sustains us.

Of course, radically accepting everything in the Universe, without judgment is extremely challenging because we don't automatically see the goodness or the jewel in the things that seem very wrong, therefore, requiring trust. To have *radical Universal acceptance* we would have to enter into the space of "not knowing" and accept the mystery of life, Herself. This is a form of blind faith. This place of 'not knowing' is actually a very high state of consciousness that involves a great deal of trust. However, being able to lean on the Feminine Universal Mother, without really understanding it in our minds, is a necessary step in receiving the wisdom of the unknowable. Stepping into the realm of the unknown allows us to move out of our minds, and into direct gnosis, to receive the wisdom. As the great Greek philosopher, Aristotle, eloquently stated: "the more you know, the more you know you don't know anything." This is the terrain we have to enter, a prerequisite for radical Universal acceptance.

Furthermore, we don't want to confuse acceptance with passivity. In other words, just because we accept that something is ultimately for our highest, doesn't mean that we aren't called to action. Perhaps the impulse that is urging to come through us might be the very impulse of action. Perhaps we're so appalled by something that it ignites a passionate service of action on our behalf, and inspires us to use our voice for good. The fact that we radically accept something means that we don't judge it, label it, nor reject it, because in that moment, we create resistance and lose our power. Our power is our power to act, to choose our thoughts, to decide the meaning we give things, that, we have power over. When we decide to go against life itself, we lose, because life is always going to win. We don't have agency over the events that happen to us... we have agency over how we experience them. So, in truth, we still have to act, and sometimes it's the action itself, the process itself that brings satisfaction and healing in an unexpected way.

Radical Universal acceptance is truly subscribing to the underlying thought that everything that happens has a purpose of awakening us to Love, wholeness, and our divinity. And so, when we're faced with something that we don't like, whether it's something that happened to us personally or whether it's the state of political climate; can we extend this idea of acceptance even if we don't know why this is happening, or don't see any good in it? Can you accept it unconditionally, while simultaneously experiencing your own personal feelings of the situation and listening deeply to what you are being asked of in this situation?

When we step into *radical Universal acceptance,* there's a level of resistance that disappears, you are no longer at odds with the Universe and life itself. You are no longer a victim of the Universe, you simply may not have the answer as to why something is happening to you, but you reap the rewards so much easier. Therefore, the prayer becomes, what is this situation asking of me? What is right action for me to take in this situation? All of a sudden, adversities become a puzzle that you haven't solved yet, but that ultimately you know; it's there to support you, to push you, to experience something new in yourself. There's no punishment, there's no room to be a victim, there's just a challenge and an opportunity to rise to another level of awareness or consciousness, however long that may take.

POWER IS SELF-RESPONSIBILITY

If we challenge our interpretation and subscribe to the *radical Universal* acceptance paradigm, we then are able to release the tendrils of victimhood that subconsciously we've been enslaved to. Even though we get to be mad, sad, or angry when challenges come our way, we get to drop the blame on others and take full responsibility. Other people certainly still have responsibility for their actions in any given situation, they are, however, not necessarily responsible for our happiness. For example, if someone calls us a name, we can get offended and say it is his/her fault that they have ruined our day, but in actuality from a *radical Universal acceptance* perspective, that person is only responsible for what they said, not for ruining your day', because you have choice. 'Ruining your day' involves the perception of how you decide to take in what they said, in which you have a choice to dismiss their remarks as silly, or to become offended, therefore ruining your day. In fact, you can even hear what they're saying, while simultaneously noticing what it's bringing up in you, without necessarily reacting. This inner emotional reaction can be later used for the evolution of your own soul, pointing directly to where you are vulnerable and in need of some healing. This is fuel for your evolutionary process and giving yourself and unconditional love to feel it, and process it allows you to be present in a way that perhaps you did not have before. You have an opportunity to mother yourself and give yourself the unconditional attention that you never received. And for the rest of your day, you can decide to continue to enjoy the present moment and go back to this emotional reaction at your convenience. That is an act of self -responsibility and also of what we would call, 'not giving your power away'. When you stand in your power, you recognize you have choice, regardless of the emotion someone has evoked within you, you still choose to respond rather than just become unconscious and react. When we blindly react from our old conditioning, we automatically give our power away to the situation and/or the person. Realizing that we have choice also entails releasing our expectation on any given situation and whole-heartedly accepting it, as well as realizing we have choice of our own responses.

Actually, reflecting on a situation that has felt offensive in the past, allows you to confront and heal the feelings that arose for you in the past. In your own privacy, you can allow yourself to deal with and look at the powerlessness, or other offensive reactions from the particular situation. In allowing yourself the space to process the unresolved feelings, you realize how much of that reaction was due to unacknowledged expectations, or lack of acceptance, or even your own shame or fear projected onto it. How much of your reaction might have been fueled by your own disappointment of the events or person? Did you have unrealistic expectations? Maybe there is a part of your still expecting them to treat you different, display a behavior that is not what they are capable of or what their norm is? All of these point to various ways in which our lack of self-acceptance, coupled with our expectations and thus disappointments, continues to create suffering for ourselves. As we reevaluate and reflect on our reactions, we're able to take our responsibility for how our expectations and conditioning are contributing to our offense, and furthermore heal from these painful experiences.

EXPECTATIONS - THE HIDDEN AGENDA

Therefore, in many of our interactions where we feel powerless, or offended, or reactive, actually stem from a hidden, internalized, unconscious expectation of the other person. Sure, we all have an expected cultural norm of how people should behave civilly, but our expectations of others are clouded by our own conditioning and past suffering, geared to keep us safe and feeling pleasant. It's as if we're having these relationship with people and situations, and in between ourselves and others, there is this unspoken rule of 'how things should be', which may include; how you should behave in certain situations, what you could say, what you shouldn't say, what you would do for me, what you should never do, etc. Most of us don't realize the unconscious agenda that we're walking around with that is forcibly projected over others and many situations. And, of course, we live in a civilized society, and there are unspoken rules that we all live by. But what happens when others do not live by these rules, and one easily gets offended? What happens when we are constantly feeling like others are letting us down, or not there for us? How much of that is really our own unconscious agenda of expectation clouding our interpretation of their actions? How much of that is really our own unconscious dependency, fueled by our need to feel safe?

When we are unconsciously very attached to how things should be, we are automatically less willing to accept things as they are. These expectations may remain within us, hidden and unconscious, until we lash out in offense to something someone has said or done. As we reflect on our reactions in moments when we feel powerless, we may find that the ways in which we are giving our power away are completely entangled with unconscious expectations of how things 'should be'. These unconscious expectations are further conditioned by our need to be liked, loved, accepted, heard. And ultimately they are derived from an internalized dependency on others to make us feel safe and good.

The truth is that, as grownups, we have to let go of depending on others to make us feel safe and evolve to become our sovereign over ourselves. The definition of sovereignty reads " Sovereignty is the full right and power of a governing body over itself, without any interference from outside sources or bodies." The idea is that we release and let go of our dependency on others or outside stimulus to make us feel good and safe, as we did when we were a child. We are not children anymore, and, therefore, much of this transformation is becoming our own sovereign being, capable of depending on our connection with our divine nature, our Essence, for all of our physical, emotional, mental and spiritual needs, in order to heal, be safe and feel good.

Clearly, we can see how easily it is to step into a constant experience of feeling powerless, if our power consists of situations that have to fit a particular code in order to acknowledge our self-worth or make us feel good about ourselves. To unwind this from our own psyche, we must take an honest look at how we're expecting others to be, unwind the underlying identification that you may with those expected behaviors and your self-worth, and thirdly realize that you have responsibility over your own thinking, interpretation and the meaning that you give events and people in your life.

When we bring in *radical Universal acceptance* paradigm into this entangled conditioning, we automatically unravel the expectations of others and how they must see you, and realize that whether someone lives up to your expectation or not, does not necessarily need to affect your sense of Self. The truth is that people only have the power over you that you give them.

Secondly, we come to the issue of how your self-value is tied into this. When people disappoint us, or fail to live up to our expectation, many times we default to a deeper self-blame or unworthy picture. When others don't validate us, we automatically default to the 'not being good enough conditioning.' As grown-ups, we no longer need to depend on other's validation of us for us to feel worthy. Perhaps this might have been true when we were young, and this kind of default behavior is clearly as aspect of learned conditioned behavior from our youth, as well as from the collective treatment of our gender, however, we are independent women now, capable of honoring ourselves, our needs and our truth.

Here, in this initiation, we're faced with the opportunity to dissolve these hidden expectations, along with the veiled invalidations of our true Self, that have been showing up as powerlessness. We have the opportunity to untangle ourselves from our dependency in others, and of the denial of our own power. Now, it's up to us to see where we're still holding ourselves captive to someone's else opinion and rise into our own sovereignty, which begins with full disclosure with ourselves.

DARE TO BE WRONG

If we realize that our power is intertwined with these aspects above, therefore, to reclaim our true power, we have to be willing to be wrong. Having the courage to be wrong about our minds, our thoughts and our conditioning, opens the door to a greater truth, that perhaps we were not able to see when we were fixed on being right. Of course, it's challenging because we may have such a sense of unworthiness that saying to ourselves that we're wrong send us downs spinning down a spiraling descent that may feel like death. Yet, realizing that we aren't our thinking, but that our thinking reflects our conditioned responses (our egoic nature of separation) and therefore, cannot perceive the Truth. Therefore, holding these two realities in our heart, of being wrong in our thinking while still feeling the beautiful sacred light of our being, is completely necessary and possible in order to walk across the bridge of reclaiming our power.

Intrinsically, we're good, created in the likeness of our creator, the Divine Mother. We're Divine and human, we aren't a mistake, but we do and can make mistakes, or we can say that at times we aren't fully expressing our divine nature but rather our limited egoic nature of separation. Is that a mistake? It's only a mistake from the perspective that we are limiting our ability to express and experience more of our wholeness, of the love, joy and divinity that we are. However, from another perspective, it's this very 'mistake' that allows us to grow and free ourselves from our limiting paradigm of our ego conditioned reality. So, in many ways, it isn't a mistake, it's perfect. However, it's in recognizing our limited response or conditioning that we can open to something more, something new. It's in our recognizing this as a mistake, because it's not expressive of our full wholeness or Oneness, that allows us to grow. But, in essence, it is only a relative mistake.

This paradigm shift of willing to be wrong, allows us to detach from our thinking and evaluate it, to see if it is reflecting our true divine unconditional nature, or some other limited conditioned mental construct.

In daring to be wrong, we radically commit to self-responsibility, and dissolve the illusion that it is up to someone out there to make it better, to take care of us, to validate us, to authenticate our existence. We begin to own the places where we had subtly and unconsciously relied upon the outer world, people and actions for our worth, value and happiness. We begin to look within, and activate the power that we have, and that we have had all along in giving meaning and in our perceptual thinking. We also begin to stand in our power, as we honor and validate ourselves.

RADICAL SELF CARE

The step that follows is to access the places where we're still expecting others to take care of us and shift to giving that to ourselves. As we integrate more of our inherent power and release the dependency on the outer for our emotional, mental, spiritual and physical needs, we realize we are solely responsible for our needs, therefore, everything we receive from the outer is 'extra.' We realize that our emotional, mental, spiritual and to a great degree, our physical wellbeing, is dependent solely on what we do or don't do with ourselves. It's our responsibility to take care of ourselves on all these levels and give ourselves the inspiration we need every day, provide the emotional support sources we crave, organize our clean food, down time, connection with nature and all that fulfills us, in order to be content. No longer do we get to blame others for our joy, or lack of it. Sure, our children and other people may bring us joy, but we actively have the ability and responsibility to surround ourselves with what we need, detaching ourselves from any dependency on others, or events outside ourselves to be fulfilled and happy. The truth is we have everything we need within, and a great part of stepping in to our power is realizing that we are this Essence in our being, the very Essence that provides the essential qualities that our soul craves for fulfillment. We are the Medicine.

This doesn't mean that we don't enjoy time with others, that we don't derive pleasure from involvement with other, people or places. Of course, we do, the difference is that we free ourselves from dependency on outside sources of fulfillment, that don't fulfill us and could never fulfill our soul. We break the cycle of dependency and disappointment, because we begin to rely on something bigger than ourselves, Source. This allows us to become solely responsible for the quality of our lives, releasing all outer blame on others and taking full responsibility so that we can engage in manifesting our greatest life.

One other aspect of being a woman is being so keenly aware and programed to take care of others, unfortunately, at the expense of ourselves many times. In this pattern, we continue to abandon ourselves, to perpetuate the idea or expectation that when everyone is satisfied and taken care of, we will then get our needs met. Unfortunately, this isn't true, and what ends up happening is that we burn out, become exhausted, frustrated, angry and even depressed. If we looked a little deeper, we could see that our inner pattern of giving to ourselves, is being reflected on the outer, and all we see is 'others needing.' It's no surprise the Universe would be mirroring exactly what we are doing. So, again, instead of perpetuating this victim stance, we have the opportunity to change the pattern by acknowledging our mental, emotional, spiritual and physical needs and making them non-negotiable. These are as important as eating and brushing our teeth (those are obvious to everyone, I hope).

Letting go of any and all victim constructs is truly part of stepping into our inherent power and sovereignty. On a practical level that looks like taking inventory and deciding what is it that I need? What is it that inspires me, that brings joy to my life, strengthens me, nourishes my heart, inspires my soul? What does it look like to honor myself in all the varying aspects of my life? What are my non-negotiable needs? Once we have established that and have made no excuses as to why we cannot have that, then we can prescribe the *Radical Self Care check list* to ourselves, setting the foundation to reclaim our power. See *Radical Self-Care Checklist* under the *Sacred Initiation of Conscious Feminine Power* section below, towards the end of this chapter.

FORGIVENESS: PORTAL OF POWER

Another critical step in reclaiming all aspects of our sense of power is releasing the victim construct of our past history. This final step allows us to release the story of victimization on all levels, by realizing that we're much more than the part of us that has experienced the pain and suffering of the past. Yes, we aren't forgetting that things have happened to us in the past that have been painful, however, if we're willing to see ourselves as much more than the hurt victim, then we can step into our wholeness in a greater way, and not be diminished nor defined by our past experience of pain.

To step into this greater realization of our own power, we must consider forgiveness. Ah yes forgiveness, most people have knee jerk reactions to this word, suddenly we have images of either having to tolerate something unpleasant that has happened in the past, or having to somehow do 'the right thing" and humble ourselves to forgiveness, even though we feel wronged in some way. However, forgiveness isn't really about any of those two things. I personally had a shaming experience of forgiveness when I was around 13; my mom asked me to 'ask for forgiveness from my step-father for my angry behavior towards him.' And not wanting to hurt her, I said yes, and I asked him for forgiveness from my 'angry, resentful attitude' towards him. She didn't know what the true motivations for my angry attitude was, but she assumed it was 'wrong of me' and therefore, in that moment, I too, made myself wrong. The underlying core of my angry attitude towards him was that I could sense an inappropriate sexual energy from him when he was alone with me, which created a feeling of unsafety in my home. My angry attitude was in fact a reflection of my inner wall, in attempt to protect myself, unconsciously. At that age, I didn't have the words to explain this feeling and it seemed much easier to just bring in this 'forgiveness and let it go.' The truth was that that incident of forcing this forgiveness and apology, didn't change the way I behaved with him. I continued to have that wall of protection for myself around him. Time did prove, after some of his journals were discovered during my mothers' divorce, that my intuitive perceptions were correct. His intentions were not innocent.

Nonetheless, my experience of what forgiveness meant was erroneously anchored in a picture of having to deny what you know feels right in order to 'be good', 'do the right thing' or even be shamed for the feelings that naturally arises in oneself (in my case - anger). The fact was that the anger was not wrong, it was a response to the penetrating inappropriate energy he was directing at me. And yet, from the outer, the anger was judged and deemed 'wrong'.

In choosing forgiveness we're really choosing to reclaim our power and untangle ourselves from the web of anger, righteousness, and pain that keeps us in victimization mode. I want you to think of forgiveness in this way, as an energetic frequency that when invited has the ability to sever the ties you have with this matter and open yourself up to what you have been wanting in the first place. In other words, when we are hurt emotionally or spiritually, we have had a need or expectation to receive the love, respect, and acknowledgment, etc., from something or someone that wasn't able to deliver. The particular issues aren't necessarily relevant here; what I want to show you is that in some way our pain and suffering in the past usually entails some unmet need, and underneath this is some expectation that it should have been met.

Collectively, we believe that mothers have a responsibility to feed and nurture the their young until they are self-sufficient. And yet when that doesn't happen, it may cause deep pain and suffering for the child. However, we can spend much of our lives in the story of what has occurred, which in this case is that the mother didn't nurture her young child. Staying in that story will only continue to hurt us. Bringing forgiveness into this story from a place of accepting that this did happen, (not that it was okay), allows your heart to be released from the binds of identifying with pain, and, therefore, open to receive the love and nurturing that didn't happen before. It opens up your ability to actually receive and heal the unmet need that is still there. In this case, the truth is that the love and nurturance was not given by the mother. The second reality was that this wasn't okay and it did hurt and create some pain. But staying identified with that reality creates an unending wound that can never heal. Instead, opening up to forgiveness means beginning to change the narrative, the part of you that identifies with this reality, recognizing that you are much more than that. Thus, realizing that the event doesn't have to define you, you can accept it (although painful), you can forgive it, and then open the our heart to the greater Love, to receive the love that you have been yearning for.

When we hold onto the pain of the past, we're still stuck in a power play, and don't realize that we're also giving our power away. Many times, we have a narrative in our minds that insists that we were right, deeply desiring to be acknowledged and vindicated. But yet, that vindication may never come from that outside source, or from the one that imposed the pain upon you. The truth is that you're the only one that can vindicate yourself, but choosing to release the pain, and the narrative of being a victim. We have a responsibility, as discussed earlier, to ourselves. As we mature, we recognize that we're the ones that have to hear our stories, validate our voice, our pain, our voices and acknowledge our heart. When we stay in the struggle of the past pain that can't be forgiven, we affix ourselves in the place of victimhood.

Remembering that we have choice comes with remembering responsibility. No longer is it up to the outer world, nor the people in our world to make things right for us. It is up to us, to care for our needs, on every level. As we grow into our sovereignty, we have to be willing to take responsibility to loosen the ties that keep us habituated in our pain. And if we truly adopt the idea that the Universe is a benevolent force, then we must let go of our original grudge with the event or person itself, and allow ourselves to open up to the blessing that the Universe is gifting us, through this seemingly painful situation. We cannot reap the rewards of the pain of our past, until we open up to acceptance and forgiveness, leading with the possibility that there may be a jewel to reap from this experience.

When we are able to open ourselves to a different interpretation, we remove ourselves from being right or wrong. At this stage, we move past our egoic duality of right and wrong and enter into Soul Consciousness of reaping the jewels of wisdom and healing. With forgiveness, we open the door to a greater perspective, than just one of being hurt, not demeaning the original pain, but often through the pain, our egoic nature is humbled and our heart is wide open to contain more of our Soul Light.

Through the betrayal of friends, we learn to count on ourselves, and perhaps to speak up for ourselves rather than to depend on the group. Through the absence of love, we turn inward and discover the true source of Love, that isn't dependent on others. Through powerlessness, we learn to access our own sacred power. Through shame, we learn to love ourselves, and so on. There are many great gems to discover through the pain of the past, but we only discover them when we lose our attachment to being right and move forward from the duality mentality in Oneness consciousness. Perhaps we are not right, perhaps we're wrong, not in the minor way of just the personal situation, but in the bigger picture. Perhaps the bigger picture is the Universe supporting you completely and creating the perfect situation for our egos to hit that wall of limitation, crack open and discover your true potential of your Essence.

Forgiveness is the bridge that allows you to rise above that level of witnessing from your egoic nature, the one that has been hurt, disappointed, angry, etc., into the soul consciousness that can accept and reap the rewards. In many ways, it's our egoic nature that cannot let go, that finds difficulty in forgiving, that needs to right, not our Essential Self (soul). The soul knows the truth of the situation, knows that you are held unconditionally in love, and nothing that happens to you is for only pain, but our Conditioned Self cannot always see the greater truth, unless we choose to be wrong and experience a greater reality.

Therefore, humbling ourselves with forgiveness, only positions us to receive the Grace from letting go of our Conditioned Self's view of the event, and open ourselves to the unknown mystery of divine intervention. And in doing this we open our hearts to receive the energy of forgiveness, restore our power and heal our hearts. The secret of forgiveness is in its ability to alchemically polish our hearts in order to unveil the true ray of light that is hidden behind the pain of the wound. Calling on Her, forgiveness will let you dissolve these conditioned places in your heart of the past and expand the true light of your Soul.

"Forgiveness is the evolutionary process of freeing ourselves
from our past identification of victimhood and
opening ourselves to the radiant LOVE of our Soul"

~ leonor murciano-luna

2ND SACRED INITIATION OF CONSCIOUS FEMININE POWER

Now, it's time to begin your Sacred Initiation of *Conscious Feminine Power*. Throughout this chapter you've become aware of the factors that have contributed to the wound of powerlessness and hopefully realized that you have the ability to restore and reclaim your power through this Sacred Initiation. Next, are a few reflections, practices, and checklists to assist you in your process of this transformation. This process helps to walk you through the three key steps of each Sacred Initiation; *Awareness* (becoming conscious), *Transformational Alchemy* (shifting from old paradigms into new ones), and *Embodiment* (anchoring these new realities in all aspects of your being). As you begin with your writing reflection, let yourself explore your relationship with power, from your heart. Take your time with each process and notice which processes may challenge you the most. Don't rush through these, because doing so may not allow you sufficient time for transformation. Sometimes, you may even need to revisit these processes multiple times until it feels complete.

At completion, you'll engage in the *sacred initiation of Conscious Feminine Power* which is the culmination process that should be done to complete the embodiment of your Feminine Power. If you feel you've experienced a lot of wounding in this area and would like to strengthen yourself in this way, then consider practicing this particular Sacred initiation processes for at least three months. Use your inner wisdom to guide you and communicate with you what you need. Furthermore, this can be part of your checklist of Non-Negotiable needs for the month. Enjoy!

RELATIONSHIP WITH POWER
WRITING REFLECTION

Take a few minutes to reflect upon your relationship with power. Allow yourself to drop in to your heart as you explore these questions. Reflect on one, two or all the questions, however, let the answers arise from your heart.

1. What are the things/ people/ situations outside of you that you consistently tend to blame?

2. Consider how much power you felt you had in your family of origin. Did you feel heard and acknowledged by your mother, by your father, and/ or by your siblings?

3. What situations/ people consistently keep showing up in your life, where you still find yourself blaming for your unhappiness?

4. Are you willing to take full responsibility for your happiness, and accept that people may fall short of your expectations? If not, why not? If so, why?

5. Are you willing to honestly look at who you are still relying on to save you, to make things better for you and to acknowledge that you are/were right?

_____

_____

_____

_____

_____

_____

_____

_____

CONSCIOUS FEMININE RADICAL SELF-CARE COMMITMENT
FINDING YOUR MEDICINE WITHIN

Self-responsibility is primary factor in stepping into our inherent Feminine Power. Assessing and becoming aware of what our needs are in order to feel fulfilled and manifest our greatest potential in our lives is not only possible, but necessary part of the process. You carry the medicine within. What is your medicine?

Self- Reflection: Take a few minutes to reflect on what you need in these various aspects of yourself in order to create the foundation to show up fulfilled, inspired and whole in your life.

Physical Body: When I tune into my body, what is it that my body needs daily or weekly in order to respond to the world? What makes my body feel good, happy, strong and lovable that that I can give to myself? Journal your responses.

Emotional Body: What do I need to be real with my emotions and feel safe enough to express genuinely? How can I give myself the support I need to explore all ranges of emotions within me and resolve past places of hurt and suffering? Journal your responses.

Mental Body: What do I need for my mind to be inspired, hopeful, creative, excited and hopeful every day? Journal your responses.

Spiritual Body: What do I need to feel like I am making a difference, to believe in my own light and to be reminded of my greater purpose in life every day? Journal your responses.

CONSCIOUS FEMININE
NON-NEGOTIABLE SELF CARE CHECKLIST

RADICAL NON-NEGOTIABLE SELF-CARE	ACTIVITY	HOW OFTEN DAILY	HOW OFTEN WEEKLY	WHAT IS THE MEDICINE
Physical				
Emotional				
Mental				
Spiritual				

RADICAL FORGIVENESS FREEDOM CONSCIOUS MEDITATION

The following items will be necessary to engage in this process:

- Three pieces of paper.
- Tin or steel container.
- Lighter.
- Journal and pen.
- Candle.

1. Let yourself sit comfortably, light your candle, and place your hands on your heart.

2. As you connect with your heart, allow your awareness to move into your breath and take a few minutes to connect your complete body.

3. Ask yourself what person/situation from your past, have you not been unable to forgive, in other words, what people or events in your life do you still feel deep anger, rage, resentment, sadness, disappointment, hurt, grief, disbelief or indignation over?

4. Identify who/ what this may be and write it down on your journal.

5. Under this person or thing in your journal, write the words that follow;

"I understand that I no longer wish to be tied energetically to this situation in the past and realize that everything in my life is material for my evolution and liberation."

6. Now, reconnect with your heart by breathing into your heart and ask your heart what is the difficulty in letting this go? Why have you been holding on to this pain, this incident, this person? What are you unconsciously hoping to receive from this person or situation; an apology, acknowledgement that you were right, holding on to non-acceptance? Allow yourself to receive the responses to these questions directly from your heart, rather than from your mind or logical answers. Write them down in your journal.

7. Dare to be wrong: Now under these "reasons" write, "I dare to be wrong!" Consider the possibility that the things you're still waiting for, that prevent you from forgiveness and release, are also where you're giving your power away. These are internalized expectations and dependency, where you're still awaiting someone or something to rescue you, to make it better for you. Consider that perhaps forgiving this person doesn't mean condoning their behavior, or that you're weak, or that you're excusing their behavior. Forgiveness doesn't mean any of those things; it means freedom to realize that you no longer are depending on an outside source to make it better for you, or take care of your needs. You are willing to let go of the dependency and the expectations on outer resources, and resource from the unlimited source of Love within your being. You are willing to take your power back and take care of your needs.

8. Take a few minutes with that consideration in your heart, as you close your eyes and breath the possibility of freedom in your heart.

9. Turn to your three pieces of paper and write on each one, a reason why you've been holding onto this situation till now. You can use some of the dependencies and expectations that you wrote in your journal about this.

10. Continue to breathe in your heart and acknowledge that you'd like to open yourself to a new reality, in which you no longer are bound to this situation and the pain that it's caused you. And when you're ready to you invite unconditional LOVE of forgiveness in your heart and continue to breathe it in... until you see the frequency of LOVE washing away and filling in all the spaces where you once held the anger, hurt, and overall wound of this situation. Trust that LOVE of forgiveness is greater than that of pain. Continue to breathe the LOVE of Forgiveness in through your breath until it becomes clear. You may repeat the words "I unplug from the internalized expectation and dependency on this person or situation to fulfill my needs, I take full responsibility over my own need at this moment and I return this need to the place of undifferentiated wholeness and Love in my heart."

11. After sitting with this realization in your heart, feel the transformation and proceed to burn the three papers, symbolizing the releasing of the old story of unresolved pain into the ethers of Love. Invite the unending Love of Forgiveness, and feel it expand in your heart. End in a silent bow of gratitude for the blessing of Forgiveness in your life.

12. You may continue to do this process daily over a three-day period if you feel this is a very ingrained situation for you. You may also use this process once a month to forgive old resentments and situations that you would like to free yourself from. It's to do during the dark moon time of the month.

13. After sitting with this realization in your heart, feel the transformation and proceed to burn the three papers, symbolizing the releasing of the old story of unresolved pain into the ethers of Love. Invite the unending Love of Forgiveness, and feel it expand in your heart. End in a silent bow of gratitude for the blessing of Forgiveness in your life.

You may continue to do this process daily over a three-day period if you feel this is a very ingrained situation for you. You may also use this process once a month to forgive old resentments and situations that you would like to free yourself from. It's to do during the dark moon time of the month.

2ND SACRED INITIATION OF CONSCIOUS FEMININE POWER ACTIVATION

1. Find a quiet spot for you to sit where you will be undisturbed.

2. Bring your favorite essential oils and mix three of them. Let your body choose for you.

3. Take a few drops of your essential oil mix and put it into the palm of your hands, bringing your hands up to your nostrils and taking a few deep breaths.

4. Close your eyes and bring your hands to your heart, letting yourself dissolve into the scent of the essential oils, take three breaths here.

5. Bring your inner awareness into your heart space and watch how your body expands and contracts with each breath. Take three breaths here.

6. Gently breathing and dropping into the wisdom of your Being where you are connected to Source Consciousness. Letting your boundaries begin to dissolve, opening your heart, and surrendering to each breath. Feel the light in your heart expanding. Take at least 3 breaths here to anchor in.

7. Next, bring your hands onto your solar plexus, half way between your heart and your umbilicus (belly button) and notice your breath gently expanding from your heart center downward towards your Solar Plexus. Breathe here at least three times until you see and feel the light vibration expanding into your Solar Plexus.

8. Continue breathing and expanding in the light, now bridging your Heart and Solar Plexus. Begin to feel the sway of your body in response to your breath, the expansion and contraction in your Solar Plexus. Notice the sensations you may feel in this area, tightness, contraction, anxiety, fear, unsettling etc. Become aware of these sensations, emotions and thoughts. Just become present with them. Breathing into this space and letting yourself sway with the movement of your breath. Take three breaths here.

9. As you continue to allow and become present with unresolved sensations that arise, let yourself fall into the rhythm that your breath is creating, moving gently with the expansion and contraction of your body. Stay here for at least 9-18 breaths and notice what happens when you become present and give yourself permission to lovingly accept what's there in your Solar Plexus.

NOTE: We may be holding many unresolved emotions of powerlessness, fear, anxiety, restlessness, sadness, grief, disappointment, etc. that correspond to your relationship with power. Let yourself be with these and don't rush through the process. Remember that you aren't doing anything necessarily, but by just allowing yourself to be present with what is there, you allow the unresolved wounds to unwind.

10. Realize that there's a new reality of how you can relate to 'power' that is possible, even if you don't know what that looks like. Let yourself surrender to the unknown and enter the possibility of feeling empowered, fulfilled, confident and stable. But to do this, you have to be willing to enter into the unknown of the Conscious Feminine matrix, where you can receive the support in order to open up to your wholeness, and release the old relationship with power. Begin to say Yes to the unknown, leaving your mind behind, and open up to the power of your wholeness. Stay here at least three breaths.

11. As you surrender deeper, let yourself see your adrenals and pancreas receiving the breath and bringing itself into greater harmony and self-regulation. Stay here at least three breaths.

12. Now, in your Solar Plexus area, become aware of who/what you have given your power away in the past, by blaming, expecting or waiting for a different outcome. Perhaps it could be from your childhood where you have unresolved feelings of expecting the unconditional love from your caregivers, perhaps from others you have been in relationship with. Notice here, in your solar plexus, who or what that has been and take a deep breath in releasing that, and accepting exactly what the situation has been, no matter how unpleasant it has been. Realize that you no longer want to give away your power, by waiting and expecting something different from these outside people or situations, rather, you will now take responsibility to take care of your needs, whatever they may be. Take a deep breath and see the cords that had been binding you with these people, or situations, dissolve as you return them/it back to the Essence of LOVE, and free yourself from these ties.

13. Let yourself feel what arises; there may be some sadness, loss, or grief perhaps, or some expansion and freedom, or both. Feel it, breathe into it.

14. Secondly, now that you've been willing to release yourself from the expectation that they/it will make it better, breathe into your Solar Plexus, and let it expand with the limitless LOVE from your Essence, directly from Source, within you. This is what feeds you, this is what it means to take care of your needs, and nurture yourself. This is what it feels like to take back your power and your sovereignty.

15. Know that your Solar Plexus is now rewiring itself with your willingness and focus. Let yourself sink into this Light in your breath, noticing you have the power to access this state of being within you at all times. Letting all old patterns of powerlessness and victim hood dissolve into the Essence of your Being. Stay here at least three breaths.

16. Let yourself know that your power is not something that anyone can take away, because it is sourced from within; from your Sacred Essence. three breaths here.

17. Let yourself integrate this new neuropathway of power, knowing that you have the power you need at all times, and it is solely up to you to honor that. See yourself saying yes to yourself and to your Conscious Feminine Power from now on. Stay here at least three breaths.

18. Continue to breathe and notice your whole body transforming the old powerlessness into the truth of your Sacred Power, let yourself bow in gratitude for all that you've been given. Stay here at least three breaths.

19. When you're ready... come back into your present surrounding, opening your eyes, and feeling the new embodiment of how it feels to discover that you have had this power all along. Write down your experience in a journal to help integrate it completely.

Sanctity of the Feminine Body

This is your body… your Feminine Body.
Your hips wide with love.
Streaks of light in your hair, illuminating your gathered wisdom.
Your face marked by the challenges of your soul.
Your breasts uniquely contoured by the ones you have nourished.
Your belly imprinted by the scars of those…
you graciously entered into this world.
Nothing left out… every inch molded by the love and compassion of your heart.
This is your body… your Feminine Body.

~leonor murciano-luna

8

3rd Sacred Initiation of Conscious Feminine Body Wisdom

The '*3rd Sacred Initiation of Conscious Feminine Body Wisdom*' activates our sacral power center and our personal womb, dissolving the veils of collective and personal shame that's impeded the full embodiment of our sacred body. Here we have the opportunity to face our internalized struggle with the incessant patriarchal model and reclaim our bodies, sexuality and life force. In this Sacred Initiation, we can dissolve the endless patterns of shame and pervasive hatred we have accumulated in our own feminine bodies. Reclaiming our virginity is all about recognizing the stream of purity that is derived from our Essence and manifests into our physical body. Here we have an opportunity to recover the sanctity of our feminine body, break through the spell of the patriarchy, and reclaim the sacredness of our body. As we organically acknowledge the innate sacredness of our Essence, allowing that embodiment to expand into the living tissues of our physical form, we intuitively regain our wholeness, returning our flesh to its origin of holiness.

Sacred Essence moves through us as life force which we biologically experience as vitality, aliveness and even sexuality. Reclaiming our virginity and purity is what gives birth to all the possibilities of life that wants to be born through us, rather than designating our life force and sexuality as a cardinal sin. The 3rd Sacred Initiation of our '*Conscious Feminine Body Wisdom*' frees us from self-deprecating shame and returns us to the inherent wisdom of our biological life force. Once activated, it gives rise organically to vitality, bliss, intimacy and sacred sexuality, rooted in the Feminine's guiding force of wisdom, within your body.

RECLAIMING OUR VIRGINITY

Your virginity isn't something that you can lose when you have sexual relations, as our religious indoctrination might have us believe. Our virginity is actually the pureness that exists in our Essence; in the secret of our Soul. It's our state of wholeness and our divine nature. The Sufi's believe that there can be wounding in our soul and some of our deepest challenges are our soul lessons, equipped with great challenges as well as great reward. However, deep in our soul, is a part of our soul that's pure and untouched by the veils of the world that we live in. This, by the Sufi's, is referred to the level of consciousness of 'the secret of the Soul'. Here, in the 'secret of the Soul', we experience our divinity with no limitations, the pure essence of our being. This is the root of our virginity.

Our virginity can never be lost, because it is our sacred origin; the perfected divinity within us, our Essential Self. However, part of the evolution of our soul coming into this incarnation is forgetting our sacred origin, our virginity. Cynthia Bourgeult writes, "the name given to the state of restored alignment – of 'singleness' or purity of being – is virginity'. [1]

We have lost our alignment with Essence and as we mature, we begin to awaken to the truth of who we really are. In this way, much of us have lost our virginity to the mental constructs and judgements in our minds. In our patriarchal culture, virginity has been used as a measuring stick in which to judge women, accessing their value according to whether her hymen (vagina's membrane) has been severed or not, due to sexual activity. Ongoingly, our degree of virginity has been equated with our value and worthiness, as a female individual. However, that's all part of the misogynistic view point that has severely undermined the worth of women, leading to a violent culture of shame, repression and femicide within our own culture.

Furthermore, our patriarchal religious culture has been pervasive in the declaration of valuing strictly the celibate tentacles that further shame our body's natural inclination to pleasure and sexuality. This underlines the subtle correlation and fascination with purity, chastity, abstinence and spirituality which has further deteriorated the sacredness of our bodies, and instigated the misogynistic views throughout the world, let alone our western culture. These religious overlays of cardinal sin projected onto women, have caused further repression of our own sexual and sensual impulses for at least the last 2000 years to avoid being judged, shamed, and ostracized to survive.

This collective culture of repression, which began as a form of cardinal sin, has developed into great body shaming for women and also a great source of violence. This body shame isn't only apparent in our relationship with our bodies, but it also interferes with the expression of our life force through our passion, our creativity, our pleasure and our joy. When we factor in that one out of every four women experience some kind of child sexual abuse in the US, we realize how much more prevalent shame has played a role in women's perception of themselves, as well as how much trauma has been contained on the psychic level to survive in such a hostile environment. As women, when we hesitate to express our passion, hesitate to speak our truth, hesitate to stand up for those things that are important to us, we're defaulting to this trauma and the shame that's been layered over it, dictating our responses and choices. Unfortunately, this is a pervasive fear and shame that's not just known to us personally, but collectively to many of the generations before us.

TRANSFORMING THE SHADOW OF SHAME

Women have been carrying shame for a very long time; it's been part of our survival dynamic. However, this shame continues to control our thinking and subdue our responses through the preponderant fear. It injects doubt into what we feel we have permission to say or not say, act or not act. Shame in itself, insidiously corrupts our sense of self and sense of worth, leaving us resigned and devoid of hope. Shame is silently woven into our subtle bodies; from the moment we are born as females. Even in this country where females don't face the fear of being drowned at birth, due to their undesirable gender and lower status, we're still infected with the collective shame of being born female.

Women's bodies are sacred bodies. The vessel through which life is birthed. There's no greater honor than to be in a feminine body, whether you have created life or not. This third sacred initiation of Conscious Feminine Body Wisdom helps us restore the honor, sacredness and wholeness in our Feminine body, that has been lost for thousands of years. She gives us an opportunity to stop the cycle of shame and the culture of trauma, blame and fear, as we step into the miracle that the feminine form is, while honoring all aspects of our being.

Our monthly cycle urges us to draw our energies within, and slow down, shifting our rhythm and our focus from the outside world, to our inner world. There's a lot of changes happening in our bodies at the time of our menses and listening to what our body needs, at this time is imperative to honoring ourselves. During the time of our menses, we release our endometrial lining along with all the other fine-tuned processes of cellularly, hormonally and physically, but emotionally, we're also releasing unresolved feelings and challenges that we've faced during the previous month. It's a time where we're usually more sensitive, and our emotions are more on the surface to consciously process what's no longer needed. It's a time of purification, clearing and transformation on all levels; physically, emotionally, and spiritually. It is said that physiologically a woman's brain releases the God molecule, during her cycle in order to receive greater communion with the divine. The molecule DMT, Dimethyltryptamine, which is referred to as the god molecule, has been found in the blood of menstruating women. This is the same molecule found in medicinal plants used by ancient medicine elders to reach altered states of consciousness and connect to Oneness/Spirit. It seems that during our menses, our body is supporting our ability to communicate and navigate these subtle realms more easily, as well as helping us enter into higher levels of consciousness.

As women, we transform the shadow of shame when we recognize that we have an intrinsic value that isn't dependent on our looks, on what we do, nor on how much money or possessions we have, but it just is. Let's untangle our value from our preconceived ideas of who we are, so that we can be free to express our greatest light and joy! Through the transformation of our shame, we open the doors to freedom of expression, and of being. This freedom and joy are what arises when we aren't limited by our insecurities, judgements and the self-shame that is so ingrained in our conditioning. This is what we've been raised in, and what is energetically in our psyches, from many, many generations back. However, we have the ability to free ourselves from feeling *'less than'*, or *'not good enough'* or any other self-deprecating perception of ourselves, and immediately step into radical self-acceptance and self-love, which we have spoken about.

This form we call our 'body' is perfection in itself and the conditioned filters through which we see our bodies needs to be dissolved so that we can see ourselves in greater alignment with the truth of our bodies. There's no need to perpetuate the conditioned perception of shame that has been grown out of a society that has rejected the Feminine, and women at large. There's no need to buy into this story and longer, even if we still crave being accepted by society. We must decide if we're willing to continue to betray ourselves in order to fit in. In the past, we may have needed to go along with the conditioned story, for our own survival. But now, for most of us in the western world, the opportunity is here for us to awaken to our greater truth. We have a choice to make; we're are faced with a difficult decision of speaking our truth, of standing up for the truth of our intrinsic value and break free the cultural norms that have been dominated by the negation of this truth.

However, to free ourselves of the shame and reclaim our true Essence, we have to say no to the norms that have been created around this story. We have to be willing to stand up for ourselves and protect the sanctity of our bodies, in all the ways that society is still unconscious to. We are riding this first wave of breaking out of a 5000+ year old story of repressed, rejected and demonized feminism.

SUBCONSCIOUSLY ENDORSING THE PATRIARCHAL FEMININE BODY IDEAL

Do we want to continue to endorse the patriarchal misogynistic view of women, our-selves? Do we want to continue to reject our bodies; to reject the sacredness of our bodies? Do we want to continue to reject our bodies, by subtly harboring feelings of wanting to change it? Do we want to continue the mental obsession of trying to fit into a particular size, weight, image, while rejecting what our body is manifesting as in this moment ?

The patriarchal view of women is that they're thin, young looking with an absence of aging, including marks of birth on the belly or breasts, and, of course, no wrinkles on the face. These are the qualities that make women attractive in a patriarchal society and simultaneously objectify the women as a whole. Women that don't fall into this category are simply categorized as not attractive and, therefore, unworthy within our patriarchal confines. The constant computerization of women's images as well as the continuous announcements of 'weight loss' programs are examples of how women are psychologically reminded daily of what is acceptable and preferred, welcomed and eternally cherished in our cultural system.

The problem is that most of us are aware of this criterion intellectually, but unfortunate-ly we still get trapped into believing that there's something wrong with us and that we must change, conform and adapt ourselves to be happy and fulfilled. Every time we think of dieting to make our bodies smaller, or we commit to a surgical cosmetic procedure to alter our body, chasing some imaginary ideal of what would be better, we abandon ourselves and our bodies. This is where we're controlled by the patriarchal norms and conditioning.

We may think that these thoughts are innocent and that we're just subscribing to what we want. The truth is that behind what we want is a perceptual reality at play, which is being informed and manipulated by the constant media manipulation of what we should be, along with the misleading pattern of 'we would be better of if', 'we would be more fulfilled if', etc. And most of us unconsciously buy into this message, believing that we have autonomy in making these decisions. These are the underlying messages that we are buying into when we follow through on the behaviors that are supported by those thoughts. Nevertheless, we shouldn't' be too quick to judge ourselves, because these are deeply ingrained patterns of survival behavior, that mostly continues to influence us, unconsciously. And so, the work is to awaken to these patterns of manipulation within ourselves, to unplug from them, and free ourselves from the control of this spell.

For example, let's take a look at the collective view of the issue of women's weight. This has been an interesting and very personal arena for myself as it has with most women. For most women that gain weight during various life changes; giving birth, menopause, etc. , there's a subtle judgment that appears where we're encouraged to lose weight and return to the weight that our bodies were at one time. There's very little regard for the process the body has undergone, rather it seems that it's usually reduced to this single idea of 'having to lose weight and return to the past', as if accomplishing this, the body would somehow be better off. What about the wisdom, the sacredness, and the transformation that the body has undertaken during this time? These things aren't valued in our society, therefore, they are usually not mentioned, even in our own minds.

Submitting to this thinking of returning to the bodies past weight, or even deciding that the body has a particular weight it should be, is in itself a denial of the state of the body in the present moment. Not only that but it is clearly buying into an arbitrary idea of what the body should look like at any given moment, making it wrong if it doesn't meet up to those standards. This is a complete denial and rejection of the bodies state, and a complete conformity to the patriarchal ideal of a woman's body. Unknowingly, we continuously give the message to our body that it was wrong in the shape and size that it is showing up. And then proceed with layering feelings of failure, powerlessness and inadequacy because we don't meet the standards of some illusionary objectified ideal.

At the end of the day, we have severed the trust with our bodies, and this is the relationship we are rebuilding as we unplug ourselves from the umbilical dependency and expectations, we have been immersed in. Is it possible to trust my body's innate wisdom, more than the conditioned norms that have been imposed on me throughout my lifetime? This is the question we are faced with every time; we consider unplugging and not following through on one of these impulses. Will we let fear stop us? We will let shame make us feel desperate enough for us to give in? This is the personal conflict we embark on when we dare to disengage from the cultural conditioned patterns.

My personal answer is that, yes, my body's wisdom is where we all have to turn to and trust, rather than abiding by some outer arbitrary rule that makes us reject what our bodies are doing in any said moment. And yet, we also have to take responsibility with our care, our health and, in this case, eat healthy, organically, and in a responsible way. There may be areas to improve, but if we're being responsible and giving ourselves the highest qualities of food and care, then the key is to trust the body and what is happening in it, even if it wants to gain weight, it may need to for some other reason. But this is an example of how extensive this Feminine rejection spell is in our society and why it is so difficult to break out of the spell.

In relation to this, I wouldn't argue that millions of people are addicted to food, but more importantly many more are addicted to dieting and losing weight. We've conformed to this idea that only a certain amount of fat is acceptable measured against this arbitrary weight chart that our systems all default to. However, this particular spell of acceptable weight is so pervasive due in part because our public health authorities have all been supporting and advertising this arbitrary weight norm and yet, surprisingly these weight guidelines that we all feel 'we have to abide by' have been based on unsubstantiated medical evidence.

According to public health authorities, we're considered at a healthy weight at 18-25 BMI (body. Mass index) and anything over that is unhealthy and "overweight". However, due to a recent study by Katherine M. Flegal, PhD; Brian K. Kit, MD; Heather Orpana, PhD; et al, [2] on weight (BMI) and mortality, of over 3000 people, statistics show that people that have been categorized at the '*overweight and obese category 1 (BMI 25-35)*' are considered to have a lesser mortality rate of 3-4%, over people that have a '*normal weight index of BMI 18-25*'. In other words, if you're overweight and even in the obese category 1 with a BMI of 25-35, you get to live 3-4% longer than you would if you're within what is currently considered to be the so-called '*normal weight category*'. What's more interesting is that our government and medical officials, continue to push the narrative of 'correlating overweight with unhealthiness', through thousands of weight loss advertisements and media, that clearly isn't true. This continues to perpetuate the idea that if you're overweight (according to that arbitrary weight chart) you should lose weight to be healthier and live longer, when the truth is quite the opposite.

Moreover, only 25% of the population falls within the acceptable weight standards. That leaves 75% of the population outside the so-called normal weight parameters. Contrary to popular belief and what officials are still promoting, there's no direct correlation between weight, health or mortality, until we reach the class 2 obesity level, which is over BMI35. It's actually healthier to be overweight and slightly obese, with a higher BMI of up to 35, according to Katherine Flagel and her associates at the CDC and the National Institutes for Health.

We can understand how the narrative that's being pushed on a collective level, whether it is true or false, affects us and manipulates us through fear, and in this case 'fear of dying, if we don't fit in, lose weight, and fit the ideal body'. And for the other 75% of the population that hasn't been successful in meeting the alleged ideal weight, there are accumulated layers of shame and failure that is poured over the perceived disappointment of failing. When the whole culture is steeped in this, it adds to the general objectification of women's bodies, and certainly adds to the underlying fear that controls our every decision. Given these circumstances, of course we would want to lose weight, it sounds like the only sane choice. We all want to be accepted, loved, admired and attractive, along with being healthy and disease free. Who would choose to be constantly judged, ostracized, ridiculed or even blamed for not conforming to the arbitrary weight regulations. However, when we buy into this idea of fitting into a mold in hopes that it will deliver our desires, we end up disappointed by the outcomes, and rejected and abandoned by our own doing. The irony is that we might be inclined to conform to avoid judgment, ridicule, ostracization, and rejection from others, and yet, in turn, that is exactly what we end up doing to ourselves. That is the paradox of this situation. When we submit to fear, and make decisions from fear, we usually end up doing to ourselves what we fear the most, in this case rejecting ourselves to avoid being rejected by a misogynistic culture that rejects the true form, sacredness and essence of women's bodies. And by doing this, we perpetuate the shame, insecurity and blaming of our feminine form.

Nevertheless, I'm not advocating being irresponsible with our bodies to the point where we disregard guidelines on what to eat, or on our physical exercise behavior, but what I am saying is that the guiding element in our decision has to shift to create health, healing and listening to our body wisdom, rather than turning our sovereignty over to the ideals of a patriarchal culture. We still have a responsibility to self-nourishment, if you eat sugar and gluten and you fall asleep right after or you notice it initiates your headaches, then we need to be responsible and adapt our behaviors accordingly. Listening is key to your body's health, but more importantly, it's about taking the power back to decide what your body needs, and honoring your bodies size and intelligence in making your choices. This is all part of clearing the shame and fear that has kept women submissive and furthermore, reclaiming your power.

OUR BIOLOGICAL BLISS

This dismissive attitude that our culture displays about women in general, women's bodies, and our vaginas, contributes to greater lack of on-going safety for a woman. This stress affects not only a women's mental state, but also our sexual responses and overall vitality in our body. Psychologically, women register these ongoing threats from our culture, which in turn cause physiological fear responses, inducing a cascade of stress hormones to mitigate the perceived danger. Our body responds as if we are facing a room of potential rapists, which by the hostile under currents of our environment, we might very well be. This constant barrage of nervous system stressors further weakens our system over a long period of time, effecting our vitality. According to Naomi

Wolf, in her book Vagina, *"The role of manipulating female stress in targeting the vagina should not be ignored. This behavior—ridiculing the vagina—makes perfect instinctive sense. These acts are often impersonal and tactical—strategies for directing a kind of pressure at women that is not consciously understood but may be widely intuited, and even survive in folk memory, as eliciting a wider neuropsychological "bad stress" response that actually debilitates women."* [3]

So, just being in an environment in which women are objectified, or exposed to subtle degradation of our feminine body, faced with constant struggle over reproductive rights, warding off the overall sexualization of our bodies, including dismissive and disrespectful attitude of our vaginas, does indeed affect our mental, emotional and physical health, via the nervous system reactions alone. In a misogynist culture, this can mean women living in a continuous state of underlying stress, due to the subtle resonance of dismissive attitudes, continuously creating a feeling of lack of safety.

By living in a world that is ultimately unsafe, we perpetuate the constant alertness in our nervous system, as we respond to the perceived threats, as well as responding internally and psychically to our collective conditioning from our not so distant relatives. Is it any surprise that our culture is addicted to substances that desensitizes us to the ongoing anxiety, depression and other feelings overall? Using societal acceptable means of lowering our stress, such as alcohol, television, gaming, food or any other common activities has given us a means to survive and temporarily mitigate the ongoing uncomfortable intensity felt daily, in our own bodies.

Furthermore, this kind of continual stress affects our vitality, our life force and our sexual responses and ultimately our ability to feel good, to feel pleasure, and bliss in our bodies. When we're under stress, our nervous system is too busy managing the cascade of stress hormones that is continuously flooding us, leaving little to no allowance for the relaxed experience of feeling pleasure in our bodies. Ultimately, this constant biological stress interferes with our vitality and quickly adds to the deterioration of our internal system, leaving us with the abundance of these common epidemics we see in women; nervous system disorders, auto-immune disorders, reproductive disorders and thyroid issues, to name a few, '*1st world feminine disorders'*. Our physical systems are designed to protect us from danger, or perceived danger, through the biological production of stress hormones paving the way for us to 'run' from danger, instead, the result of living under constant underlying threat and fear, is that our bodies become over exhausted, taxed and dysfunctional, all in the name of trying to protect us.

It's impossible to feel fully alive, fully activated, fully in joy and bliss if our nervous system is engaged in survival and fear. The fact is we need to feel safe to feel good. Our ability to feel the true joy and bliss that is sourced in our bodies becomes unreachable under the cascade of this stress hormone response. However, through deliberate awareness, transformational alchemy, and our own willingness to change the story in our bodies, we can move past the unconscious cycle of fight or fight in our bodies and reunite ourselves with our true nature of bliss that exists in our bodies.

Therefore, we must try to stop the automatic response, even if we find ourselves surrounded by a lack of safety. We must shift our awareness and break through the conditioned response that has made us repress, and live in constriction, rather than in relaxed pleasure of our true nature. We do have choice, and the first step in shifting this dynamic is engaging in the process we began in the 1st sacred initiation, and continuing to unwind the conditioning and wounding that is found here in this sacral center. This is the work of re-mothering ourselves. Giving ourselves the unconditional love and acceptance, so that our unresolved needs are met with what they need, to heal. Through this 2nd Sacred Initiation, we will expand your sacred power and allow it to completely reorient yourself to living in joy, pleasure and the wisdom that is sourced from your Essence.

As we turn our awareness and consciousness inward, we continue the journey of detaching from the conditioned responses of our nervous system, and begin the process of igniting our body's innate biological bliss. Breaking the unconscious dependency on any outer source to fix us, make us feel better, honor us, etc., offers us only a false sense of temporary satisfaction. Our bliss, our ability to feel good, and our internal physiology is all sourced from within ourselves. Any dependency on the outer to feel good, tell us our worth, or make us feel safe is unreliable and transient, and will never fulfill us. Paradoxically, the acknowledgement that we're looking for when we repress and concede ourselves to other's will in order to stay safe.. is within us. We have to acknowledge ourselves, and find our strength as women, compassionate nurturers, mothers, sexual beings, and furthermore, as sacred beings, before we can have the outer world acknowledge that for us. The support we're looking for in the outer world, shifts when we support ourselves; it's a shift in consciousness and it begins with us. Frankly, the fact that we're marginalized, objectified, and overall repressed acts as a catalyst for us to honestly explore the context in which we hold ourselves, and what we stand in for ourselves. It's an opportunity to return to our source of power within and reactivate our deeper truth. Without this dire situation, we may never ignite this process, instead choosing to stay in mere survival, rather than thriving of our fullest potential.

Once we have turned our awareness inward, relying on our cultivated sense of Essential Self, that which is connected to the ocean of Eternal Source Consciousness, we must then shift our awareness to follow our bliss and our pleasure, instead of our pain. Through the many generations of collective survival, our nervous system is highly attuned to protect us by following and guarding against pain. However, as we discussed, this overall management of our system eventually breaks us down, and is no longer needed. Changing our direction to uncover and follow our joy, our bliss, may feel uncomfortable at first, but it is the way to step deeper into our truth. At first, shame may arise, questioning whether we should be feeling this good Our minds might ask, "what about our other feelings, don't they need more attention?" Following our bliss may also make us feel vulnerable and unsafe, because we aren't using the same energy to guard ourselves against pain; emotional or otherwise.

Another way that we may resist feeling our true Essence of joy is in self-criticism and self judgement, which may have kept us safe in the past, but is no longer supportive to our evolutionary consciousness. We may think that it's distasteful to feel our sensuality, we may judge ourselves or others, we may criticize ourselves, or think we are wasting time, or entertain an array of other excuses that keep us away from fully merging with the innate wisdom of your body. Face these challenges straight on, don't shy away from them, and allow the shame to continue to control you. Let the shame that is underneath rise, whether its shame, fear, inadequacy, judgement of our bodies; whichever way your old programming is protecting you, let it rise into the container of your true Essence, Love, where She will dissolve it completely. This is the repressed remnants of our survival conditioning, which has undoubtedly protected us for thousands of years. Thank it and then move right through it. You don't need to maintain the walls that have kept you incarcerated in the body of pain; you can free yourself completely through the rise of the Feminine, Love.

Making the decision to release the grips that shame, guilt and fear have had on us will shift our sense of who we are, and create the space to feel the freedom of our being. This process allows us to appreciate our bodies for the sacred vessel that they are. We no longer allow the restrictive conditioning to continue to dictate our state of being, even though we may continue to feel unpleasant feelings as they arise. However, we no longer believe the narrative of shame, guilt, or fear tell us about our bodies, our sexuality, our ability to feel good, or about our self-worth. We have enough space cultivated to see them for what they are, a filter, produced by our culture, and taken in by our minds, against some perceived danger. This is how we break free from the collective pain of the generations that have come before us, and rebuild a new story based on truth, rather than fear. This is the process of believing in truth more that we believe in fear.

Bliss is a biological response in the body that's possible when we move past the emotional and mental memories of the past, and reconnect with our energy body sourced in consciousness itself. This state of being is present, whether we're aware of it or not, and it isn't something we only feel with sexual union, even though it's certainly possible in that case. The sensuality of our breath interacting with our body, and the subtle sensations of presence in our energetic body, all hold the deeper qualities sourced within consciousness Her Self. These are accessible to you; it is you. In this pure Essence of our being, we find the universal light source qualities of our soul; unconditional love, peace, joy, bliss, safety, justice, all sourced from within. Just focusing on your breath opens up the pathway to your soul (your Essential Self) and can be a sensual experience. Once you are in the terrain of your Essence, the joy and the bliss, you are in connection with the fountain of your wisdom, the wisdom that is sourced in your body. This is truly your guiding light. This is the key of embodying the Feminine within you and reclaiming the sanctity of your body.

The Feminine wants us to know that our bodies are sacred and that one of the gifts of having this body is to be in love with it, to feel the love, not just for other or between yourself and other, but within yourself. When you awaken to the Feminine, you enter into a relationship of Love, with all of life. You fall in love with Her, and because She is Essence in form, you are in love with all of Life. This is the love of the beloved and your-self. Shifting your orientation to one of pleasure and bliss, shifts your perspective to be grounded in Source. It allows you to shift from a hyper vigilant nervous system reaction, based on fear and using fear as your fuel, to being in safety, in love, in presence moment to moment. Here, we can feel the presence of the Feminine, as She is rising through you, around you, and within you, feeling Her viscerally, as sensation, as love, as bliss. We open our bodies up to the sensation of pleasure, to the sensation of feeling good, and return home to an experience that we have long forgotten, and that we confused with momentary pleasure of the flesh. We aren't talking necessarily of the sexual act, even though this awareness and embodiment of enlivening your senses can expand your sensations greatly. We're talking about the sensuality that is innate in your body, the aliveness of your cells, the awakening of the Feminine in your body. This is where you can lose yourself in Love, and where you honor your body, because it is the vessel created from this source of Love. When you open to your Essence of Love, the biology in your body shifts. No longer releasing the cascade of stress hormone, but one of 'feel good' hormones and neurotransmitters, that accompany the enlivened sensation in your body. This is your body biologically being turned on by the Light of your being, the Feminine Essence.

POWER OF OUR SACRAL WOMB

As women, our womb is the center of our creativity, the place that unites the Essence of being, with the power of creation and manifestation. Our womb is also where we hold the past memories and identifications of what it is to be a woman. The great power of our pelvic cavity houses our Sacral center that exists as a bridge between the worlds, connecting unmanifested reality to manifested reality. This particular bridge of the sacral center is the root of where the creative power of the Universe is templated in our bodies, root aspect of our Feminine Essence. As we unravel the restrictions and pain body associations from this sacral center, we begin to unveil our core essence, as we see ourselves as the creative beings that we are, birthing life into this existence through our expressions of words, thoughts, and actions, and, of course, living human beings.

As the womb is the essence of creation itself, it's also where women have deposited their inner feelings and wounding of being a woman. In our society, the miracle of birthing Essence into life has become an ordinary act, and somehow the sacredness and holiness of it has been stripped away. By association, the sacredness of our female bodies has also been stripped of its wonder, mystery and awe. In this very ordinary lack of sanctity and dismissal sits the deeper influences that have contributed to women's negative shaming and rejection about themselves, leading us to the visible deterioration of the corresponding female reproduction system and hormonal system.

In an earlier chapter, I mentioned how at least 80% of women around the world experience pain with their periods. Furthermore, infertility, polycystic ovaries, hormonal imbalances, and thyroid dysfunction is all on the rise, affecting more and more women every day. Where do the feelings about ourselves as women end up? For each negative thought about how our bodies look or should look, shame-based feelings, fear driven inadequacies, there are hundreds of bio-chemicals produced that affect the delicate hormonal balances of our system. Put aside the fear and stress bombardment flooding our system because we don't feel safe, and consider the chemical response to our inadequacy, shame or self-rejection we feel in our bodies. Where do all these bio-chemicals end up? Well, if it's to do with our bodies and our value as women, it will probably affect our womb and womb related functions such as hormones, reproductive system and endocrine system as a whole.

What does that mean exactly? It means that as women, what we are feeling about ourselves, our bodies and our gender can be disruptive to our hormones and contribute to the rise of undiagnosed infertility, the rise in pelvic pain with our periods, thyroid and other endocrine disbalances and much more. We have to understand that our bodies are one entity with our thoughts, our emotions and our chemistry. And when we think something, whether it's conscious or unconscious, our physiology responds by sending out chemical signals in accordance. Our thoughts are important, and the stories we tell ourselves are incredibly important, because the rest of our self (our body, our emotions, etc) is responding to these stories and where we put our energy. So, there's a good chance that if there's an imbalance in your pelvic cavity, your period, your thyroid, hormonally, or in your reproductive organs, there may be an underlying psycho-emotional/ spiritual relationship to these discussed issues of shame, inadequacy, self-judg-ment, self-rejection, self-blame, from the collective and personal culture. The key is to embrace your Feminine Essence completely, especially honoring your womb wisdom and your body wisdom, which in turns alchemizes, dissolves and metabolizes all the calcified conditioning you have believed to be true till now.

Your virginity can only be lost when you deny the truth of who you are.
You are a pure Essence of Light in a physical body.
Your virginity is the Essence of your Being.

~leonor murciano-luna

3ʀᴅ Sᴀᴄʀᴇᴅ Iɴɪᴛɪᴀᴛɪᴏɴ - ᴄᴏɴꜱᴄɪᴏᴜꜱ Fᴇᴍɪɴɪɴᴇ Bᴏᴅʏ Wɪꜱᴅᴏᴍ

We begin our descent into the 3ʳᵈ Sacred Initiation, through which we commit to surrendering all the patterns of conditioning, along with our wounds of shame, insufficiency, and inadequacy, rooted in fear. Here, we turn our hearts to the Essence of our being, where we can be guided through the deep wisdom that is innate within us. Along with this process, we invite the bridge of trust, safety, and faith to accompany our transformation and help us anchor in truth.

Tʜᴇ Mᴇᴅɪᴄɪɴᴇ ᴏF Rᴀᴅɪᴄᴀʟ SᴇʟF Lᴏᴠᴇ

The medicine for healing our Sacral Womb begins with Radical Self Love. When we open our hearts to the truth, while hearing the pain from our unresolved past, we invite forth the process of transformational alchemy that's needed for us to ground in our being of light. We're led to open ourselves to understanding and offering compassion to our own hating judgments within, which in turn, allows these layers to dissolve into the deeper Love. Don't reject your judgments, instead, acknowledge them, wrap them up in compassion and meet them with your Essence of love. Recognize that these judgments about yourself aren't true, however, you can understand how they have become part of your defense mechanism to stay safe. You can now see them for what they are, without added judgment on yourself for having them. These conditionings no longer dictate your actions, however, you continue to acknowledge them and love them, because after all it has been the catalyst to your awakening.

Secondly, it's important that in this process of radical self-love, you affirm the fact that these statements of inadequacy or judgment that have been living in your mind, don't actually define you. These judgements simply reflect how your egoic nature has identified you up to now, but it isn't truly who you are. Don't limit the idea of who you are to these judgments about yourself, instead, opening yourself up to acknowledge your Essence, your divine nature, and the Love of your being to dissolve these judgments, rather than letting them define you. Let's look at how we can unwind these judgments, particularly shame, from your body/mind.

SPIRITUAL ALCHEMY OF SHAME
WRITING REFLECTION

Awareness is the first key of Feminine Healing to unveil your conditional judgments of shame.

What are you subscribing to?

1. Make a list of what you are subscribing to.

You can start by listing how you feel about your body, judgments about yourself, and anything about you that's clouded with shame.

2. Then, side by side, go back and write what part of yourself are you rejecting with those internalized statements.

3. After you have written this list, become aware of how often these statements cloud your mind, pausing after you become aware of each one, and making a mental decision to radically love yourself and stop subscribing to these judgements. It is an exercise in awareness and free will.

Examples

Statement:	What are you Rejecting and Subscribing to:
I am overweight. I have to lose weight.	I am rejecting my body and the shape that it's presenting, right now and subscribing to society's rule of what is acceptable weight.
I have to put on make-up to go out.	I am rejecting my face, my features and my natural beauty and subscribing to societal idea of what beauty should be (something other than me).
I should have more money, and be subscribing to more successful.	I am rejecting my abilities, and myself and subscribing to culture's idea determine my value.

Now, try your list and become aware of how these levels of conditioning are underlying your thinking about yourself and shaming you in the process.

CONSCIOUS FEMININE BODY WISDOM ACTIVATION

1. Allow yourself to sit quietly to begin your 3rd Sacred Initiation of your Conscious Feminine Body, gathering your essential oils and breathing them in. As usual, you may want to record this ahead of time and then just lead yourself through this process.

2. Begin by slowing down your breathing, bringing your awareness into your heart center and breathing into this space. Notice the rise and fall of the breath gently moving your body. Take at least 3-6 breaths here.

3. Next, bring your awareness from your heart into your womb, your sacral center, right below your belly button. And as you begin to notice the expansion and contraction of the pelvic area in response to your breath, allow yourself to relax even deeper. Continue to activate this pelvic area by sounding the OOOO sound deeply, slowing into the womb, letting the womb be filled with this sound. Notice how the OOOO sounds penetrate right into the womb, releasing old tension and all the old patterning that may be there. Breathing into womb, pelvic, activate with OOO sounds, vibration throughout. Stay here at least 10 breath cycles.

4. As you continue to connect with your womb (sacral center), place one hand on your womb and the other on your heart center. Invite the Love... the love that you are and the love that is surrounding you. Notice that in one level there is only LOVE, that is the source that life is created from and that you are created from. And you are LOVE, your Divine Essence is LOVE, it is your sacred nature. Let this LOVE which is You expand as you continue to breathe into both centers. Continue to breathe here for about six breaths.

5. As you feel the love in your heart and in your womb, let yourself also feel the LOVE holding you, supporting you, from the chair or surface you are sitting in, to each breath, notice that this is Source of Love, the Feminine Mother holding you, as she does with all of creation. Feel yourself being held, by gravity, by the surface you are on, by life itself. Stay 3-6 breaths here.

6. Now, notice your Love expanding through your whole body, feeling the vibrational frequency of Divine Mother's Love moving through you... realizing you are never separate from the Mother Essence of the Feminine, you are made from Her. Feel this vibration of Love throughout your whole body, expanding from the inside out. Stay three breaths here.

7. As you expand in Love frequency, you consciously bring the love frequency to each part of your body, first your internal organs in your torso, your heart, lungs, spleen, liver, gall bladder, stomach, large intestines, small intestines, vagina, and all reproductive organs, and then into your head, brain, eyes, ears, nose. Then continue to see the Love penetrating all your extremities and outer features; your shoulders, arms, hips, stomach, breasts, legs, thighs, feet, toes, neck and any other area that feels needy of the love. Breathe here for 6-9 breaths.

8. Let yourself fill completely with the Love that you are, letting it break through any place that has been holding any other vibration of shame, fear, inadequacy, unworthiness etc. See the vibration of Love dissolve everything else. Take your time, until every single cell and body part is vibrating in the Love that you are. (This might require a few repetitions to be completed). Stay here at least 6-9 breaths, until you feel complete with this process.

9. Now, as you sit with your body vibrating with Love, notice this vibration or tingling that you may feel as Love itself, originated by Source, the Feminine aspect of source, the Divine Mother. She is the creator of life, and she is in you as She is in all of her creation. You are an extension of Her, you are the Love, and you are never alone; that is only a perception. You can choose to see this truth about yourself and about who you are, it just takes a few minutes to consciously move into this subtle realm of perception, where you can feel your body of Love and Light and where you can feel the oneness of your Essence. This is the level of consciousness that dissolves everything else that is not vibrating at the level of love. Your initiation is needed here, you have the choice to turn it on or not, depending on what you choose to consciously focus on. When we are outwardly focused and, on the go, we sever our power that we carry within. It is up to you to make the time and awaken to this level of consciousness. Let yourself completely immerse in this LOVE Essence that you are. Stay here for at least 6-9 breaths or more.

10. Bow in gratitude to the Love that you are and that sustains you. Peace.

9

4ᵗʰ Sacred Initiation of Conscious Feminine Union

The illusion of separation from Source is the root of the greatest wounds and deepest source of fear and terror that women carry in their being. The 4ᵗʰ Sacred Initiation of *Conscious Feminine Union* allows us to transmute the fear and terror deriving from the shadow of abandonment and illusion of separation, as we restore our knowing of who we really are. However, it's through the surrender and full embodiment of the Conscious Feminine, that we're able to bridge the Oneness Source with our form, and restore the spiritualization of matter. It's She that can restore us back to Oneness, it's She that lives in matter, and that never loses her Essence. It's She is that is eternal and returns us to our eternal being.

As powerful as this initiation is, it does require us to take a leap of faith, and face our deepest darkest fear, our fear of death, abandonment and the illusion of separation. This requires us to trust in something bigger than ourselves, even as we're exploring the deep recesses of the unknown in the underworld of our psyches. Just like the journey of Innana into the underworld to save her sister, Ereshkigal, in the old myth of the "Descent of Innana", [1], we must surrender and bare ourselves. We must surrender all illusions that we have held onto for safety. We must enter the unknown, naked and empty, leaving behind everything that we have known to reclaim our wholeness, our complete Self. We must surrender and trust that we will be resurrected, we must be willing to surrender all sense of self to be reborn in our wholeness.

If we're willing to face the places within us that hold the imprint of abandonment and separation, we enter into the holy union of Oneness, through the grace of the Conscious Feminine, restoring the light in your being. This union with the Conscious Feminine allows us to restore the spiritualization of our form, and experience the light in our form, heaven on earth. The culmination of this 4th initiation is to anchor in union with the Conscious Feminine, where we feel deeply safe, in peace, and at one with the Universe. Here we can feel constantly part of life, and 'in the flow' because we know life is not against us. Through this initiation, there's a deep sense of trust that's restored in your being, because you can see through the 'maya' of the world and all of its moving parts, although it's not your intellect that you rely on. It's a visceral experience of Oneness, that you can feel, that literally dissolves all sense of separation between you and life itself. Here, you blindly surrender your life to the greater 'field', of Oneness. This is where you realize that you're part of something much bigger than yourself and that you have always been. Here, you realize that in actuality, it was your limited perception that limited you and confined you to your experience of life. You realize that you've never been separate, but that through various levels of consciousness, you can appear to be separate, abandoned, and alone. You realize that the key to living in your bliss, is to continue to embrace the truth of your being, as you open up to these divine level of consciousness within your being.

Here you realize that you've always been part of Her, and She is you and, therefore, surrendering to Her is really surrendering to the divine consciousness of yourself. This is the gift of the 4th Sacred Initiation of Conscious Feminine Union.

FACING OUR DARKNESS

To come into full union with our wholeness and Essence, one must face our greatest challenge of death. Moving through this Sacred Initiation is the invitation to die before you die, as the Sufi's would say. It's about facing your inner darkness and all the unresolved pain of feeling abandoned. The paradox is that the one that is facing the death, is the separate part of yourself, your egoic nature, the Conditioned self, and your Essential Self, the one that is merged with the Divine, knows that it's eternal, therefore, does not fear. But to live in that reality, we must dissolve all of our identification with our egoic nature (our separate self). The layers of conditioning that make up the egoic self must be transformed, and this may feel like a death to that aspect of ourselves. As one engages in this transformational evolution, we release emotional and mental patterns that often induce feelings of fear and terror of the unknown. Now, I must clarify, this isn't about death in the physical sense, it's a death of our state of mind and may feel like a death or a loss of some kind. I'm simply using the phrase 'die before you die' to signify the transformational process of our egoic nature, that goes through an evolutionary process of dying to resurrect our true nature of our Essence.

So, what happens when we 'die before we die'? In reality, we let go and separate our attachments and identifications with thoughts, things, or even people. That includes the roles that we play, or the outer things that we erroneously attribute our value to, as well as our deep-seated fears and pain. The 'I' that we identify with, becomes something much greater, and yet much humbler because we realize the great potential of our spirit in connection with the intelligence and creator of all. We recognize at a very deep level that we are an expression of the One Consciousness, and as such, we are constantly expressing thus, everything that we have depended on for meaning of who we are that we based on something outside ourselves begins to dissolve.

As we know, our darkness and our pain leads us to our light. It's in our commitment to move through our darkness and our deepest fears, that the layers of separation begin to dissolve. As we enter this initiation, we become focused on one thing, which is our commitment to our Light, expressing of the One consciousness in the most aligned way possible. When we fall short of that, we allow ourselves to return to the truth by entering into forgiveness, and continue to pursue our highest state of unity consciousness. In this state, there's no judgment, only presence and awareness of what state you're reflecting. We recognize that if we cannot be in alignment with the highest vibration of Light; unconditional love, unconditional mercy, compassion, joy, peace, there must be some veil of separation that is conditioning our ability to be in union with Oneness. We realize that in our conditioned state of ego, we distance ourselves from experiencing this oneness reality. Yet, when we aren't in the love, or able to default to the state of Love in union, then we take the time to process, what is arising within us, because this is the unresolved conditioned experience that has separated us from the state of oneness, to begin with Oneness.

Now, we understand that this is a process, although there are some beings that have been able to transcend and stabilize in Unity consciousness effortlessly. This is usually the terrain of masters and enlightened ones that have been graced, in this way. For most of us, it's a process of transformation over this lifetime and many others, that results with us stepping into full realization of our being. However, I feel through the shift in consciousness of the Feminine that our planet is undergoing at this time, more and more of us are able to sincerely open up to embody and live in unity consciousness, through the grace of the Feminine Spirit.

Now, as we continue to face our darkness, and release the attachments to outside things, roles or even our own victimization mentality, we can still enjoy the fruits of the outer world and all of its creative endeavors. The difference is that we don't get attached, or derive meaning for ourselves from that which we engage in. In other words, we may be a wonderful cook, or an excellent lawyer, but we do not place our value on our accomplishment, or on our relationships. We experience our sense of value from within our light. Furthermore, we always return to realize that the challenges we may be facing; mentally, physically, or emotionally, are rooted in our psyche, therefore, we always have the opportunity to address it on the inner levels and allow a new creation to emerge.

By facing our deepest darkness, we're able to completely surrender the final illusion that separates us from Truth, the illusion of separation itself. By our willingness to enter into this 4th Sacred Initiation, we can shift our paradigm from one of suffering to one of being consumed by the deepest mystery of all, the Feminine Herself. We finally realize that She has never left us, it's us, that have left Her state of consciousness. It's that us, that have forgotten Her "unifying light in creation"[2]. It's us that have turned away.

Illusion of Separation / Shadow of abandonment

In our illusion of separation, we experience the other side which is the shadow of abandonment. No one escapes it, we all have this programming. Many of us attribute this deep pain to our early caretakers, parents, etc. However, this is a deep wound in our soul that we're all born with as we come into existence and 'forget' that we are an expression of the Oneness consciousness.

As a soul, we come in simultaneously as our egoic nature starts creating a separate identity. This separate identity passed on from generation to generation in our collective disconnection from spirit, creates the space for the wound of abandonment. We inevitably feel a deep level of abandonment that is inherent in the formation of our identity. The formation of our egoic nature and, therefore, our separate identity, is a necessary process to survive and experience life here on this planet. However, it also requires us to forget our Truth, only to start the journey of reclaiming it before we die. I believe that we're on the precipice of a paradigm shift in our level of consciousness on the planet, in which we will not experience the complete veiling of separation, as we have been for thousands of years. The consciousness on the planet is awakening us to our true wholeness; fully divine and fully human. That is the great transformation of the Feminine, to realization of the light within matter. I believe that even though we must still experience some separation in the creation of our egoic nature and individual self, we will be able to retain some of our consciousness of truth of our divinity. Nonetheless, this is the process we're engaging through these sacred initiations of the Feminine. The work begins with us.

However, most of us remember as children that we felt still the wonder and the joy of oneness, until it slowly starts to fade and we experience the abandonment of the love in our lives, mostly through having caretakers or parents that were not awakened to limitless love themselves. How can one love unconditionally, if we're still unconscious to that level of consciousness? Even though most parent and caretakers might have done the best they could, they have also been functioning from the collective wound of separation and abandonment within themselves, unable to connect and merge with the source within. Naturally, it's impossible to imprint this state of limitless love in others, if we don't have the imprint ourselves.

Moreover, throughout our evolution in childhood and the progression of our egoic nature, we have further separated from our divinity through our cultural patterns and family norms that were demonstrated and taught to us. The outward focus required from in the ego's development, further disconnects us from our source within. We may have learned what we needed to say, be and do to receive the love that we experienced as being absent. Our egoic nature determines what we like, what we don't like, what we should do and what we do not want to do in accordance with the rewards, safety and ultimately love that we receive in accordance. This turning outward of ourselves is crucial for the development of the ego and our 'identity'. This turning outward into illusion, magnifies the separation paradigm of being alone, not being supported and the overall abandonment wound that is so painful. Nevertheless, the fact is that, that love, the limitless, unconditional love that our souls yearn for, could never be fully satisfied from another, because it is within you.

DEATH AS A CYCLE OF LIFE

We must remember that what's dying is the illusion that our egos have been operating under. Nonetheless, it feels real, because when we're in illusion, we cannot see the other side of reality. This requires our blind trust into the space of 'not knowing'. Not knowing becomes the bridge for something new to be birthed. We cannot know it before we have experienced it.

We might have a conceptual idea of what we're talking about; I may say to you the sun looks like this and feels like this, but until you see the sun you have really no idea, and much less a visceral experience of it, until you feel it in your body. If I say the sun warms your body, but you've never had your body warmed, you will not know what that is, even if I describe that it feels like it hugs you, and feels safe, you will still not know until you experience it. This phenomenon is the same when we are talking about an awakened state of consciousness. You really don't know how it feels to be loved fully and experience the union of your Light, until you have died to your old reality, and experienced fully in your being.

Death is a natural part of life, and yet the perfected soul, our true Essence, is eternal. But, of course, we don't really know what that means, unless we have experienced being in union with the eternal level of our consciousness. When we enter this level of union, many of us have closed this root center due to the illusion of being in separation. Furthermore, this root center is also closed due to our fear of sexual trauma and sexual abuse that women have experienced personally and collectively. And even most spiritual practices preference the higher centers, disregarding the lower centers as something less valuable. However, this root gateway allows us to anchor in our Mother Earth which sources us physically on this plane. If left unaddressed, it prevents us from greater union with Oneness and disconnects us from our divine nature. Essentially, it keeps us stuck in the original wound of being a separate entity acquired during our initial experience of incarnation, in the womb. We stay in the illusion of feeling separate, perpetuating the feeling of lack of safety in our form, if we resist the power of this root gateway.

There has been great abuse with this root gateway; we have collectively chosen to close it in an attempt to stay safe and protect ourselves from further sexual and physical abuse. Of course, the paradox is that closing off this gateway, also closes off these other factors I mentioned above of feeling safe, and experiencing the union with Oneness consciousness in a complete way. It closes the door to our ability to fully merge with the eternal. This root center houses our deepest fears, terrors, and even traumas of being separate, lost and unprotected. While it's true that all three of these centers, from the solar to the root can be blocked with fear, it's here, in this root center, that we hold the cumulative patterns of our deepest fears, beginning with our initial fear of separation, acquired in the womb, along with the accumulated survival fears of being in a feminine form. Our fear of abandonment, being alone, ostracized, and separated, gathers at this point of the root, causing dysfunction and constrictions in our physical structures of the perineum, the pelvic floor, the cervix and any of the muscular structure in this area, contributing to dysfunctions in our reproductive system, as well.

During my near-death experience, I went through the dark space that houses our fears and our horrors; this place is also known as the dark astral field, where we can experience heaven, as well as hell. I continued to move through this place and into the light Essence of Oneness, God, and Unity consciousness. However, upon my return, I've always felt a deep sense of fear and terror in my physical body. I realized my root gateway was still connected with this Astral level of darkness, allowing for the frequencies of fear and terror to resonate here. What I realize is that when we die, we either move through this field, or are held in this field, depending on our perception of death itself. If we die in fear and trauma, then we may have a part of our soul still connected to this place. This is why many spiritual traditions, from the Sufi's to the Tibetan's insist on breaking through the illusion of death itself, in this lifetime, by dissolving the perceptual realities of the ego. However, even though I didn't die, I still entered that state of possible death in a panic and great fear, and when I returned, the opening to this dimension remained, allowing the energetic resonance of great fear and terror, which further contributed to the lack of safety in my body.

I believe this is the level of panic and terror that many women, and ancestors have died in, therefore, leaving this doorway open to a collective field of fear and terror. As we heal our own abandonment separation wound, we're also able to continue to heal the collective abandonment/separation wound of the Feminine, in all those that have come before us, and that are still on the planet. Our work on this level is critical in bringing the light and spiritual release to these souls that haven't died in peace. To release them from this state of confinement on the astral level can be done by our intention and prayers that I've included in chapter 10, on 'Healing the Ancestors'. This is part of releasing the collective negative energies of fear and darkness that accumulates on this astral energetic level around the planet.

I think it's important to see this level of collective darkness, and realize it's there, so that we're aware that this veil of fear and illusion is operating and blocking our ability to access our divine nature of Light and Oneness. Freeing ourselves from this veil in our root gateway, also frees us from the collective planetary veil of darkness, fear, terror, and horror that exists.

Serena's Case #3

I worked on Serena when she was laid out from a leg injury, where she was immobilized for six weeks of healing. The injury had been on her right leg, although her whole body was affected due to the severe fall that preceded the injury. On this particular day, about eight weeks after her injury, I began to do healing through the Soma Presence work. She reported that her right leg was in excruciating pain and that she hadn't been feeling well since the day before. She mentioned that the previous day she had to confront the unwanted situation of facing the person that had been living rent free at her rented apartment for years. Until now, she hadn't had the courage to make them move, and had been absorbing the financial burden for them. This pattern of taking care of others and feeling emotionally, physically, and otherwise responsible for them, was a common and strong pattern in her life, keeping her from speaking her truth out of fear of causing suffering in others.

As I worked on her leg, guiding her to move deeper into her subtle bodies of heart and soul, she began to see herself as a baby in her mother's womb, and then she remembered that her mother, at the time of giving birth, had faced a great tragedy in her delivery, which resulted in her right leg being moved out of socket to progress the delivery. She was told that her mother was between life and death, feeling excruciating pain and fear as she endured this procedure during the contractions with no anesthetic relieve. She realized that she could feel the trauma that her mother experienced, while she was still in her mother's womb, and she could feel the deep fear and terror that her mother was feeling. However, she'd merged with this emotional reality, feeling it as her own pain, rather than her mother's fear and pain. Furthermore, she also felt responsible for her mothers' suffering because it was related to her birth, leaving her with an uncomfortable sense of being responsible for someone life. In her mind, she had internalized this trauma as her life and her expression was at the cost of someone else living or dying, and even though her mother lived, it caused her great pain and suffering. Therefore, she carried the burden of knowing this and unconsciously compensated by withholding her true expression, if it meant causing someone else pain and suffering.

Interestingly enough, her mother didn't die, but yet carried the scar of having entered the portal of death as a separation, along with fear, and terror that's associated with the tragedy itself. This astral plane was opened for Serena also, because as an unborn child, she was merged with her mother's consciousness, not really delineating what was her truth, and what was her mother's consciousness. When we're in the womb, our mothers' consciousness becomes our own consciousness and our experience of reality. Therefore, her mother, even though she didn't die in terror, still carried the fear and terror of moving through that dark astral field. And interestingly enough, the leg that the mother was tragically affected was the right leg, the same as Serena's injury, that triggered all of these memories to surface. Serena realized that she'd lived all of her life feeling guilty and responsible for others, and afraid of causing others to suffer and even die. Her unconscious fear caused her to stay in relationships that didn't honor herself, and prevented her from speaking her truth, most of the time. She deeply felt that if she spoke her truth, others might be so upset, that it may cause them to die. As irrational as that may sound, I for one can tell you that there are many people walking around with this underlying conditioning, which inadvertently causes great levels of co-dependency to others, as well as co-dependency to substances or situations, that make this death like pain manageable.

Serena also realized that her loyalty to others, in spite of her own wellbeing, had been derived from this pattern as well. The inherent guilt that controlled her kept her loyal to everyone outside of herself. This caused deep pain within her own heart and soul, a deep level of betrayal to herself. When she could unravel and bring consciousness to this deep unresolved memory that was still operating in her being, she could realign herself to the Truth of her being, the Light that she is. She realized that she wasn't and isn't responsible for anyone's else's life, other than carrying out and honoring of her own, and that all she could be aligned to is her Light, allowing it to further dissolve the places within her of fear and terror of separation, the places that were doubting her worthiness, her desire to live for herself, her guilt, her over-responsibility, her illusion of inadequacy, and guilt. Furthermore, she was able to restore that unborn, newly born child to her inner Light which had been severed, in consciousness, by the extreme traumatic experience her mother was experiencing. And in recalibrating her Light and Truth within herself as an unborn and newly born child, she then transmitted the light to her mother's spirit, which in turn allowed her to also heal her mother's soul, which was still caught in the tragic trauma of that moment.

As we heal our soul trauma of the fear and terror associated with the illusion of separation, we are able to also stand in our light, expand our light, and shift the collective consciousness of this astral accumulation of fear, terror and tragedy, for all living souls. This process along with our ability to anchor into this earthly plane all reflect in our root gateway.

4ᵀᴴ SACRED INITIATION OF CONSCIOUS FEMININE UNION

CONSCIOUS REFLECTION

CONSCIOUS FEMININE UNION

Take a few minutes to reflect on the principles of the 4th Sacred Initiation. How do those concepts feel in your body? What aspects stuck with you? What does your heart want to explore?

_____

_____

_____

_____

_____

_____

_____

_____

_____

_____

_____

_____

_____

_____

_____

_____

_____

Now, let's reflect on your bodies root gateway, in the area specifically of the perineum. Bring your awareness there, and take a few breaths, just taking the time to feel; physically, and emotionally. Simultaneously, bring your awareness to your heart, staying connected to both places; root gateway, and heart gateway. Take some deep breaths, just being and noticing. Notice your feelings of being alone, separate, perhaps lacking support or feeling unsafe in general. Call these feelings up to your attention and let yourself reflect and write about these feelings, anything you have always wanted to say. Say it now to the Great Mother of the Universe, She is here listening.

_____

_____

_____

_____

_____

_____

_____

_____

_____

_____

_____

_____

_____

ACTIVATING FEMININE UNIFYING LIGHT

READ THESE INSTRUCTIONS THOROUGHLY BEFORE ENGAGING IN THE ACTIVITY.

1. To engage in *Conscious Feminine Movement,* wear comfortable clothing and find yourself a space on the floor where you have room to move as you please.

2. There's a unifying light of the Feminine that is alive in your body. It's not only alive, but it's what gives you life. This light is the primordial Light in your being, sourced from Oneness (Great Mother), Creator of the Universe.

3. You can activate this Unifying Light of the Feminine through your breath. So, let yourself breathe, notice your breath, and how your body rises and falls in response to it.

4. With each breath, you will see the Unifying Light of the Feminine, activating each and every cell, becoming alive in your body, energizing you, nourishing you and expanding through your whole physical form.

5. As you continue to breathe, you will close your eyes and start to move, stretch, rock, vibrate and follow the signals of your Light in how it wants to move your body. It may be fast, it may be slow, it may be stretches, or rocking, or anything at all. The only thing you have to do is stay connected with your breath, feel the light moving you and your body from within as you breathe.

6. As you continue to do this, you will feel the Unifying Light of the Feminine all throughout your body and you will experience your body of Light, moving, activating, nourishing, loving and bringing you into bliss. This is what you can count on, depend on and lean on. Continue this practice for about 20-60 minutes. Afterwards, end in gratitude and journal your experience.

SURRENDER INTO THE WOMB OF THE GREAT MOTHER
(THERE YOU ARE ONE WITH ALL)

PLEASE DO THIS PROCESS AFTER THE PREVIOUS TWO, IN ORDER TO RECEIVE MAXIMUM BENEFIT.

1. Take a few minutes to center yourself and breathe into your sacral womb at least 9-27 times. As you breathe into your sacral womb allow all sides of your lower pelvic cavity to expand in all directions, forward, backward and sideways. Inhaling, receiving, exhaling, releasing and letting yourself merge with the Earth beneath you.

2. Begin to visualize your sacral womb and lower pelvic area as a great big balloon carrying the light of your being and with each breath it expands even more.

3. As you allow your pelvic region to expand, notice your whole body releasing and surrendering slowly and deeply into the container of the Great Mother all around you.

4. The Great Mother has given birth to you and has sustained you on this plane with life force, and with everything that you need to survive and evolve. She is the invisible field of Love that is always there, watching you, listening to you, and synchronizing your soul's needs at every moment. The Great Mother is holding you with Love; She is omnipotent and omniscient and carries the quantum field that all wisdom is stored. She is the matrix that sustains your every breath, every thought, every impulse; every inspiration comes from Her.

5. You are not separate from Her. She is not separate from you. You can access this place of Oneness, in Her Cosmic Womb and allow your Self to surrender completely and restore your vitality, rest in Her womb.

6. As you continue breathing, let yourself surrender even more, letting all your fears, and preoccupations dissolve into Her field of Love.

7. How does it feel to be completely surrendered? Where you know that you are being taken care of on all levels and that every step of your path is lined with Love and caring from the Great Mother.

8. Take in another breath and feel the trust, the bridge that allows you to surrender deeper into Her womb, Her field of Love. This is the Universe you live in, even if you can't understand everything that happens in your life, you can begin to trust and feel the matrix of Love that surrounds you.

9. How does it feel to trust and surrender? That there is this invisible field of Love of the Great Mother, rest with each breath you take. There is nothing to do but recharge in Her womb. Let yourself continue breathing here for about 15-20 minutes, allowing your nervous system to shift from sympathetic to para-sympathetic, where you are able to return to the innate rhythm of the Universe.

10
5th *Sacred Initiation of*
Conscious Feminine
Transcendence/Inner Marriage

ANTHROPOS REVISITED

Anthropos is the word for human being, but not just any human, it's rich meaning consists of the integration of Feminine and Masculine (yin and yang) within that transcends into a new creation of human, one that is fully divine and fully human. In Jungian interpretation, it means to integrate the opposites of the Feminine and Masculine principles of our psyche, thus actuating our wholeness. This, as we recall from the beginning chapters, is the meaning of the complete human being, Anthropos.

It's the integration of these two fields within us, feminine and masculine, that causes a fundamental shift into a third level of consciousness, the trinity, which I spoke about in chapter two. This trinity refers to the unitive level of Oneness that can be experienced when we unite these two forces within us and expand our consciousness to a new level of awareness, the Essential Self.

As we come into our final initiations of anchoring and reclaiming the Feminine, we realize a level of integration where the Feminine within us has been activated. This unifying light of the Feminine is in essence the immanence that exists within every form; it's the sacredness in our being, and thus all of creation. As we move into this 5th Sacred Initiation, we have an opportunity to merge the Feminine with our Masculine, and transcend our limited expression of any of these two separately, thus creating a new creation, a new consciousness, and a new expression of ourselves that is rooted in Essence, in Oneness, in wholeness.

This 5th Sacred Initiation of Conscious Feminine Transcendence offers a path to the realization of our wholeness, leading us from the duality, into the secret of the trinity consciousness. Stopping with the 4th Sacred Initiation of the Feminine only, wouldn't allow us to realize our true potential as human beings. We need to go further into union with Oneness and Source. This is the sacred marriage your Soul has incarnated for. Adam Gainsburg defines sacred marriage as, "The unifying of opposites. 'Sacred' implies alignment with larger forces including time, cosmos and evolutionary urges and 'Marriage' implies an alchemical transformation into something 'new', which isn't possible through a simple combining of the parts."[1]

UNRAVELING OUR IMPRISONED MASCULINE

What is the Masculine and how do we experience this force within us? We may have a conceptual understanding of what the Masculine is, and I know we covered it in Chapter 2, but let's take a deeper look at how the masculine manifests within us. As I mentioned previously, for us to experience our greatest potential as Human Beings, it's not enough to stop at reclaiming our Feminine Essence, we also need to heal the wounds of the Masculine within, which reflect in our outward expression and manifestation of our inner power. One without the other is incomplete and CFM (*Conscious Feminine Medicine*™) bridges these two aspects of our being to move into wholeness and transcendence.

Because of the trauma that we've lived in, the advent of the patriarchy culture, the trauma that most women have experienced has created deep seated wounds of the Masculine. As a result of these wounds, an internal disconnection from our own masculine (yang) energy has occurred. Disconnection from our inner masculine may manifest as a deep feeling of being unsupported by life itself, feeling disconnected from our vitality, feeling disempowered, alone, and incapable of succeeding. However, there may also be an over compensation of using this yang energy excessively and without pause, which is also a dysregulation our masculine energy. This pattern may manifest as exhausting our vitality and running on empty, which seems to be the norm in our modern western culture. Our sacred masculine shows up and helps us actuate in the world. It empowers us to do, to achieve, to produce, to succeed on the outer, and to 'feel' productive and equipped (enough) to be productive. Our Masculine is closely related to our relationship with accomplishing and achieving in the outer world, as well as expressing our true selves, our uniqueness, and our creativeness.

This internal disconnection of our own yang masculine energy may not be obvious to ourselves, but to survive our pain and suffering, many layers of fear and disconnection have buffered us against the perceived threats of the distorted masculine shadow. These patterns within us continue to disconnect us from our own source of masculine (yang) energy.

Intellectually, we may know that not all men pose a threat, of course, nor do they represent the ideology of a misogynist, sexist culture we live in. However, as women, because of the deep level of insecurity and lack of safety that we been assaulted with, there is a rejection of this collective distorted masculine shadow that we must face and come to peace with. This deep rejection of the masculine shadow, which is usually unconscious, originates from our own deep need to survive.

To survive in a distorted masculine world, our first instinct has been to protect ourselves from what we perceive as unsafe. Throughout history, men as a whole have played out this distorted masculine shadow creating a world that presents a misogynistic, sexist, abusive, threatening and unsafe environment for women. This collective distorted pattern has imprinted in our psyches a link between all men and the distorted masculine shadow, causing an unconscious need to reject men to feel safe. Furthermore, the incessant infiltration of the masculine God associated with shaming and punishing, we perpetuate the unconscious rejection of men or the masculine principle. However, this pattern also affects our own ability to embrace our masculine within.

It isn't that we're rejecting men on the outer, many of us love men and enjoy being heterosexual. However, unconsciously, because men have been the greatest vehicle for the distorted shadow of the masculine, there's a place within our psyches where we're in conflict with men as a whole and more importantly with the masculine energy. Until we've made this conscious and worked it out, this inner conflict may show up as rejection with the 'male GOD', masculine power, men in general, conflict and power struggles in our relationships. etc. Furthermore, this imprint affects our inner relationship with our masculine yang energy, as it relates to our ability to accomplish, to do things, to stand in our truth, to act, and the confidence level behind all these relationships.

I recently did a somatic healing, Soma Presencing, that accurately personified how we internalize the masculine wound within ourselves as women through these various layers of fear, blaming, and judgment upon ourselves. Below is the unwinding of this mapping of her (patient's) experience during the healing session. Please keep in mind these statements represent the patient's perceptual reality and not necessarily the Truth of who she is.

THE MASCULINE WOUND MAPPING:

- It began with the feelings of disappointment, deep disappointment in herself.

- The disappointment led to uncover feelings of inadequacy and failure. She felt she was a failure in life and had failed others.

- The failure led to hopelessness in which she felt alone and unable to change anything in her life. She felt deep sadness and hopelessness, she felt she couldn't be saved from this feeling and she felt abandoned by Life, by Source itself.

- From this place, she saw the image of a Male God, the same God she would pray to when she was little and receive no response, and her conclusion was that 'she didn't receive a response because He (God) didn't want to give her what she wanted'.

- She felt deep disillusion, rejection, and unworthiness from the male God that wouldn't answer her prayers.

- She believed that the fact that she wasn't getting what she asked for over the years, from the male God meant that she wasn't good enough, and that there was something wrong with her. She made herself wrong, because she knew it couldn't be the male God that was wrong.

- She then saw how she began to reject the male God, not wanting to hear anything about the male God, because it would remind her of her rejection and her unworthiness. The male God now started to represent unworthiness to her.

- She felt the hatred for the male God and the anger she felt because of how alone it made her feel, especially because everyone was still praying to this male God. This in turn made her feel even more ostracized and rejected, because she felt not understood by anyone, she felt different and made herself feel even more wrong.

- Due to her anger, hatred, and ultimately deep pain and rejection underneath that, she closed off her ability to receive masculine energy because of the perception and meaning she gave her experience with the male God. The male God and the masculine was perceived as something that made her feel rejected, wrong and unworthy, primarily from her personal interpretation of not having her prayers answered, not being seen, heard, and responded to. From this particular experience, she concluded (quite erroneously that she wasn't important and that she wasn't even worthy of divine intervention. She concluded that she'd been forgotten and that it was from being wrong is some way, or at least not being 'good enough' to be responded to). However, this was one experience that was still unresolved in her psyche, that surfaced in relation to the conflict of the masculine wounding. In addition, it's important to know that just like this one experience, we carry many layers of this conflictive masculine wounding within that derive from the culture that we live in.

Once she was able to see how her perception of the male God and more importantly, her conclusion about herself being wrong or unworthy, she could start to clear these painful conditioning patterns and restore the vitality of her inner masculine. Reclaiming this vitality supported her, allowed her to feel included in Love, rather than excluded. Furthermore, it opened up the creative flow to be expressed outwardly in the world and restored her sense of her ability to act in the world.

By working all the way through this masculine wounding pattern, she was able to see the origin of her 'failure' feelings within and help dissolve her lifelong feelings of disappointment, unworthiness and inadequacy related to the conflict of her perception of the masculine. More importantly, she could then also begin the reclaiming of her masculine energy and her relationship with power. Reclaiming her own masculine dissolved her distortion of the male God, opening her up to receive the true essence of the masculine male Essence, Father God, as a supportive masculine yang energy from Source that reconnected her with the source of vitality, safety, and boundaries. She was able to shift the internal meaning of limits and boundaries from something painful and restrictive to something necessary and helpful as a containment. She could also feel a greater containment from the Universe and from Source, breaking through the pattern of 'having to do it all by myself', now she felt the Universe supporting her in many ways.

OUR MASCULINE WOUNDING

We've all been raised with a father God that is stern, judgmental, and shaming, whether we personally related to it or not, it's in our collective unconscious. As such, we carry this unconscious distorted masculine wounding within us. When we feel into this masculine wounding, instead of making male father God wrong, we have the tendency to make ourselves wrong first. Wherever we have inner feelings of failure, etc., we turn it back onto ourselves, because logic tells us that it possibly can't be God that is wrong. We've been indoctrinated to fear God, therefore, rendering ourselves powerless to speak our true opinion. The truth is that neither is wrong, nor you, nor God. The key to unwinding and dissolving these paradigms of masculine wounding within us, is to see that it is our perception that creates the meanings that we give things, and unfortunately we have all brought into the distorted masculine patterns, but do have the power to free ourselves and heal this masculine wounding.

In essence, we're wrong, but not for the reasons you think. We're wrong, because our perception is wrong. We as people aren't wrong, our self-worth isn't wrong, we aren't faulty, but the way we're seeing and interpreting it is wrong. The meaning we've given this situation is wrong. The meanings that we give these incidents become 'truths' that we live by, they become imprints, that becoming conditionings to our Soul. Our thoughts entrap us and control our behavior and trap us in a world of illusion.

Sure, that isn't to say that we aren't horrified at the things that have happened at the hands of the distorted masculine pattern. Of course, we are, and yet even in those events, we must be diligent about not blaming others, nor ourselves, and not judging ourselves with erroneous perceptual realities that create more illusion for us, trapping us in the world of meaning that isn't even true. The point is that we carry the divine light of truth within, and no one, nothing outside ourselves, can every take that away, regardless of the challenge that these events may contain. No one can make us feel wrong unless we allow ourselves the thought that says 'we're wrong' and then believe it as 'truth.' We have that choice.

Marriage of our Feminine and Masculine

In an ideal conscious world, we may have the opportunity to be nourished and supported by the conscious Feminine represented in our mothers or other motherly figure. When faced with disappointment, restrictions, boundaries or limitations of the masculine in our father figures, we would still receive the unconditional love we needed and avoid the self-blame and self-compromising effects that is assured with conditional love. The interplay of the masculine (father) and feminine (mother) in our young lives would naturally bounce off each other, never leaving us void of the experience of love.

However, most of us didn't have the unconditional love of either, the mother or the father, most of the generations before us have been unconscious to the reality of the unconditional love realm. Therefore, by not having it actualized in our caretakers, we weren't shown access to it. Most of our caretakers might have been there for us in many ways, but most feel unseen, and unsupported due to a deeper absence of Essence. This absence further blocked our ability to resolve feelings of disappointment, limitation and boundaries when encountered, resulting in deep wounding and repression of these in our body/mind. Furthermore, in order to cope, we may have turned those feelings against ourselves, judging ourselves and adding to the embedded layers of shame.

Furthermore, these repressed feelings, mainly due to the lack of nurturance when needed, are easily projected towards the masculine, reflecting on the men in our lives, manifesting as distrust of the masculine and even distrust of the feminine. These unresolved feelings are imprinted in the neuropathways that become our habituated patterns, defining our experience of life. Ultimately, we may go through life with a deep distrust or disappointment, or powerlessness feeling, due to these unresolved situations of the past.

For myself, the constant inability to receive what I asked for or wanted in my life created an unconscious perception of deep disappointment and failure. I created a pattern of believing that '*I don't get to have what I want*', '*I don't get to be happy*' - all equating to '*because I am unworthy*'. From a child's perspective, it's easy to understand how we go from '*I don't get what I want*', to self-blame of '*I must be unworthy*'.

Therefore, like so many other women I work with, the meaning that I gave the fact that I wasn't receiving what I asked for was that '*I was wrong*', and this became my unconscious filter through which I lived my life. And after working with thousands of women, I see this pattern very, very often. The default for women is '*I am not good enough*', or '*I am not worthy*', or '*I am to blame for this in one way or another*'.

Along with self-blame and failure, we also carry a great degree of unresolved anger, resentment, and even hatred towards that which we have learned is all powerful (masculine). We may question ourselves; why hasn't life been fair? Why do I have to suffer? Why isn't the Universe, God, Source or (fill in the blank) giving me what I need to end my suffering?

And so, underneath our self-blame, failure, inadequacy, shame, and/or powerlessness, there's resentment, anger, and hatred projected at what we feel restricted by, abandoned by, or what we blame for our suffering. These destructive feelings keep us stuck in perpetual blaming and furthermore keep our energy stuck in an unending game of illusion and defeat.

We free ourselves from this pattern when we face the wounds of the relationship between our Feminine and Masculine within and become conscious of the power struggle between them; this is where our power is energetically locked up. Our early experiences in childhood set up the playing field of our consciousness with exactly the perfect conditions for our soul to encounter the outer conditions needed to heal this wounding within us and, ultimately, have the perfect ground laid out, to embody our power. But yet, we may not see it that way; we may still feel that the painful restrictions were our enemies. Moreover, because the perfect scene is set up for our soul to evolve through our identity here on Earth, in this lifetime, there's no need to go back into past lives and resolve our issues there, even though I'm not denying that our challenges are limited to only this lifetime. We have to remember that there's only the present moment; the past, and the future are not here, they exist in our minds. The conditions we are experiencing in our life right now already contain within them the perfect scenario in form of: thought forms, perceptions, and dynamics, that is perfect for our soul's evolution. Therefore, by becoming conscious of our wounds and exploring our power struggles with our Feminine and Masculine, we can truly reclaim the power inherent in both of these aspects of consciousness; yin and yang.

To recap, if we don't have an experience of the strong Feminine mothering qualities modeled in our early childhood, it's challenging to integrate the masculine force within us. We need the Feminine within ourselves to offer the compassion, the safety and the ground we lean on to open up to the Masculine and the places of fear that it has produced. It's extremely challenging, given the survival issues and repression we've experienced as women, to open up to our Masculine energies unless we have healed the wounds of the Feminine, to a great degree. Therefore, it's why it's important to move through the previous Sacred Initiations of the Feminine before jumping into the inner marriage of the Feminine and Masculine. Once we are well established in our Feminine qualities, and have dissolved the self-blaming, shame, and self-rejection from our Feminine wounds, then we can safely address the all-powerful, magnificent expansion of our Masculine. Our deep connection with our Feminine creates the safety and trust, that facilitates the process of facing the wounds we associate most with the masculine, power, survival and death. The Feminine provides the ground and trust to face these directly.

UNWINDING THE RAGE OF HERSTORY

Unwinding the pain of being abandoned and feeling betrayed by the masculine, mainly in our fathers, our male God, etc., has created many layers of rage that haven't been safe to release. The rage from the powerlessness that has been in the collective history of women, dictated by a misogynist culture, isn't something that we can just brush over. The destabilization, the obliteration, ostracization, and persecution continues on in our cellular memory. Undoubtedly, women have received much abuse in the hands of the distorted masculine which is still operating in many parts of the world.

Treading these waters requires extreme amounts of compassion, patience and acceptance to acknowledge the painful places of disappointment, disillusion, grief, sadness, anger, rage, and even hatred. Recognizing and unraveling the anger and rage we may feel without direct causation, is a necessary part of the process if we want to clear the imprints we've taken on of the distorted masculine to heal and be open to our true masculine energy.

Due to our need for survival, there are many places where we have automatically taken blame for other people's irrational behaviors, which typically adds layers to the unconscious rage we contain. Unwinding this self-blame is a key factor in reclaiming our power. This isn't an easy task. It's important to be honest with ourselves and allow these feelings to surface, knowing that on one level they are thought forms that have come from our perceptions, and yes, while we have faced real danger, pain, and death as a gender, we also need to be able to release our hatred and rage of the past to move forward and let go of the story.

Allowing ourselves to feel the rage, bringing some healing to the injustice of the past, doesn't make these events in our lives, or in our ancestors lives any less real. Whether we physically have been raped, or whether we've just lived in fear of being raped, the rage of the past is real and must be faced. Releasing the emotional charge doesn't not change the facts that you have been wronged, and that it has been painful to live with.

However, if we stop with our pain, and move no further, then we stop our ability to heal from the past errors of man and we also become a slave to our pain and to our rage, perpetually creating more rage. When we live our lives this way, in continual feelings of rage, anger, and injustice, we perpetuate the wound and choose the pattern of injustice and suffering, rather than the amazing light within our being.

It's important to realize that moving on and healing doesn't lessen the reality of the injustice that we've lived through. What it does do though, is moves us past victimhood and into empowerment. We can admit this happened, and yet are so much more than that, and you choose to be more than that, rather than staying stuck in an experience of victimization. It's helpful to realize that the definition you give the experience is what keeps you stuck. Because truly the light that you are and what you carry in your heart cannot be changed by anyone else outside of you, regardless of what is done to your body. Your spirit continues, and we get to choose the magnificence of our spirit, over pain.

So, how do we begin to face the rage? We do so with honesty and compassion with ourselves. We begin by realizing the meaning we've attached to these experiences are completely subjective and are relative to your perceptual reality. Remember that everything is stored in our bodies, all the ancestral memories, and your past life memories that are relevant to your evolutionary process in this life time. By making space to hear these imprints of mental and emotional conditioning, we begin the process of transformation and dissolution of these veils.

This process is about freeing ourselves. Our brain can create new neuro pathways based on the environmental stimulus that it receives, proven by studies in neuroplasticity. We have the ability to choose. We can stay operating in the neuropathways that are based on our past experience of fear, victimization, and powerlessness, or we can choose to step into the present reality and reclaim our power. We can create new neuropathways that support a greater understanding of who we are, neuropathways that support our wholistic view of our Essential Self along with our Conditioned Self. We can open ourselves to the aliveness and goodness of unitive field of Oneness and open ourselves up to the unlimited ability of creation. We can let goodness be a factor, as well as leaving room for the unknown to be a factor and allow ourselves to envision a new reality, thus imprinting it in our neuropathways. Once we create new neuropathways and continue to support that reality within us, our brain dissolves our old neuropathways, thus releasing the old pain with it. Our bodies support our healing, along with these shifts that are created in our brain. All we have to do is be willing to release our anger, moving beyond the paradigm of right and wrong and free ourselves from the pain of the past. We don't need to hold on to the anger to justify our pain. Instead, we can hear our pain, acknowledge it and witness it, and then be willing to heal our hearts and move beyond it. And even though anger and rage are difficult to walk away from, what we have to realize is that by staying justified in our anger and rage, we also stay stuck to the pain of the past. Anger requires us to acknowledge where we have been wronged, however, we have to release the expectation that others 'should' do right by us, or that they owe us something. Instead, we acknowledge our pain and our anger, and then choose to let go of our expectation of others, and to free ourselves from the past. We have to be willing to let go of the identification of victimization fully.

EMBODYING THE BELOVED WITHIN

Without healing the masculine, we cannot embody the beloved within. We have to clear the conditioned pictures that are entwined with our version of the masculine, whether they are associated with the Father God, or our fathers, or any outer male version to open to the true power of the masculine within us. The Masculine is the complementary energy to the feminine, it provides us with structure, boundaries, outward movement of energy, and manifestation into creation. To feel the whole of ourselves, we need to unravel our wounding and limited experience of the Masculine from the true aspects of the masculine.

Embodying the beloved within is, in reality, what we do when we embrace the divine aspect of ourselves and this includes our wholeness, both feminine and masculine qualities. We fall into the sweet love of life itself, and we find our true beloved within. Uniting these two aspects of ourselves is like falling in love with the Essence of Love itself. Our life becomes magical, and we're able to see the mystery and light of Essence within every manifestation, every action, every challenge. We're in love with Love, that lives within ourselves. However, to embody the beloved, we have to transform the thoughts that are creating separation within these elements within ourselves. This union is the harmonizing of our left brain and right brain. It's the reclaiming of our power, and the transcendence beyond the Masculine and the feminine, into the unified field of wholeness where there's no separation.

Following are some simple embodied practices that will guide you in the process of reclaiming your Feminine and Masculine within, reclaiming the Beloved, thus initiating the Conscious Feminine Union within you.

CONSCIOUS REFLECTION WITH YOUR MASCULINE WOUND

Take a few minutes of reflection and consider how you feel about these themes. Before beginning, sit down in a quiet area and connect with your heart, breathing for a few minutes. As you read these questions below, see which question feels more charged, or which one elicits a response in your body or emotional field, then take a few minutes to write about it and become aware of the varying aspect of your masculine wound. You can come back and write about a few of these themes, before moving on to the rest of the 5th Initiation to bring this wounding into your conscious awareness.

How do you feel about having power?

How do you feel about the men in your life?

How do you feel about Father God?

Do you ever feel like you are forsaken by Father God?

How do you feel about your own vitality?

Do you ever feel like you are running on empty?

What is your relationship with disappointment?

How do you relate to your ability to create?

How do you relate to your ability to manifest in the world?

How do you relate to your ability to achieve?

How do you relate to your ability to be successful?

How do you feel about your ability to realize your dreams?

Do you hold yourself back from saying or acting because you judge yourself as too strong, too forceful etc.?

How much of the time do you feel anger, resentment, disillusioned?

Did you grow up with a male father figure? If so, what were your feelings about this male father figure?

How did you reconcile the suffering in the world with the male father God figure?

UNWINDING THE RAGE OF HERSTORY

1. Sit quietly with a journal nearby, slow down, become present, and breathe.

2. As you bring your awareness to your inner world, let's reflect on your relationship with anger; how you experience anger, when it shows up, and how it shows up. Choose a recent moment or look at the pattern of how you experience anger in your life. Take some moments to feel the sensations in your body of perhaps when you have felt undermined, unheard, dismissed, or any other situation that is related to feelings of being mistreated, or undervalued because of your gender. Allow yourself to feel the sensations of anger arising as you breathe and allow. Just choose **one** situation in this process and begin to feel it cellularly, the sensations related to what you call anger.

3. Continue to feel these sensations of anger in your body. Let yourself feel the anger with total acceptance and without any judgement or shame. Let yourself feel all the energy of the anger as if it was a force that has been suppressed and bound up in your body, without being able to express itself. Continue to breathe as you feel the power of the anger.

4. Feel the energy of the anger, this intense energy that wants to move outward and upward. While you breathe into it, seeing it moving like millions of energy cells moving in your body, feel it moving, feel it shifting, giving it some space. Now, add the sound SHHHHH with each exhale, breathe in and exhale SHHHHH, breathe in and exhale SHHHHH. Slowly continue this breathing as it allows the movement and release of this powerful bound up energy in your body.

5. Continue with the SHHHH sound with each exhale, however, make sure you're being gentle with yourself and staying connected to your inner sensations. Do at least 10 minutes here or until you feel much more space and release in your body. Can continue for 10, 20 or 30 minutes.

6. Now, let yourself feel what's under the anger, the part of you that the anger had been protecting all these years. Perhaps there is sadness, grief, hurt, aloneness, hopelessness, or just a deep sense of space and vulnerability. No need to label it, just be with the sensations of that vulnerability. Breathe 10 times.

7. Meet these sensations and feelings in your body with Love, through each breath, you're meeting them with Love, no shame, no judgements, no story, just Love. Know that you can count on yourself and on this all-encompassing

field of Love, that has always been here. You no longer are at the mercy of 'other' as you might have been in past situation. You also do not need the approval from 'others' and whether they acknowledge you or not, you can acknowledge and value you now. You can acknowledge your feelings, honor your truth and give yourself what you need. You can count on you and the Universal field of Love that is always with you and is you. You have access to this dimension of unconditional Love, and can stand in that truth now, no longer dependent on other's truth. Continue to breathe while you continue to recalibrate your heart, (middle womb) mind (upper womb) and womb (sacral womb) to the truth of Love, at least 10 breaths or more breaths here.

8. When you feel full and merged with the field of Love, then ask your heart if there is an action that is needed on your behalf now. Is there something for you to do for yourself, in response to this situation of anger? And allow the inspiration to reveal itself and rise up in your heart. Sometimes it may be immediate but sometimes it may come in later on as you journal, or as you contemplate other things in your life. Trust that you will know when and what there is for you to do.

9. To close, bow in gratitude and take a few minutes to journal your experience of this process, starting with the situation that had triggered the anger in you, what you felt as you faced your vulnerability to any wisdom or revelations about following steps. Sometimes, allowing these places to unwind without judgment is enough to heal these old wounds, no action may be required. And sometimes, we may have to assert our feelings, boundaries or even believe more in ourselves and take a risk in the outer world, by showing up confidently. Just listen to the wisdom that arises from your heart, rather than imposing your 'ideas' on what to do, if anything. Peace.

RECLAIMING OUR INNER FEMININE & MASCULINE

Take out your journal and let's begin with reflection on the following:

1. Choose a time where you allowed someone else to determine what was right for you, either because you were scared to make a wrong decision, or you felt not capable of choosing, or for any reason at all, you asked someone else to choose for you.

2. Write down your feelings around this situation, how you felt about it, and what the fear was. Was there a fear of disappointing anyone? Did you feel afraid of making a mistake, speaking your honest opinion or hurting other people's feelings? Write down your reasons.

3. How often do you find yourself resorting to someone's idea of what you should do, even in the simple things in life where you'd rather have them choose because of whatever reason it's uncomfortable for you to choose? Write down how often or what percentage of the time you find yourself doing this.

4. After writing about these things above, sit down and envision these situations in your heart. Let yourself see/feel these situations in your heart and the feelings that are underneath the reasons why you continue to give away your power this way. Let yourself feel these feelings, breathe into them and accept that this is how you have been feeling about yourself. No judgement, no blaming, no criticism, just pure acceptance and love for what you have been believing about yourself. Continue to breathe and accept these ideas of the past.

5. After letting yourself bring Radical LOVE to these unresolved feelings, let yourself make some choices and commitments to Self. Realize that you have a choice and you can choose to face these fears and other feelings about yourself, because in actuality, you're much more than that. You don't have to continue to choose the fear, you can choose the LOVE. You can choose the LOVE of loving yourself and daring to challenge these feelings of the past.

Are you believing the fear, the judgment of yourself? That you aren't good enough? That you're going to mess things up? That you really don't know, but someone else might? Here is your choice... Do you choose:

Fear above LOVING yourself

Inadequacy above LOVING yourself

Giving your power away above LOVING yourself.

Now, you have a conscious choice so, do you want to choose OTHER or LOVING yourself?

You have the choice, but here is the key; that if you choose yourself you will have to face the fear, the shame, the inadequacy, or take the chance that someone may be disappointed, or that you can make a mistake. The good news is that you'll also be supporting yourself, and choosing your side instead of the fear, shame, disappointment, disillusion that has made you give away your power in the past. These are all part of life and part of taking our power back. You have choice, and now that you see how you've been giving your own power away, you have the conscious choice to face those loud voices within yourself of the past, and reclaiming your power by choosing You. Now that you're choosing you, you're reclaiming the power to do your agency and your masculine power.

6. Now, let's continue to expand the Feminine power within you. Let yourself feel the love surrounding the past fears in your heart. Let the love of the Feminine expand in your heart and continue to alchemize the fears and inadequacy of the past by breathing and being present with all that is, within you.

7. Let yourself continue to expand the Love within your heart then towards your whole torso, your arms, your legs, your head, your neck, and your feet, all the way down into the Earth and all the way up out of your head.

8. Let yourself be supported by the Earth and the yin energies you are receiving from the Earth and let yourself receive the yang forces into the crown of your head. Notice that you're a vessel, between Heaven (yang) forces and Earth (yin) forces. And you carry both in your being. This is the power that fuels you, the LOVE of the Feminine, and the ability to express that power of agency of the masculine. The key is to support yourself and to say Yes to choosing you, rather than choosing other, this is the reclaiming of your Feminine and Masculine Power.

9. Continue to sit quietly and breathe in these forces within you, feeling how they support you. Realize these forces are you, and there is no separation. Let yourself integrate these for a few minutes. Thereafter, journal your experience.

YOU ARE THE VESSEL
DANCING WITH SOURCE

1. Take a deep breath and find a quiet place to dive into the mystery that you are.

2. Begin by feeling your Light body in your vessel. This is the Feminine Unifying Light of your soul, the expression of greater Source Consciousness. Breathe into your Light body (soul) and invite it to become present in your consciousness, so that you may feel the vibration of your Light body. Do this at least 9-27 times.

3. Now, as you continue to breathe, begin to feel the tingling and energizing aspect of your Light, your Essential nature, that is continuously moving through your physical body. Feel the tingling vibrational quality first in your hands, then in your feet, then throughout your limbs and finally, all throughout your complete torso and three wombs. Follow your body signals if it's different than what I am describing.

4. Let each breath expand your Light body. Breathe here 9-27 times or until you a strong vibrational quality to your Light body. Take your time, no hurry. Just breathing and allowing through your intention.

5. Once you feel the vibrational quality of your Light Body, allow it to continue expanding, until it meets with field of consciousness all around you, the field of Love that you're swimming in and that is always supporting you. Breathe and allow.

6. Now, realize that you're the vessel (soul and form) that is continuously expressing the eternal Consciousness of Oneness in a unique way. This consciousness comes through you, sustains you, and nourishes you as it animates you into your own individual expression. This is the dance between you and unmanifested consciousness. You're the expression of Source.

7. You're the dance, dancing with the beloved. The beloved is within, it's source consciousness, Herself, as She moves you, inspires you, and supports you. Envision yourself expressing and dancing this dance of life with Love and Joy. Continue breathing into this realization until you feel the dance within you with every breath.

11
Birthing the New Collective Story of the Feminine

After moving through the *Sacred Initiations of the Conscious Feminine*, we've loosened the collective wounds that have been in place for thousands of years. As we look forward, we have to ask ourselves, how do we integrate ourselves into the outer world of multiplicity, without losing our Self and our center, especially when we are immersed in an outer world that actively rejects the Sacred? The answer is simple, yet challenging. What I've noticed is that we have to be willing to be the keepers of the light, and pioneers, anchored in our unwavering commitment to Truth. Undoubtedly, we will be challenged in our expanded consciousness of light, but ultimately, we choose whether we want to continue to buy into the collective unconscious wounding or whether we dare to challenge the status quo and live by the inner guidance of Her mystery, Herself. Do we have the courage to be different, to go against the social collective flow of the egoic manifestations? This becomes the moment to moment challenge of walking in the world, but not being of it.

Do we have the ability to continue to dissolve into the mystery, awakening to more and more pure consciousness in our being, remaining unattached to the outer attraction of addictive social norms? Will we have the wisdom to lean on our inner unending foundation of Light, and remain disconnected from criticism and judgments of others that may not privy to our expanded experience of reality? It becomes a tall order, and we may fail many times over, however, the success isn't in whether we are able to continue in a linear progression, but rather in returning, day after day, to that unwavering commitment of being present to the ever spiraling evolutionary process of our soul, with all of its ups and downs. This is the threshold where our perceived failures become the very fuel for our walking, and our continued Self Realization process.

Mahatma Gandhi famously has said, "become the change you want to see in the world". Heeding this advice, we move in the trajectory towards awakening and begin to see that we're the medicine that we need. As we continue to hold this refined frequency of Light, we realize that it's our inner work of transformation that resurrects the sacred Feminine within ourselves and into our world. As we dissolve our separated egoic natures, we become the vessel for the Conscious Feminine to rise through us and disseminate these frequencies of greater consciousness, so greatly needed, into our world. When we perceive the outer world as a reflection of our inner world, as so many mystical teachings point to, then we remember that the only real work is within our own consciousness, that is what holds the key to the changes outside ourselves. This chapter details how critical and valid the awakening of yourself is to the whole and what it may look like to live consciously, until the outer world catches up to us. As Einstein remarked, "No problem can be solved with the same consciousness that created it". The inner evolution of our consciousness is crucial when shifting the condition of the world we live in.

What does the medicine of the Conscious Feminine look like as we continue day to day, in our world? How critical is it to recognize that we're the healers and the medicine? The transformation that we're all experiencing, and desiring is directly anchored in our own personal state of consciousness. This is the medicine that we all need; we are the medicine. The change happens through us. Let us take a deeper look at how the outer transformational changes take place through us, as the Conscious Feminine rises in each one of us.

CONSCIOUS FEMININE RISING

The Conscious Feminine is rising for all of us, even though our experience of Her, and how She shows up through each one of us will be unique to our soul. We each experience her individually, like varying colors of the rainbow. Of course, and for those that are aware and conscious of the transformational shift happening, will also experience Her radically different than those that are still caught in the illusory nature of survival.

Our evolutionary process doesn't stop; we'll continue to grow into greater and greater levels of consciousness, however, when the Conscious Feminine is awakened within us, our foundation shifts. We begin to live from our Essential nature, rather than from a place of powerlessness and fear connected to our survival history. We continue our evolution, but there's a deeper trust, a knowing and a ground to lean on within. This is the shift that's possible when we're willing to dissolve the calcified conditionings that prevent us from living from our Essence. This is an experience of breaking away from the unconscious grip of fear, and feeling an expanded sense of freedom in our being. Deep in our cells we realize we're no longer a victim, because it's our egoic state of separation that is the victim. There is a sense of empowerment, and of safety that begins to grow within us, regardless of the physical circumstances we find ourselves in.

When we awaken to the Feminine, our foundation becomes one with Her, as we continue our engagement in the ongoing process of returning to the Essential sacred nature of Love, Power and Wisdom within. Even when we drift away temporarily, caught by some painful experience of the past, we return, because now the Feminine is conscious in your body, heart, and soul. It seems like the process of cultivation which we have explored through the sacred initiations takes on a life of its own, as if consciousness is now awakened to consciousness itself. Therefore, we don't necessarily put more effort into the cultivation, because it automatically is alive within us, and continues to awaken within us, overriding all the old paradigms of fear that were once our reality. Thus, our very foundation shifts from survival, fear and separation to union with mystery, Herself. And we recognize ourselves as the mystery, Herself. The Feminine is now woven into our consciousness, reflecting our inner world onto our outer world.

What is the result? Women initiating the change of the collective story of the Feminine, from one of oppression and suffering to one of empowerment in our Sacredness. As we dare to break the silence and honor the sacredness in our being, it honors us and we change the world. As the Dali Lama stated; "the western woman will save the world...", this is the rise of the Conscious Feminine within us and through us onto the world.

RETRIEVAL OF OUR FEMININE SOUL

By now, we see that what the rise of the Conscious Feminine is offering us is a door to restore and surrender our minds to our hearts and souls. It's an opening to balance the right brain of creativity with the over emphasized left brain of reasoning and logic. It offers us an opportunity to live life with mystery, allowing ourselves to be led, while we continue to strive forward. It's the shift from objectifying our bodies to living kinesthetically in our bodies, ultimately honoring all the realms, not just our physical reality. It's an opportunity to restore the radical Love, source of the Universe, and to restore the Love story that has been forgotten, rejected and refused.

The rise of the Conscious Feminine is essentially a process of retrieving our Feminine Soul personally and collectively. As I mentioned at the beginning of the book, we have lost our nature of Essence, the unseen, and mystery of our lives, and we have pretended that we, as human beings, are in control, as we live truly disconnected from the source of life. In our efforts for survival, we have shut down our hearts and souls, repressing the ability to hear wisdom. These are all the places where we have given our true power away, the power that comes from our sacredness and our divine dimension. And now, the opportunity is available to retrieve these lost parts of ourselves that we've left behind, our Feminine Soul. These are the very parts of our self that have posed a threat to the religious order and culture of our time, therefore, we hide them until they became so unconscious through the generations, that they have been forgotten. As a collective, we've become used to living without our Essence, and yet the yearning grows louder with each day.

Our Feminine Soul has been lost in our calcified beliefs of shame, fear, oppression and powerlessness, that make up our collective story or repression. This is the story we've all taken for granted, unless you've been chosen to awaken through the rise of the Conscious Feminine already. And as we heed to the call of the Feminine, there's a great shift that happens when we each start standing in our truth, supported by something greater than ourselves. We see and feel how the Universe is supporting us and become aware of the great synergy that moves us forward, in lightning speed. It's like the 100th monkey theory, where all it takes is a particular number of people awakening, for the whole world to move into a consciousness shift. We're reaching that critical mass, as each one of us awakens to Her voice in our hearts and recovers their Feminine Soul, or just soul, as many call Her.

While we continue to move towards critical mass, one Feminine Soul retrieval at a time, the conscious Feminine is present rising through us, using our vessel to become the voice, the honoring, the acknowledging and the action, with which She moves in the world. Through each and everyone one of us, women and men, we restore, resurrect, and retrieve the *collective Feminine Soul* of the planet and restore the foundation of radical Cosmic Love.

What does this look like? It looks like a field of Cosmic Love descending down from the Heavens, weaving itself through every manifestation on the Earth. It looks like the spiritualization of matter, realizing that in every form, there is light, there is soul, and there is no separation. This field of Cosmic Love is ever extinct, yet it cannot evolve in our world, unless we become conscious of it. We have a choice, as humans. And we can stay in our cages of darkness and deterioration, or we can break free and live in the Cosmic Love of Truth. This return of our spiritualization looks like Earth restoring itself, being honored, treated with respect as we listen to, rather than imposing our egoic desires upon it. It looks like us making economic, political and world decisions based on compassion, community and greater good, rather than on competition and greed. It looks like women being honored and on the same playing field as men. Women's physical bodies being respected and honored for their inherent sacredness, for their ability to give birth, for their mothering compassion, for their emotional intelligence, intuitiveness, and natural abilities to commune with the Divine dimension. It looks like a paradigm shift where we honor ourselves as sacred, along with all of creation, and thus the Sacred is restored as the primordial Essence of all.

Personally, giving birth to the new story of the Feminine within ourselves births the end of the story of separation, survival and fear. It's an awakening to the beauty and essence that we are. It motivates us towards connectedness, compassion, and generosity with all other beings in the world. It's a story where I recognize my dislikes or judgements of others, as an inner conflict with myself. It's a new story where we can live our lives experiencing the magic of the ourselves, rather than the dread of fear and separation. It's a story where we trust more in Love than we do in fear.

This is the possible paradigm shift as we retrieve the lost Feminine Soul within ourselves and within the world. This is the evolutionary course and the trajectory of consciousness that is awakening us, especially at this time. As we awaken to the possibility of it, we create space in which it can take place, within our psyche, therefore transforming the collective metamorphic field of humanity. As Richard Rudd states, "Energetically speaking, it is the feminine that carries the vision of synthesis and the masculine that will build it. This is the generalized blueprint of future society – it will be a world in which the masculine principle serves the feminine principle." [1]

COLLECTIVE FEMININE WOUND

As we review our history of the fall of the Feminine in the last 5000+ years, we're well aware of the atrocities that have been experienced by women on the planet. Unfortunately, these atrocities continue to happen around the world, minute to minute. However, there are some of us living in the west that are somewhat free of the direct consequence of these atrocities. Although we may still live in collective misogynist culture, our day to day psyche isn't concerned with immediate survival of death, due to our gender. The fact that we aren't necessarily in gender survival, gives us an edge in awakening, even though our memories and nervous systems might still feel the reverberations of the trauma of the past.

Nevertheless, we must realize that the effects of the repression of the Feminine still continues behind the scenes, lurking in institutions, behind closed doors, in the board rooms, in the hidden interactions between men and women, operating in full force in the unconsciousness. This is the ongoing resistance that the Feminine rising is met with. And as the Feminine consciousness continues to rise within each person, the resistance gets louder, evident in the hostile political climate we are experiencing in the United States and around the world.

The resistance can be a distraction, a force that lures us into anger, hatred, self-doubt, fear, and into a fighting mode. If we're caught by these distractions and pulled into further resistance, we continue to perpetuate that which we are intending to dissolve. What we resist persists, as the adage goes. So we must ask ourselves every moment and at every crossroad, what do we want to be in service to? When we're caught in the anger, hatred, or even disappointment, we're in service to something other than Love; we aren't expanding Love. We want to take our time, to anchor ourselves in Love, and from there, act in the world. If we resort to negative behavior, even if justified, then we've lost our ground and are no longer transmitting the Love into the world. It's important to take the time to work out the parts of ourselves that are in resistance, that are triggered into anger and other painful emotions. Then once we've worked out our reactions, we can then act out in the world, in service to Love. We can continue to seed from our Essential Self, rather than from our Conditioned Self, thus continuing to be an agent for the awakening of consciousness.

We know that these wounds continue to surface, as we continue to expand ourselves further. The wounds of the Feminine have survived atrocities throughout lifetimes. The collective wound has created a field that many of us feel and live from day to day, just by witnessing one woman being abused in anyway. This is because the pain of the ancestors is still living in the collective wound field and we can access that unconsciously and consciously through the unified field of Oneness, as we each face our own pain.

One women's pain is all of our pain, and many of us are sensitive to this collective field on a continuous basis. Many times, we don't know why something insignificant is felt so deeply in our hearts. There's a possibility that the particular issue that we're challenged with is also connected to similar issues that have been experienced by many women before us, and this imprint of pain is held in the collective field. Most of the wounds that we experience on a soul level is collective in nature, meaning that the women before us or our ancestors experienced them as well, and that the origin of this challenge isn't exclusive to us. Many of humanities wounds are collective in nature, it's just expressed in a particular form through us. Also, particular groups of people and cultures experience their own collective group wounds, which they may become loyal around, not realizing this loyalty keeps them bound to the suffering itself. When we're birthed into a family, the collective and group wounds of the ancestor lineages come through us and become part of the calcified conditioning that we hold in our psyche, until we awaken and become conscious of it, freeing ourselves and our ancestors.

Here, in this book, we've been working through the particular collective wounding that has shown up in women in the past 5000+ years, however, each particular group, whether it be gender specific, religion specific, culture specific, or any other identifying factor, will have collective wounding that is specific to that group of people. If you feel a kinship or even a belonging to a particular group, then it is possible that you will also unconsciously adopt their collective suffering patterns, until you become aware of them.

HEALING THE ANCESTORS

Therefore, it's no surprise that we can bring healing to our ancestors, when we're healing deep collective wounds of our lineage, that have been residing within us. I truly believe that our ancestors have been waiting for this great transformational time, where we can each come into full realization of ourselves and our divine natures within. We have an opportunity to free our ancestors, especially the women that have come before us, from the places of fear, tragedy and trauma where their consciousness may be stuck in.

When I had my near-death experience, I moved through a space that was dark, where there were many entities moving around trying to scare me and frighten me. This place, an aspect of the astral realm, holds what we refer to as heaven and hell, however, I was able to continue to move through and experience the Light of Oneness. This place of darkness that I traveled through has been reported in many near death experiences and tracked by many. The astral realm is a place where our personal and collective fears gather and exist, they become personified and are seen as entities and other phenomenon. This is the collective field that we also refer to darkness, and evil. According to the Sufi's, the state of consciousness that we die in, we may possibly become trapped in, finding it harder to navigate through the denser levels of consciousness into the higher realms. Thus, the Sufi saying, 'die before you die', means learning how to move through those denser layers of consciousness now, while still alive, to ascend into union with the purest level of light. This points to the process of purification of our egoic states of separation while we're alive, helping us to experience a 'death' to these states and awaken in the truth. Also, in many spiritual traditions, we pray for the souls of our loved ones upon their death to help them through the denser states of consciousness, and help them become closer to Divine consciousness. Helping our ancestors move through various levels of the 'barzak' (veils of separation) upon death is something that we can do now, once we reach these levels ourselves in this lifetime.

While it's true that once we clear our soul level wounds, we're also clearing these wounds for our ancestors, I also believe that we can directly impact the state of consciousness that our ancestors are experiencing in their soul, directly. Those women in our lineages, that have died in tragedy, in fear and in pain, living through the horrors of the past 5000 years, may be waiting for our awakening to be liberated themselves.

Sometimes we can feel some of our ancestors, waiting around for us to 'get something' and change the course of our evolution, not just for ourselves, but for them and for all the generations that come from us. They say that living in this body, at this time, on Earth, is a great privilege at this time of the flowering of divine consciousness on the planet. The truth is that at the unified consciousness level, there is no time, everything is happening now, so our awakening is their awakening. Sometimes, when I do a healing through the Soma Presence work, myself and the patient can feel their ancestor waiting for them to break through a particular pattern, as if the ancestors were waiting for the present family member to break the spell of the whole family, through this one moment of choice. Many of us think our ancestors are guiding us, and many might be, but there are many that have come before us that are waiting for us to awaken to the higher levels of consciousness so that we can all be free.

When we each retrieve an aspect of our Feminine soul that has been lost and hidden within ourselves, if it's a lineage wound, then we're also returning that aspect of the soul essence to the ancestors, that also experienced that wound. However, sometimes we may stop the progression of our own healing, and that of our lineage, because we deeply feel we're betraying our family of origin, or our ancestors, in daring to change something culturally or personally. The truth is that there is something greater that we can align to, in our loyalty, that goes beyond the wounds and cultural patterns of the past. Let me explain.

Many of us have a deep inner response of loyalty to our mothers, and to the feminine lineage we come from. And it's this very perception of loyalty that enslaves us to reactive patterns that no longer serve us. At the center of this concept of loyalty, there is the fear of betraying our ancestors in some way. This feeling of loyalty actually confuses us into an illusory sense of commitment to old patterns of thinking, which translate into staying loyal to unworthiness, victimization, scarcity mentality, or other similar forms of suffering that have been passed down through our ancestors, sometimes only because they have suffered to.

For example, if our mothers passed on a pattern of being sacrificial and putting everyone before themselves, we may lack the willingness to change this pattern out of an idealization of 'loyalty'. In turn, we may feel that taking care of ourselves and dissolving this pattern is in some way a betrayal to our mothers and ancestors, because it's changing the belief or simply the way things were done. Feelings of guilt and betrayal may come over us, urging us to stay in the same patterns of our ancestors, justifying it by our need to honor their suffering. Sometimes misery loves company. Furthermore, we may feel that if we change our paradigms, we are saying 'no' to our ancestors; saying 'no' to what was taught and to the unspoken family beliefs that we have lived by. We may also feel that we're leaving them behind and moving on to better things without them, leaving us with a disrespectful and even ungrateful feeling to contend with. However, these are all our minds' way of keeping us stuck in the same limited reality of separation, this is all resistance of our ego's. Our ancestors all want us to evolve, and move into greater levels of light, and as we do, they do also.

First of all, we aren't saying 'no' to them personally, but rather ending a pattern of suffering that has been passed down from generation to generation. We mustn't confuse the patterns of unconscious wounding and behaviors that have resulted in them, for 'who' they are/were. We can rest assured that we aren't abandoning them or causing them any pain because in reality they are beings of light, and by transmuting the patterns of suffering, we're honoring their light and our light. Furthermore, what we're doing is ending an illusory pattern that unfortunately, they too have been caught in. We're breaking free into a greater level of consciousness and truth for ourselves, but in reality, for all of us. When you're willing to break through those veils of illusion, you're offering a paradigm shift to yourself, and collectively, to all those on the planet, that have suffered with these patterns. Consciousness becomes alive through you and you become the agent of Light and healing for the world. Our loyalty to our ancestors becomes anchored in Love and truth of who they are, rather than in pain and suffering.

Rebecca Case #4

Rebecca came to me to help her with her grief after the passing of her mother. As she began her Soma Presence healing session, she realized that she was blaming herself for her mother's death in a very subtle way, supported by her justification that 'she wasn't' able to save her'. Unconsciously, she was also judging herself as 'unworthy' due to the same reasoning, of 'not been able to save her'. Consequently, as she became present to the unconscious patterning within her, she realized this unworthiness was also passed on from women to women in her lineage. She noticed this unconscious thought of 'not being able to save her' was just another way to continue the dysfunctional pattern of self-blame, judgement, and unworthiness that was so common in her family. She also understood that the deep-rooted feelings of inadequacy she felt were all being held in place by this unrealistic unconscious expectation of saving her mother.

Rebecca recognized the strong bond of loyalty that held her hostage to the patterns of self-blame and unworthiness. It became clear to her that the thought of even releasing these patterns felt like a deep betrayal to her mother and her ancestors, thus adding more layers of guilt to the original feeling of guilt about not saving her. It felt to her as if there was no way out of this endless cycle of suffering.

However, as she continued to bring presence to her feelings of inadequacy, self-hatred, self-blame, etc., she felt the alchemical process of dissolution happening and felt the light coming in and her heart feeling lighter. As she then embraced the feeling of betraying her mother and, furthermore, the underlying feeling of failing her in some way, she found the deep grueling grief that she'd not completely processed, along with unresolved feelings of fear around 'who she was now that she didn't have her mother any more'.

As she faced her deepest fears and grief, the feelings alchemized and were met with the all-encompassing healing love, which ultimately are what we're all yearning for. Rebecca was could return all these unresolved frozen aspects of her being into her Essence of Love, and then could clearly choose what she wanted to be in service to; love or the dysfunctional patterns of pain.

Rebecca choose to be in service to Love, rather than to the dysfunctional patterns that had been passed down to her, and she also choose to break free from the imprisonment of these patterns. Thereafter, she experienced her body opening and transmuting, metabolizing the heavy dark cloud-like substance with light, in her solar plexus, heart gate, and then down her legs, which had been feeling blocked and heavy and out the rest of her body, through the center of her chakras. Her sense of Self was being completely recalibrated in her solar plexus, because she was able to restore and retrieve this aspect of her Feminine soul that was clouded and buried by this 'conditioned loyalty veil' to her ancestors.

Once Rebecca was willing to listen deeply and be present with her intense pain, she allowed the unraveling of the energy field of inadequacy, self-hatred, self-blaming, etc., that was enmeshed with her field. These feelings were underlying a deep pain of sadness and grief from the death of her mother. As the grief began to metabolize and dissipate in her field, she began to feel her Essence and her light body again. She could see her patterns clearly, and was no longer bound to them unconsciously. Her mind was keeping these patterns in place by her unconscious self-blame for her mother's death. Her unconscious pattern sounded something like this; " The fact that my mother died, and I couldn't save her shows how unworthy and inadequate I am, because I should have been able to save her, after all I am in the health field. The least I can do now is continue to be loyal to her by continuing to suffer, as she did through this pattern of inadequacy, rather than betraying her and having a good life. I don't deserve more than her, she gave her life for me and now she is gone. It is all my fault, I have should have done better, as she always told me. She is right, I am wrong, therefore, I do not deserve to have freedom or even a better life than she did. I have to suffer and continue to be loyal to her by never leaving her, or her 'ways'.

When we're dealing with a loved one that has passed away, it's easy to get caught up in this kind of unconsciousness guilt, blame, and martyrdom to some degree, because most of the time, we aren't aware that we're even thinking it, we're just caught in deep pain and sorrow. These patterns are ways that we unconsciously deal with the deep pain of separation from a loved one, hiding our pain temporarily under these enmeshed and self-deprecating mental constructs.

At the end of her session, Rebecca felt herself reclaiming her feminine soul's light that was occluded by this illusory veil of inadequacy and unworthiness. And more surprisingly, she saw the healing light of compassion, mercy, and sacredness that moved through her, was also available to her ancestors, allowing them the choice to also reclaim their truth. By willing to be present with the unresolved pain within herself and surrendering it to the Light, she was able to heal her soul, and also offer this Light to her ancestors, becoming the bridge for the healing of others. This is how the consciousness wakes up in us, and in others. We are the healers, serving as the bridge and conduits of consciousness Herself, waking up to truth within us.

Here we see how powerful our unconscious beliefs are, and consequently how powerful our unconscious ties are to our loved ones. At this time, I do believe that as women, we are being asked to not only heal ourselves, but to also bring this healing to our ancestors through our direct intention and healing prayers. I've shared a couple of healing prayers that are used in the Sufi tradition, to bring this light to our ancestors. These healing prayers that are chanted quietly or out loud, in a designated holy night of prayer, serve as transmissions of light that break through the frequencies of illusion, awakening us to greater consciousness. Whether we're living in this body, or whether we have passed, ancient teachings point to the soul's elevation by performing said prayers in night vigils focused on those that have passed. Bringing our awareness and consciousness to these places, helps us restore the fabric of the feminine and the suffering of the present and the past. As we continue to shift the suffering in the collective field of the Feminine soul, we have to consciously include the souls of our ancestors that might have suffered in these ways. This is all part of the spiritual purification that is part of the collective shift. The practice of the Light prayer I have included at the end of this chapter, was passed down directly from my guide, in the Sufi tradition.

As we continue our work in returning to our Essence, we begin to enliven the reality of what we are and who we are, within ourselves and our world. And so, in this process of remembering, we can read about the women that have come before us, that were seen as Healers, and begin to build the bridge within our own consciousness of what is possible. In the appendix A, at the end of this book, I have included an extensive article from the superb work of Max Dashu;[2] a researcher and expert on ancient female iconography in the world of archaeology, female sphere of power and matricultures; patriarchies and allied systems of domination; medicine women, female shamans, witches and witch hunts. This article helps us to open up to the reality of our ancestors and to begin to resurrect the disowned sacred power of the Feminine, through ourselves.

DREAMING INTO THE QUANTUM FIELD OF POSSIBILITIES

We spent most of the time witnessing linear time. This is time as we know it, with a past, present and future. We live in this reality and see things from this reality when we are witnessing from our humanity. However, we know that time is an illusion on many levels, and that in reality there is this greater field of timelessness, existing in the quantum field. This is a hard concept to imagine for our minds, but if we suspend our need to understand it for a few minutes we can enter into this dimension.

In the quantum field, all possibilities exist. What has happened in the past, still lives in memory within yourself, what is happening in the future can be seen by those that can easily move into timelessness. When we see the lights of stars in the sky, we're seeing the light from stars that have long gone and fizzled out, yet because of the duration of light years and distance, we experience that reality as if it's happening now. In many ways, timelessness in the quantum field is an experience, rather than a concept.

Within us all is the access to this timeless dimension of unmanifested consciousness, which gives birth to all, call it, Oneness, the Eternal or even the Quantum field of possibilities. Many of us experience this space when we turn inward to access our Essential Self, our divine nature. This space of timelessness is also the Cosmic Womb of possibilities, what we call in Quantum Science 'the wave', the field where everything is existing at all times.

The Cosmic Womb of all possibilities gives rise to our experience, known as 'the particle'. Within our own lives, one of the factors that gives rise to the activation of our experience is our consciousness and awareness. Our awareness matters, what we focus on matters. As the old axiom says, "what we focus on, expands." While we realize that we're created from unmanifested Essence consciousness, which is our divine nature, in actuality, it's consciousness itself that creates the awakening within us and allows us to wake up from the illusory veils of separation. Therefore, what frees us from the experience of pain and suffering begins with a shift in our awareness (consciousness) to be able to 'see' the unseen realities of Oneness (consciousness itself). It's, therefore, our consciousness; our ability to 'see' a new reality and become aware of it that brings a new reality into conscious awareness and manifestation, even though it is always operating in the background.

If we extend this understanding to the consciousness of ourselves, and notice that there's a filter of unworthiness, then we continue to experience life as if that filter is truth until we awaken to the reality of our worthiness, underneath that veil. Awakening to that reality of truth, of that which underlines all of life itself, is the process of where and how we use our consciousness that we have been working through the past few chapters.

As we've awakened through the Sacred Initiations to deeper levels of consciousness within us, we realize that when we're witnessing and experiencing life from our soul, it's very different than when we're experiencing life from our heart or even from our mind. Most of us experience life from our mind with all of its calcified mental conditioning, and believe those paradigms as Truths. Some of us experience life from our emotional body and take everything personally, adding meaning to experiences that aren't completely true. And in the soul, we can also experience the veils of conditioned filters that continue to define our reality and our truth. However, there's a place in our soul, that is pure and pristine and that experiences an aspect of the unmanifested consciousness, Oneness, in its reality. This is our Essential Self, the aspect of us that is Divine. And hidden within that reality is the reality of complete unmanifested consciousness, which we call the Eternal. We are the breath of the Eternal manifested into physicality.

Within these varying levels of consciousness, we access this quantum field, and can experience ourselves as carrying all of the possibilities within us. Experiencing ourselves in the realm of endless possibilities, we can dream into the possibility of what we want for ourselves, what we are yearning for in our hearts, and what we are willing to imagine into presence.

Furthermore, you can remember all time within you. Can you remember your laughter and joy at the age of three or five? Can you remember your anger and rebelliousness in adolescent? Can you remember your fears as a child? Many of those are still alive within us and easily accessible. As a hologram, all realities and possibilities are existing within you right now, and your consciousness, along with Oneness itself, has determined which version of you is showing up, manifesting.

In many ways, the journeys through the Sacred Initiations that we've traveled through have served to break through the calcified conditioned filters and freed our calcified patterns to choose our reality more consciously. And now, we come to the full hologram of who we are; the manifestation of ourselves that is choosing every minute, consciously and unconsciously.

Through the activation of the quantum field of possibilities we have the ability to choose also, what we want to invite into our lives, what we want to dream in and weave into our present moment. Please take the time to engage at the end of this chapter with our *Conscious Feminine Manifestation through our Trinity Womb Activation.*

ENCOUNTERS WITH THE DARK MOTHER

How do we walk in the world of multiplicity, centered in our Essential Self, the Essence of who we are?

As we continue on this dance of living in the multiplicity, while centered in our Essential Self, we undoubtedly continue our journey of awakening. We consciously enter the dance of life. Life that comes through us as pure consciousness, that which we experience in moments of being fully present fully with no agenda, interplaying with our personality, our persona, our humanness and just creating.

We move through these varying states gracefully and not so gracefully, sometimes being in our Essence, detached from our identification as a form. And sometimes, we come back into our form and momentarily forget our Truth, getting caught up in our egoic states of separation in our mind, emotions and thoughts.

As we awaken, we continue to dance through these two states of awareness and allow them to come closer and closer together, where we forget less and less who we're supposed to be and we remember more and more our Truth and our Essence, living from joy.

Once we've moved in to our Essence, we begin to detach from our form and our identification with it. We continue the process of dissolution, where we increasingly experience ourselves as light, as consciousness and also as greater light (unmanifested consciousness) expressing itself through us. This is the purpose of consciousness itself, to express itself and be known through our experience. And thus, in our journey of awakening, we have an opportunity to do that every moment that we are aware.

In the process of dissolving our egoic nature of our conditioned Self, we inadvertently will move through the dissolution of our ego states, those places within us that we've identified so well with, as if it's us. Sometimes our egoic states have been calcified in an excessive way, telling us we are the best at something, feeling arrogant, right, and obnoxiously overconfident and sometimes, our egoic state is calcified in a deficient way, feeling that we are unworthy, shameful, underserving, etc. Either way, these are states of the ego that are meant to dissolve as we cultivate our Essence more and more.

However, it's important to say that in this journey of cultivation, we do visit what many refer to as the underworlds of darkness. The deep crevices of pain and unresolved emotional states that maintain hidden in the underworld of our subconscious. When we're constantly inviting the higher frequencies of light, we might be surprised by the pouring of light that happens. I can honestly say that my experience is that when we invite the divine in and become conscious of the higher frequencies at play, they are always there supporting us and eager to break through our conditioned reality. However, the breaking of reality can be a bit shocking at times, and can also invite us onto a wild ride through the darkness of the underworld, as I have experienced many times.

This wild ride is what one of my teacher calls riding the Dragon. For me, it's taken nearly a decade to learn to trust and ride the dragon, instead of the typical slaying of the Dragon or even being fearful of it. The Dragon takes us through the underground of our emotional field, through all the unresolved wounding to allow it to dissolve. The Dragon is all of our suppressed material that finally breaks free and comes rumbling through. The Dragon takes us into the underworld of the Dark Mother.

The Dark Mother, representing the fierce fire element of the Feminine that pushes us through the places of limitation, fear and old constructs of our mind, into a whole new world, if we're ready. She's the primordial, wild, intense, feminine energy that dissolves, purifies, and destroys to let new life be born. Sometimes represented by Kali, Dark Moon, Lilith, or many other names, She is the transformer where all of life comes from. We consistently project our fears unto Her, fearing Her fierceness, her destruction, her dissolution. However, She makes room for new life, clearing whatever is no longer needed. In our ignorance, we've grown up distrusting the natural transformational forces of nature, even in our nature. We hide these intense elements within ourselves; our rage, our hopelessness, our grief and our terror, until She finds them and forces us to face them to make room for something new. She escorts us into our underworld, where we face our greatest darkness of challenges.

In the face of our darkness, our mental constructs sometimes melt away easily and gently but other times it may feel like an intense earthquake shaking up our reality, as our old patterns are broken up by the Dark Mother, Herself. Simultaneously this transformational process also blasts us with light, which further promotes the dissolution of the old calcified patterns, hidden in the basement of our psyches, to collapse. This is the death of our egoic state, one state at a time, sometimes many states at a time. Our sense of separation and the mental patterns of insufficiency, failure or scarcity come tumbling down as we watch our egoic nature dissolve and our Essential Light become more established in our reality.

One must be willing to face the darkness that we hide in our lives, our deepest fears, our worries and what we would be too embarrassed to own. In facing these states, we realize they're all figments of our imagination, but yet they present so powerfully, that within these levels of consciousness, we make them real. The pain is real, the fear is real, the grief is real, both physically and emotionally. And as I have mentioned, they're real on one level, but in a deeper level, they are calcified patterns we're limited by. If we believe that we're 'not good enough', we continue to live life through this veil of not feeling good enough, and everything is interpreted through this filter. If we have the great honor of being blasted by the Dark Mother and riding Her dragon, we may experience the veils flushing up, sometimes too quick to even take note. We may feel confused, fearful, unable to decipher because we're caught in the whirlwind of our emotional hurricane and the earthquake. Everything surfaces, spirals, and dissolves. And this is the journey typically called the dark night of the soul, where the Dark Mother has paid you a visit and taken you into your underworld, through the crevices of the darkness of your psyche, now poised at the door, waiting for you to say Yes and ride Her into dissolution.

So, when we're visited by the Dark Mother of transformation, at night or at any time, we hold tight to our breath and to the reality that we're born and exist in a field of Love, even if we don't feel it at the moment of our transformation. You hold tight to the endless possibilities of Love, knowing that She is visiting because somewhere in your being you have said Yes, and yearn for greater intimacy with Joy, with Love and with the primordial Essence of Creativity that you are. Somewhere in your being you have invited Her and asked Her to free you from the chains of pain and suffering. Through Her journey, you can let your preconceived ideas of yourself be dissolved, along with your limitations and restrictions. This is also the process of Fana, that the Sufi's refer to, which is to be annihilated, to be dissolved, to die before you die. And when I say die here, what dies is our ego states of separation (conditioned Self) so you can be born into the eternal Oneness within you, your Essential Self.

In our continued process of the evolution of our Feminine Soul, all we lose is the identification with our personality. We're are the same person, however, we grow space between our attachments and find that we aren't as attached to our personality nor our likes and dislikes, as we once were. We recognize that while we may have preferences, we aren't attached to them and they aren't enmeshed with our value. We can feel the world of all possibility within us. We can feel the reality of the unmanifested, unconditioned consciousness coming through us, coming through our Trinity Womb, as we give unmanifested reality expression through our choices, actions, words and feelings. We see ourselves as a continuity, not ending with the disintegration of our physical body but rather feeling the continuation of our soul. And although this doesn't happen all at once, it does happen. And whether you are visited by the Dark Mother often, or only on rare occasions, She will open you up to birth greater joy, love and manifest your deepest souls yearning! She will open you up to living your true destiny, while meeting your fate!

An Act of Service- to Love

Ultimately, this is a journey of service, for each person on the planet. Whether we recognize it or not, we're all in service to something, consciously or unconsciously. Some of us are in service to our ego, finding our identity in the world, searching for our place in the outer manifestation. Some of us are in service to the power and superiority, over and above anything else. Some of us are in service to Love, to the transformation of the world and to the realm of all possibilities. This is the group of us that might be hearing the call of the Conscious Feminine, rising through us.

At every moment of our day, we're in service to something. When we act out of our unconscious patterns of fear and survival, we're essentially in service to that. When we act out of love and compassion, we are in service to that. Our choices at every turn determines what we are ultimately in service to. And even though many of our choices are made automatically, unconsciously becoming aware of each choice and realizing that we have choice is a necessary step in awakening and living from an empowered place in our being. Of course, on this journey we will continue to dance between unconscious behaviors of old patterns within us and the unencumbered freedom of Love, from our Essential Self, our True nature. This is a journey and we must give ourselves the room to move back and forth, as we continue to awaken to all of ourselves in full realization.

However, once the Feminine begins to awaken within you, it's as if, She has chosen you. When we feel the deep yearning and longing in our hearts for the deep intimate love, She is calling you. She is what awakens within you. And even though we experience it as two things, Her and you, it's really one. It's Life awakening to itself, it's Love awakening to itself, through you.

And yet you are that Love, that Essence and that unified Consciousness awakening to Herself. She is the one that whispers in your ear that there is more, that inspires you to continue your search, and that continues to stream in the vision of wholeness, of love, of bliss. She is the one, within you and as part of you that yearns for the real Love, because She knows that it is possible.

When you awaken to Her, you awaken to the Truth within you. Through your vessel awareness is the catalyst that awakens Her. When we say Yes to Her, we say yes to Life itself. This takes great courage and great trust, because sometimes it's easier to stay in our comfort zone and not risk anything, especially into the unknown. This is a constant saying Yes to the unknown, as She opens up our horizons to wider and wider possibilities of embodied Joy.

Ultimately, this is a journey of service, of consciously choosing to be in service to Consciousness, Herself. Choosing to live every action, every word, and every part of your living experience as a devotion to Her, and simultaneously to the consciousness of eternal intelligence of wisdom, Love, and sacredness, that are your Divine nature.

This is a path of living through Joy. When we embark on this path of evolution, our actions, words, and thoughts are continuously sourced from the deeper Essence, Herself. We become merged with our Essence of Divine light, and we see ourselves more and more whole. This is a journey of Love, but also of living through Joy. We access our joy through our expression of the creative flow of the Feminine through our creative flow in art, dance, drumming, chanting, journaling, writing and many more creative endeavors. These are true expressions of the Feminine, where we can lose ourselves to the direct Essence moving through us, more importantly create. This is what we're here to do, to create while experiencing our full divinity and full humanity. This is truly the path of falling in love with life itself and living in our joy.

The Feminine Consciousness isn't just awakening, but quickly accelerating on the planet at this time. It's a path of Love, sacredness, and compassion, but not the Love we know. It's not the needy, dependent, conditional version of love that we've experienced in our limited egoic nature. It's the Love where all of life is created, it's the Love that gives birth to itself and has given birth to you. It can be experienced as fierce, yet gentle, blissful yet daunting, courageous, intense, powerful, tenacious, determined unconditional Love. It's the giver of life and the taker, the compassion and the severity, the mercy and the illuminator. It is that very light, that is awakening within you. The light that is You is awakening to its own Light, through you!

Consciousness needs us, it needs our vessel to awaken to itself. We're the ones we've been waiting for and She is rising through you this very moment. Yet we have been given choice, choice reflects in what we put our consciousness on what we become aware of and ultimately in what we choose to be in service to.

And when we say Yes to Her, we're ultimately saying Yes to ourselves, not the small egoic identity of our conditioned self, but the unlimited divine nature of Essence that lives through us and is us.

As the Conscious Feminine is rising, we're awakening to the hidden, part of ourselves, that is life itself, and breaking free from the darkness of the limited paradigm we've been living in.

As the Conscious Feminine is rising, you have the unique ability to change the story of the collective and transmit more of the awakened state through you, through your vessel. You and you alone, can make a difference, each time you choose Yes to Love, you're helping to create the conscious loving planet, that exudes the deeper states of mystery Herself.

CONSCIOUS FEMININE EMBODIED PRACTICES
GIVING BIRTH
DISSOLVING INTO THE DARK MOTHER
DYING TO OUR EGOIC STATES

*Please be aware that this process has the capacity to trigger trauma related events or unprocessed and unconscious challenging psycho-emotional material. If this process becomes too intense, please seek professional help and support through an embodied Somatic Healer or a qualified professional.

1. Before we give birth we need to die. Dying is part of the cycle of living. Here we are dying to our old self, to the limited thoughts of who we think we are and opening up to more of our true Essence. Take a breath while acknowledging this reality and surrendering to the transformational journey of the Dark Mother. Breathe....

2. Bring your awareness to you lower sacral womb, placing both hands here, breathing gently and slowly into this area. Breathe – 13 times.

3. Start to feel the darkness of your pelvic bowl and let yourself step into the unknown of the dark Mother. This is the space that we surrender whatever challenges we are facing, surrender the 'problem' that you are dealing with, and let yourself be in the 'not knowing' space of the darkness of the underworld. You are safe here, you are just releasing your power of your mind and your need to figure things out, diving into the mystery of the Dark Mother. Breathe here for a while into you settle into the darkness of your sacral womb. (Be aware that if we are dealing with strong emotions that arise, it is important to drop any judgments about whatever you are feeling, and allow yourself to move slowly through the emotional terrain that may arise; there is no need to 'understand' anything at this moment. Just feel the raw emotions if there are any.)

4. Once you feel settled in the darkness of your womb, let yourself surrender any thoughts about your behavior, what you must do, how you should act/ be, any moved through the stormy emotional wave. (This is where we ride the dragon... let the Dark Mother take us into the underworld of our unresolved emotional terrain and let our egoic attachments to how it should be or what's best, or what went wrong dissolve.

5. Feel the Dark Mother moon energies circling you, holding you in a matrix of Love, compassion, mercy and grace. These are all there for you as long as you surrender and let go of directing the process of your life. Trust in the Dark Mother of transformation, trust in the Universal intelligence and into the Light of your own soul, these are the factors that are directing your process, if you allow it. Breathe and allow, surrendering... breathing... surrendering... breathing... surrendering. Continue to breathe in this place until you feel the Light coming in, uplifting you and gently loving you through your whole body, from the inside out.

6. As you begin to feel the shift in your being, from darkness to light and expansion, ask for any guidance or wisdom for your next steps. Is there anything being asked of you concerning this issue or situation in your life? Let the wisdom or inspiration arise in your heart, then take a few minutes to write it down. (Take your time integrating the Light in your body, and feeling the wisdom that comes through. Do not rush this process.) Breathe and bow in gratitude.

DREAMING A NEW STORY OF THE FEMININE: HOW GOOD CAN IT GET!

1. Sit quietly and bring your awareness within.

2. Connect with your Essence, emanating in every cell of your body. Breathe deeply.

3. Once you feel the light of your being, let yourself relax and dissolve into it, surrendering all your thoughts and emotions into the vibratory, activating sensations in your body. Breathe...

4. Now, see yourself expressing and acting in your life with confidence, love, peace, safety, inspiration and with joy... imagine how that would feel in your body to live from your Essence every moment of your day.

5. Let that feeling in your body expand, whether it's joy, peace, love, as you feel yourself living from this full place in your being, from your Essential Self. Breathe...

6. Now, see yourself in your day, and image how it would feel if you were supported by the Universe at all times. Breathe into that feeling and let it expand into every cell.

7. Now, invite the Universe to support you and say yes to all that the Universe is bringing to you, whether you realize it or not. Breathe...

8. Now, ask yourself, how good can it get, how good can my life be, allowing yourself to break through any limitations or habituated patterns of limitation that you have experienced till now. Anything is possible... let yourself open your heart to that reality. And invite the Universe to support you and surprise you in manifesting the goodness that begins from within... Breathe and allow yourself to anchor in the Essence of your Self and all of its sensations.

9. When you feel complete, bow your head in gratitude and continue to tune into to your Essence, during your day, to activate the truth of your being and the possibilities of manifesting from this reality. Remember, Spirit has no limitations, it only exists in our minds.

CONSCIOUS FEMININE MANIFESTATION THROUGH OUR TRINITY WOMB ACTIVATION

1. Sit quietly in an undisturbed place and become aware of your breathing. (five breaths here).

2. Next, become aware of your body, how it feels, sensations, emotions, thoughts, etc.. Continue to breathe into your body and become aware, slowing down and noticing while you breathe. (5 – 10 breaths here).

3. As you start to relax even more, connect with the floor under your sitting bones, under your feet and invite the Earth Mother and Her Yin, nurturing energy into your body's field. Allow yourself to merge deeper with Her, and Her gravity, feeling how she gently holds you close to Her, as in a mother's embrace. (5-10 breaths here).

4. Next, let yourself feel the top of your head, the crown chakra, and invite the Yang forces of Heaven into through your head, at this top point of DU 20. Let it open, and feel it gently washing down into your body's field, inside and out, as it merges with the Yin energy within. (5-10 breaths here).

5. We will begin in your Heart Womb, center womb of LOVE, breathe deeply into this area and feel the love arising from your Heart womb. Let yourself receive the unconditional LOVE of the Universe, directly here in your heart womb, letting yourself be filled with this LOVE, and then letting this LOVE expand into the UNIVERSE through you. Notice that everything in the Universe is created from LOVE and everything in your world is created from LOVE. This is the same LOVE that you are receiving and transmitting into your world, right now. Continue to do this until you feel an enormous level of LOVE, coming over you, being you, feeding you and supporting you. (10-20 breaths here).

6. Let yourself connect with something that your heart is yearning for and would like to manifest in your life. As you are letting this yearning arise, let yourself feel this manifestation, and see the image of it. Place this image deep in your sacral lower womb, surrendering it completely to the Great Mother. Here in your lower womb, you let it merge with the forces of unmanifested consciousness... asking Her to support your manifestation if it is in alignment with the highest. from Breathe here for a few minutes, letting your vision expand in your sacral womb gather vitality for manifestation.

7. Now, if you feel your vision expanding in your sacral womb with the light of consciousness, then you may continue to the next steps. If you don't, it may not be time to bring it forth at this time. Continue to do step 1-7 surrendering the timing to the Universe and waiting for the expansion of Light to be there, before you continue to move it through your other wombs.

8. Middle Heart Womb – Breathe from your sacral lower womb into your vision and invite the light of this manifestation to come into your heart womb. Here you can **feel** your vision manifesting. How does you feel when you see your vision manifesting in the outer world? How does it feel in your body? Hone in on the feelings and let them expand in your body. Continue this process with your breath until your heart womb is full of light and the feelings have expanded throughout your whole body.

9. Upper womb – Next, feel the fullness in your sacral womb and your heart womb, giving birth to this new vision. Allow the light of this fullness to move from your heart middle womb to your head upper womb. See the creative thoughts and inspiration being birthed from your head womb. Let yourself receive creative thoughts and ideas related to bringing through this vision. Take a few minutes to allow this process to take place and then continue to journal the inspirations that may be coming through. You may want to reflect on what they next actions steps are to manifesting this new vision.

10. Finish with bowing in gratitude.

You may want to do this process every morning before sitting down to work to receive guidance on a new project or vision.

CLEARING ANCESTRAL COLLECTIVE KARMA

1. Sit quietly and light a candle for those that you would like to bring light to, preferably a white candle.

2. Begin by taking some deep breaths and becoming aware of your heart space. Breathe into your heart space, with the intention of activating the heart gateway, and the unconditional Love of the Universe. Take 5-10 breathes here.

3. As you breathe into your heart and allow the unconditional Love fill you, inside and out... start to bring your loved one that has passed into the circle of your heart.

4. Feel all the feelings here, that may arise as you do this. Perhaps there is sadness, unresolved grief, maybe even anger, resentment, guilt, etc... Expand your heart enough to feel all the feelings here, without adding any more guilt to yourself. Be as honest as you can with your feelings for this person.

5. As you feel the feelings, continue to breathe... letting the feelings move through you... whatever was in the past can be left to the past. You no longer have to hold on to these feelings. Let yourself continue to feel and breathe, until you feel open and more settled.

6. Now, gently chant this prayer of light, to return this person and yourself, to the Light of conditional love. This is a powerful prayer used by the Sufi's to return us to the Love, the Essence of Love. It is in Arabic. Repeat for at least **100** times, while feeling the vibrations of the sound in your body. Let your heart open... knowing that you are releasing their pain and your own into the Love of the Divine. Let the chant's vibrational frequency purify your heart and theirs.

   " Astig fir Allah La Dhim"

   " Astig fir Allah La Dhim"

   " Astig fir Allah La Dhim"

   " Astig fir Allah La Dhim"

   " Astig fir Allah La Dhim"

7. After you have repeated this at least 100 times, you will feel a softening, perhaps more emotions will come through, perhaps more images of the past will come through. Nonetheless, continue to chant this powerful sounds until your heart feels complete.

8. When you are done, bow in gratitude, feeling the light in your ancestors heart. You may want to repeat this process every month, on the dark moon to clear your own and your ancestor's karma.

CONSCIOUS FEMININE WORDS OF WISDOM

· Take time to go within and listen, allowing yourself to unplug and unwind.

· Make decisions from your heart, using visceral wisdom and then consult your mind.

· Be willing to be in the not knowing, the bridge to the Unified field of Oneness.

· Remember the wisdom is in your body.

· Feel everything and then decide, never make decisions from a place that is other than LOVE.

· When challenged by something or someone, address the inner first, process your feelings and dissolve the veils of conditioning, then address the outer.

· Remember there is always wisdom available, you are not alone regardless of how alone you feel, underneath there is always radical LOVE, it is your nature.

· Remember that your feelings, thoughts and actions are all layered over your Truth, and many times are coming from conditioning. Try to align your expression with your Truth.

· What triggers you is never the real issue, look deeper, the conflict is within your consciousness. Everything outside yourself is a reflection of your inner state of being.

· What is your truth? When you don't know, take the time to go within and listen, clear all the impressions of others, and let yourself feel your Truth in your heart and your soul. It will feel peaceful and aligned.

· Everyone has their own unique journey and truth, they are each working it out, be patient with others and yourself.

· Each soul carries unique qualities, and the idea is to be in alignment with your truth, and allow others to be in alignment with their truth. We get to change our reality, not theirs.

· We are completely responsible for our state of consciousness and ourselves, it isn't anyone else's responsibility.

· Create your own Sacred Witnessing Manifesto and use it as a reminder to align with the Conscious Feminine within.

· Celebrate each breath, each moment, knowing that it is a gift of Cosmic LOVE and look for the magic underlying everything in creation.

- Trust your true nature of Joy and Love, it's there, underneath the pain and confusion.

- Trust more in Love, than you do in Fear.

Appendix A

Our Feminine Women Shaman Ancestors

Our ancestors have created the fabric of the Women Shamans throughout time and history. There are entire names of women that have not survived "the boring orthodox histories" as Max Dashu refers to it, and unfortunately, we continue to have a skewed view of the truth of our history. However, Max Dashu has created a living library, "Suppressed Histories Archives", gathering thousands of digital slides, documentation and articles reviving the truth of the hidden female cultures and the roles they played in society. With her wonderfully committed work, since 1970, we find the female spheres that although they have existed all throughout time, have been hidden by the patriarchal culture.

Since the beginning of time women have been Shamans and Healers, this is nothing new, however, it is new to us and the rest of the world. Women as healers show up in oral traditions as shamanic journeyers, shapeshifters, invokers, diviners, seers, ecstatic dancers and messenger of the ancestors, according to the archives of suppressed histories by Max Dashu. This is what we are resurrecting, this is what is possible, as we restore our Feminine Soul and reclaim our deepest Truth.

Below is a wonderful summation of Max Dashu's article on Women Shamans printed with permission from Max Dashu, Suppressed Histories Archives. [1]

WOMAN SHAMAN

Max Dashú

This is a brief summary of a visual presentation, first shown in 1986, which was given in September 2005 at the Shamanic Studies Conference in San Rafael, California. It has since expanded into seven visual talks as well as a video DVD, *Woman Shaman: the Ancients* (see http://www.suppressedhistories.net/womanshamandvd.html for trailer and information). For more on the healers Pa Sini Jobu and Nishan Shaman, see the 2013 article "Raising the Dead: Medicine Women Who Revive and Retrieve Souls" https://www.academia.edu/11646356/Raising_the_Dead_Medicine_Women_Who_Revive_and_Retrieve_Souls.

A Chukchee proverb declares, "Woman is by nature a shaman." [1] Yet the female dimension of this realm of spiritual experience has often been slighted. Mircea Eliade believed that women shamans represented a degeneration of an originally masculine profession, yet was hard put to explain why so many male shamans customarily dressed in women's clothing and assumed other female-gendered behaviors. Nor does the masculine-default theory account for widespread traditions, from Buryat Mongolia to the Bwiti religion in Gabon, that the first shaman was a woman.

In fact, women have been at the forefront of this field worldwide, and in some cultures, they predominate. This was true in ancient China and Japan, as it still is in modern Korea and Okinawa, as well as among many South African peoples and northern Californians such as the Karok and Yurok. There are countless other examples, including the machi of the Mapuche in southern Chile and the Babylon and Catalonian of the Philippines.

Images, oral traditions, and historical descriptions show women as invokers, healers, herbalists, oracles and diviners, ecstatic dancers, shapeshifters, shamanic journeyers, and priestesses of the ancestors. The Chinese Wu were ecstatic priestesses who danced to the music of drums and flutes until they reached trance, receiving shen (spirits) into their bodies, healing and prophesying under their inspiration, speaking in tongues, swallowing swords and spitting fire. The power of the shen gathered around the whirling dancers was said to cause objects to rise into the air, to prevent wounds from forming when the dancers slashed themselves with knives. Similar descriptions were recorded by Greco-Roman visitors to Anatolia: "At Castabala, in Cappadocia, the priestesses of an Asiatic goddess, whom the Greeks called Artemis Perasia, used to walk barefoot through a furnace of hot charcoal and take no harm." [2]

Certain female burials from ancient Central Asia have been designated as shamanic priestesses by archaeologists Natalia Polosmak and Jeanine Davis-Kimball. The priestess of Ukok (fifth century BCE) was buried in a three-foot-tall framed headdress adorned with a Tree of Life, with gilded felines and birds on its branches. Similar finds have been excavated at Ussun' in south Kazakhstan, and from the Ukraine to the Tarim basin, with recurrent themes of the Tree of Life headdress, amulets, incense, medicine bags, and sacramental mirrors. Such mirrors are also seen in the Bactrian region of Afghanistan, held facing out against the body, and they still figure as initiatory devices wielded by female adepts in Tibet. The overwhelmingly female mikogami of Japan also kept the "sacred mirror" of the sun goddess Amaterasu.

My visual presentation Woman Shaman includes a sequence of women shapeshifting into animal form or riding on the backs of shamanic steeds. These themes recur in many shamanic traditions, and are vividly illustrated in modern Arctic carvings. An Aleut ivory (circa 1816) shows a woman shaman wearing an animal mask. Other examples from the mid-20th century include "Woman Riding a Bear" by Cecilia Arnadjuk, Repulse Bay, Canada; "Woman/Polar Bear" by Odin Maratse, Greenland; a walrus-tusked "Woman Shaman" by Nancy Pukingrnak of Baker Lake; a half-woman, half-walrus piece titled "Woman Shaman Transforming Herself"; and "Medicine Woman" by Kaka of Cape Dorset.

The darwisa or maraboutes of North Africa bear Islamic titles, but practice much older North African customs. Among the Tunisian cave-dwellers, the darwisa cures sick people from possession from the jnun. In the ritual, she plays drum rhythms to discover which jinn caused illness; when she hits the right one, the person begins to dance. Then the darwisa talks to the spirit about what caused the illness and what is required to cure it. [3]

Codices produced by Aztec artists shortly after the Spanish conquest show women presiding over the temescal (sweat lodge). One of the invocations sung by such a priestess was recorded: "Mother of the gods and us all, whose creative and lifegiving power shone in the Temezcalli, also named Xochicalli, the place where she sees sacred things, sets to right what has been deranged in human bodies, makes young and tender things growing and strong, and where she aids and cures." [4]

Invocatory chants have remained an element of Mexican Indian shamanism. One of the great masters was Maria Sabina, "the woman who knows how to swim in the sacred," whose incantations seem to have acted as a means of entering into deep states of consciousness. Laying on of hands was part of her healing practice. Further north, in California, Bernice Torrez of the Kashaya Pomo, healed by touching and removing spirits of illness from the body of the sick person. She was the daughter of Essie Parrish, the great yomta, a title which means "Song." This prophet-seeress carried chants for ceremonies, healing, and control of the elements.

Chant and shaking a sacred rattle are important elements in the practice of Katjambia, a Himba medicine woman in Namibia. As she shakes the rattle, she calls out Njoo, Njoo, in a "secret language from Angola." After absorbing the negative energies into her own body, Katjambia returns to the sacred fire of her ancestors, who release them. A song by the Chilean composer and folklorist Violeta Parra celebrates the powers of the Mapuche machi, describing how she presides over the guillatún ceremonies and how her shamanizing cures the sick and brings a crop-threatening rain to an end.

The healing power of female shamans was occasionally stated to have been so far-reaching that they were described as being able to restore life to the dead. So it was told of Pa Sini Jobu, great Tungutu of the Bosso people in the middle Niger region. Her method of dancing to ecstasy and shifting into the form of a great bird echoes the story told of Isis. Both the goddess and the Tungutu are described as beating their wings over the dead (a ram, in Pa Sini Jobu's case) and bringing them to life. (The Colchian sorceress Medea is also pictured bringing a ram to life, using a cauldron, herbs, and incantations.) In western Africa, the sorceress Kulutugubaga has the power to heal all and bring the dead to life. She is the last of the legendary Nine Sorceresses of Mande.

Reviving the dead was one of the marvels performed by Yeshe Tsogyel, a foundational figure of Tibetan Buddhism. In Lady of the Lotus Born, she says, "... In Nepal I brought a dead man back to life... My body journeyed like a rainbow in celestial fields..." [5] This 8th-century poem is loaded with shamanistic content, recast in a Buddhist mold. The shamanic Bönpo religion is known to have contributed many elements to Tibetan Buddhism.

A Manchurian epic, Nishan Shaman, turns around the story of a woman who is the most powerful shaman in the country. She is called upon to revive the son of a rich man after countless others had failed. She beats her drum, chants, and sinks as if lifeless herself while journeying to the Otherworld, where she meets up with Omosi-mama, the "divine grandmother" who "causes leaves to unfurl and the roots to spread properly," who is the giver of souls and protectress of children. It was she who ordained that Nishan would become a great shaman.

Of course, Nishan finds the soul of the dead boy. But she is pursued by her long-dead husband, who demands to be saved as well, but she calls for a great crane to seize him and throw him back into the city of the dead. The shaman is hailed as a heroine when she comes back to the upper world and showered with riches. Later she faces repression from Confucian authorities who accuse her of not being an obedient wife, and they burn her shamanic regalia and drum. [6]

In much the same way, Spanish colonials persecuted women shamans in the Philippines, calling them "devil-ridden old women" and "witches," and destroying their shrines and sacred objects. [7] Maya oracles and shamans faced the same treatment; the Tzoltzil priestess María Candelaria raised an insurrection in Chiapas in 1712 to resist the repression of the indigenous religion.

Several hundred years ago, the Jesuit Acosta wrote that Peruvian witches were shapeshifters who could journey through the skies and foretell the future "by means of certain stones or other things they highly venerate." He and other Spanish sources agreed that the witches were mostly old women. [8] The colonials imposed their own preconceptions on Peruvian shamans, notably that of the devil and flying ointments, and persecuted these Quechua and Aymara women shamans as witches.

The Peruvian Inquisition forbade seeking knowledge through dreams or signs in the sky or through vision quests: "the said women other times go out to the country by day and at night, and take certain brews of herbs and roots, called achuma and chamico and coca, with which they deceive themselves and numb their senses, and the illusions and fantastic scenes which they experience there, they think and claim afterwards as revelations, or certain news of what will happen." [9]

Inquisitors tried the curandera Juana Icha for healing with the power of the old Quechua gods. She had offered corn meal, coca and chicha to the mountain spirit Apo Parato. An Indian informer told the monks that she "worships the earth and the stars and cries to the water." [10]

This is necessarily a truncated synopsis of a presentation which has not yet been committed to writing, but I hope it conveys a glimpse of a very international spectrum of women's shamanic experience – and leadership.

Notes

1. Czaplica, M. A. (1914) Aboriginal Siberia, a study in social anthropology. Oxford: Clarendon Press, p 243

2. Frazer, James (1955) The Golden Bough: A Study in Magic and Religion. London: Macmillan, Vol. XI, 14

3. Early Modern European Witchcraft: Centres and Peripheries (1988) ed. Henningsen, G, and Ankarloo, B, Oxford: Oxford University Press, p 211

4. Nuttall, Zelia (1901) The Fundamental Principles of Old and New World Civilizations: A Comparative Research Based on a Study of the Ancient Mexican Religious, Sociological and Calendrical Systems. Cambridge MA: Peabody Museum

5. Dowman, Keith (1996) Sky Dancer: The Secret Life and Songs of the Lady Yeshe Tsogyel. Ithaca NY: Snow Lion

6. Nowak, Margaret (1977) The Tale of the Nishan Shamaness: a Manchu Folk Epic. Seattle: University of Washington Press

7. Brewer, Caroline (2001) Holy Confrontation: Religion, Gender and Sexuality in the Philippines, 1521-1685. Manila: Institute of Women's Studies

8. Silverblatt, Irene (1987) Moon, Sun, and Witches: Gender Ideologies and Class in Inca and Colonial Peru, Princeton: Princeton University Press, p 171

9. Contramaestre, Carlos (1979) La Mudanza del Encanto. Caracas: Academia Nacional de la Historia, p 204

10. Silverblatt, p 183

BIBLIOGRAPHY

Introduction

1. Marion Woodman, Elinor Dickson, Dancing with the Flames: The Dark Goddess in the Transformation of Consciousness, P58, Shambala, 1997.

Chapter 1

1. Demetra George – *Mysteries of the Dark Moon*, P71, Harper Collins, 1992.

2. Demetra George – *Mysteries of the Dark Moon*, P89, Harper Collins, 1992.

Chapter 2

1. Rudd, Richard, *Gene Keys* (Kindle Locations 4924-4925). Gene Keys Publishing. Kindle Edition, 2011.

2. Bruce Lipton, *Biology Beyond Belief*, Hay house, 2016.

3. Harvard Health Publishing, Harvard Medical School, Harvard's Women Health Watch, '*Anxiety and Physical Illness*' 2008, 2018.

4. Adam Gainsburg, Chiron, the Wisdom of Deeply Open Heart, P17, Soulsign, 2006.

5. Rudd, Richard, *Gene Keys* (Kindle Locations 432-433), Gene Keys Publishing, Kindle Edition, 2011.

6. IBID, (Kindle Locations 464-470).

Chapter 3

1. John T. Caccioppo, et al., *Foundations in Neuroscience*, p 664, MIT Press, Cambridge Massachusetts, London England. 2002.

2. Adler, Margot, Drawing Down the Moon: Witches, Druids, Goddess-Worshippers, and Other Pagans in America, New York, NY: Penguin Books, 1979, 2006.

3. Bergman & Brismar, 1994; Lumina, Thorner & McGinnis, 1994).

4. MacKinnon, Mark, *In China, a Matriarchy Under Threat*, in *The Globe and Mail*, Toronto, Ontario, Canada, 2011.

5. Mukherjee, Sucharita Sinha, Women's Empowerment and Gender Bias in the Birth and Survival of Girls in Urban India, in Feminist Economics, vol. 19, no. 1, January, 2013.

6. Turley, William S., *Women in the Communist Revolution in Vietnam*, in *Asian Survey*, vol. 12, no. 9, September, 1972, p. 793 n. 1 (DOI 10.2307/2642829).

7.   Schlegel, Alice, "Hopi gender ideology of female superiority". *Quarterly Journal of Ideology: "A Critique of the Conventional Wisdom"*. VIII (4). 1984.

8.   George-Kanentiio, Doug, *Iroquois Culture & Commentary* (New Mexico: Clear Light Publishers, pp. 53–55, 2000.

9.   Tracy Elise, "American Indians... Shamanic perspective: Oklevueha Native American Church Medicine Woman and Elder medicine Woman for Onac Mother Medicine Wheel.

10. Cynthia Bourgeult writes, "the name given to the state of restored alignment – of 'singleness' or purity of being – is virginity'. Pp137, *The meaning of Mary Magdalene*, Shambala, 2010.

Chapter 4

1.   Candace Pert, Molecules of Emotions-The Science Behind Mind-Body Medicine, Simon & Shuster, 1999.

2.   Bonnie Bainridge Cohen, Sensing, Feeling and Action, pp1. Contact Editions, 2014.

Chapter 5

1.   Marija Gimbutas, The Living Goddesses, 2001, University of California Press, California, USA, 2001.

2.   Max Dashu, https://www.suppressedhistories.net/aboutmax.html, 2017.

3.   IBID.

4.   Alexander Marshack, The Roots of Civilization: The Cognitive Beginning of Man's First Art, Symbol and Notation, McGraw-Hill; First Edition, 1991.

5.   Eisler writes in her right hand the figure holds a crescent moon notched with thirteen markings: the number of lunar cycles in a year. Her other hand, as if to instruct us of the relationship between the cycles of the moon and women's menstrual cycles, points to her vagina. Riane Eisler, *Sacred Pleasure: Sex, Myth and Politics of the Body*, p.61. Harper One; Edition 1996.

6.   Neil Douglas Klotz, *Prayers of the Cosmos*, Harper One; Reprint Edition 2009.

Chapter 8

1.   Cynthia Bourgeult, *The meaning of Mary Magdalene*, Shambala, 2010.

2.   Katherine M. Flegal, PhD; Brian K. Kit, MD; Heather Orpana, PhD; et al, #2 https://jamanetwork.com/journals/jama/fullarticle/1555137.

3.   Naomi Wolf, *Vagina*, Ecco; Revised Updated Edition 2013.

Chapter 9

1. Sylvia Brinton Perera, *Descent of the Goddess, A Way of initiation for women*, Inner City Books, First Edition, 1981.

2. Marion Woodman, Elinor Dickson, Dancing in the Flames...The Dark Goddess in Transformation of Consciousness, p.22, Shambala. 1997.

Chapter 10

1. Adam Gainsburg, *Chiron, the Wisdom of Deeply Open Heart*, P17, Soulsign, 2006.

Chapter 11

1. Richard Rudd, *Gene Keys*, p292, Gene Keys Publishing, 2011.

Appendix A

1. Max Dashu, https://www.suppressedhistories.net/articles/articles.html, 2017.

ABOUT THE AUTHOR

Leonor Murciano-Luna, PhD, IMD, AP is a spiritual healer, teacher and mentor, author, integrative doctor and acupuncture physician. She has spent the last 25 years dedicated to guiding women to step into their true Essence, and to reclaim and heal themselves physically, mentally, emotionally and spiritually. Dr. Murciano is the founder of *Conscious Feminine Medicine*™, a non-profit organization dedicated to healing women on the soul level, the *School of Conscious Feminine Medicine*™, and *Nourishing Women*, her clinic in South Florida.

At the age of 6, Dr. Murciano experienced an extremely traumatic experience resulting in a near death experience. This experience has proven to be a powerful awakening in her life, opening the path to her own personal healing and discovery of the Feminine Essence of all. This transformational healing journey has inspired her work, yielding a very distinct healing formula, dedicated to the evolution of our Feminine soul. This is the foundation of *Conscious Feminine Medicine*™ a transformational healing system committed to the awakening of women, through the embodiment of Feminine spirituality. Dr. Murciano, mother of three beautiful young women, has been initiated into two healing mystical lineages which deeply penetrate all of her work. For more info. or a complete bio, please visit: ConsciousFeminineMedicine.com.

BOOKS AND OTHER WORKS BY DR. LEONOR MURCIANO-LUNA

Evolution of our Feminine Soul Journal
~a transformational journal for women awakening to the Feminine.

Feminine Wisdom: Rise of a New Creation
~a wholistic spiritual guidebook for women facing infertility challenges.

Dr.Murciano's 7 Keys to Conscious Feminine Body
Blueprint Activation E-book

Initiating the Feminine

The Feminine listens...
The Feminine feels...
The Feminine seeks to include not exclude.
The Feminine sees the wonder in togetherness...
rather than the strength in one.
The Feminine tunes in to Her body and asks how it feels...
rather than following an agenda.
The Feminine leads with compassion and empathy in any situation.
The Feminine asks the heart before asking the mind.

~ leonor murciano-luna

Join our Feminine Wisdom Circle

Join our Conscious Feminine community and be part of the movement of
women all around the globe,
that are changing the story of the Feminine on the planet,
by awakening, transforming and embodying
their true magnificence and power.

As a **Feminine Wisdom Circle** member,
we will gather several times a month,
explore Feminine teachings and activations,
embodied meditations and forge the new path of the
Feminine Era of Sovereignty.

For more information, visit our
Conscious Feminine Medicine™ Wisdom Circle,
membership page at
ConsciousFeminineMedicine.com.

If you have read this book... I am sure you understand the importance of
raising the vibration on our planet... and supporting women all over the world
to move into their Sovereignty.
Therefore, please join me in spreading the word
by leaving a review for this book.
Your opinion is valuable and can empower many more women on the planet!

Amazon.com for reviews.

Thank you.

Made in the USA
Coppell, TX
08 July 2020